The Heart Thing

The Heart Thing

Jack Freedman

sitaram PRESS

20% of all profits from this book will go to a non-profit organization that Jack supported: The Trevor Project.

FIRST EDITION

ISBN-13: 9781981745609
ISBN-10: 1981745602

INTERIOR LAYOUT AND COVER DESIGN BY CREATESPACE.COM
EDITING BY PARVATIMARKUS.COM

Dedication

To the Trevor Project, for the valuable help they provide
to the LGBTQ community of young people.

Founded in 1998 by the creators of the Academy Award®-winning short film *TREVOR*, The Trevor Project is the leading national organization providing crisis intervention and suicide prevention services to lesbian, gay, bisexual, transgender, and questioning (LGBTQ) young people under the age of 25. Their trained counselors are available on the Trevor Lifeline—a nationally accredited, 24/7/365, toll-free, confidential suicide hotline at 866-488-7386. They have also begun TrevorText, TrevorChat, and TrevorSpace. Go to https://www.thetrevorproject.org for more information.

Table of Contents

Foreword

Sorry folks, I'm not the famous someone Jack wanted to write his foreword. But I am the editor, as well as a good friend, that helped him fashion the manuscript over the years.

Jack and I first started working on this book before his open heart surgery (when he wanted to write it as fiction), and then really got into it as a memoir in 2005. Jack had years and years worth of journals, since he wrote everywhere, all the time. He would pull sections out of the journals from which we cobbled together an initial manuscript. (If you think you might have been embarrassed by whatever was in those journals, don't worry, I never read the journals themselves, only whatever Jack pulled from them.) Then, as years went by, we would meet occasionally to discuss "the book," but he was always reluctant about publishing and would ignore the manuscript as assiduously as he had ignored his heart condition.

Then in 2015 something shifted, and we started making plans once again to meet in New York or L.A. or Florida to wrap it up, but that never happened. Maybe if I had suggested Paris . . . Oh, well. Then Jack's "heart thing" reasserted itself one final time, with hypertrophic cardiomyopathy. On December 31, 2015, minutes after posting a New Year's Eve update on Facebook, his heart suddenly gave out.

There are so many ways a heart can break. There are many who loved Jack. In his too-short life, he touched deeply everyone he met with his wit, charm, intelligence, compassion, and fabulousness—from his extended family, to his countless friends, and to the many Facebook "friends" who wrote thanking him for posting his coming-out letter to his dad and his courageous commentaries concerning the LGBTQ community.

After his death, it was clear that he would not be finishing what was to be the final edit on the manuscript. But his is a voice that needs to be heard. Heaven only knows how he would have changed what you will read here. Please enjoy his humor and insight as you wipe away your tears, and may your heart grow wiser and stronger thanks to his imperfectly perfect heart.

Missing Jack,
Parvati Markus

Preface

December 7, 2000, 7 p.m.

IT'S THE NIGHT BEFORE MY open heart surgery. I am to be at Cedars no later than five o'clock tomorrow morning. I go into pre-op at six and my surgery is to begin at seven. I have told everyone that I want to be alone tonight. It is the last time I will be able to be alone for a long time. I know that everybody is worried about me. I feel guilty that they are worried even more because I have insisted on being alone tonight, but they wouldn't really know what to say and I don't think I can handle that kind of energy. We're not quite at the point where they realize that human touch is better than the human voice, and I don't think I can explain it to them. They love me, but tonight that isn't enough. Besides, I also know I will fall into my pattern of reassuring them that I am okay despite the fact that I am truly terrified.

I have prepared for my death. I wrote goodbye letters this morning to Mom, Dad, Nick, Linda, Roy, Eric, and Babba, and hid them in various places. If I die, they'll find them eventually. If they were here, I would try to tell them that I understand that it is hell for everyone, not just me. Tonight I need to sit in my own hell without worrying about theirs. Perhaps it is selfish, but there is a tiny bit of strength in allowing myself to be selfish right now.

I am in my jammies—old, grey sweatpants and a white t-shirt, which are now very loose since I have lost so much weight. Standing on the deck, I'm watching the lights of the city start to twinkle in the wind. My head is full of so many emotions that it is almost blank.

At 7:30, my doorbell rings. I am instantly angry because everyone has promised me, absolutely promised me, that they will leave me alone. No phone calls. No emails. No voicemails. The doorbell is followed by a loud, insistent knocking at the door. I decide not to answer it. If I have to deal with my hell, they have to deal with theirs. The knock gets louder and does not relent. I go to the door and fling it open ready to be angry and hurt and defiant against anyone being here, invading my one last chance to sit in my terror.

Roy and Jack

It's Roy. My irritation dissolves immediately. He is carrying a brown paper grocery bag and barges right past me into the kitchen and starts unloading the bag onto my kitchen counter. Before I can even say hello, he says, not looking at me, "I know you want to be alone tonight, but I don't give a shit. I'm staying." Then he stops with the groceries, looks directly at me because I am still standing with the door open, stunned. Before I can even try to say something, he cuts me off. "We are not talking about your surgery. We are going to sit and eat junk food and chocolate and ice cream until our stomachs hurt. We are watching videos of *Absolutely Fabulous* until we laugh so much that our sides hurt. Then you are taking a Xanax and going to bed. At 4 a.m. I am waking your ass up. You're going to shower, get ready and we're driving down to the hospital to meet your family. You're having your surgery. I'll be there with everyone else holding your hand when you're done."

I start crying. Huge, uncontrolled sobs. My chest and shoulders heaving. Tears are spilling down my face. Roy continues to put huge amounts of junk food of all varieties onto the counter. I slowly close the door and walk into the living room and plant myself on the couch. The tears don't stop. Roy does not rush to hug me. He knows he cannot try to make me feel better with words. I'm beyond that. I'm alone with my terror and he lets me sit in it. Anything else would be false. I know I cannot tolerate any bullshit if I am going to get through this.

We eat so much junk food that I am sick. We watch *Absolutely Fabulous* and I laugh—true, thoughtless laughter like I haven't done in months. We play. It's not that I am suddenly fine or that my perspective is suddenly any different. I do not think to myself, "This is okay. I can get through this now that I know I can still laugh." I don't think at all, which is as joyous to me as anything that could have happened tonight. Even a moment, a second of not thinking about it, is all I can hope for right now.

It is a little after 10 and I am standing at the edge of my kitchen counter where all my pill bottles stand, including my recent Xanax prescription, sixty .5 mg pills in the bottle. I plan to take 30 tonight and 30 in the morning. Later, when people figure out what I've done, they will wonder if I tried to kill myself. Fifteen milligrams of Xanax would kill some people, or at least put them into a coma for a very long time. My tolerance is this high since I've been taking so much for so long. I am taking them as quickly as I can because Roy is in the bathroom and I have to hide this from him. He wouldn't hesitate for a moment to call the whole family, get them up here, take me to the hospital. Roy does not feel sorry for me. He does not look at me and feel pity. He simply feels horrible that I must go through this. I am so grateful for this I can barely express it. I realize only later why it is okay for him to be there: I don't look into his eyes and see pity.

He comes out of the bathroom and I have finished taking all 30 little pink pills. In fifteen minutes I begin to feel it. It's not the usual euphoria I get from them. It's not peace. It's simply nothingness—exactly what I hoped for. My fear is that if I do not drug myself into total incoherence, that I will not go through with the surgery in the morning.

I get into bed quickly so I don't pass out on the couch or start slurring my speech. Roy crawls into bed next to me and puts his arms around me like I am a baby. I have always been able to sleep comfortably in the same bed as

Roy. There has never been even the slightest moment of sexuality with us. I am facing the floor-to-ceiling windows that look out onto the lights of the city twinkling in the wind. Roy is spooning me from behind. I can't feel anything inside. It's safer this way. This way, I think I can actually go through with it tomorrow.

This is the last thing I remember before passing out for a dreamless five-hour sleep.

CHAPTER 1

Twists and Turns

ONE MOMENT I'M WALKING DOWN the street, the next I'm lying on my back on the sidewalk. My right leg is bent, foot flat on the sidewalk. My left leg, however, is bent in the air at a 90-degree angle, knee toward my chest. I have absolutely no idea what happened. Tiny tissue paper-like snowflakes are falling to the ground, melting against the dark grey, wet sidewalk, falling gently onto my face. I begin to put my left leg down and the pain is so excruciating that reflex alone causes me to leave it hanging in the air. The first thing I think is that I just fell on my ass outside of The Big Cup in Chelsea—the only part of New York City with people who are more critical than on the Upper East Side. A thought that immediately evaporates when I feel, again, the excruciating pain.

Something is terribly, terribly wrong. This is pain like I have never, ever felt before. Not the time I split open my head when I was eight, jumping off a brick wall to prove how brave I was. Not the time I split my forehead open from jumping up and down on my bed and landing head first into the corner of a very large, very heavy, antique wood desk. Not even the time I broke my wrist from slipping on terra cotta tiles while jumping out of the bathtub when I was 16 to urgently answer the phone (of course, I told everyone that I broke it while skiing). I have a history of really lame accidents. This, however, will prove to be the worst how-on-earth-did-you-do-that-just-walking accident ever.

The pain is awful, numbing everything else around me. I quickly become totally incoherent. The little snowflakes continue to fall on my face. Little

1

pricks of cold. And I start to cry—from the pain, from being totally helpless, flat on my back alone on a sidewalk at 9 a.m. on New Year's Day.

Two cops are peering down at me. I can't speak. I look at them, helpless, mind blank because of the pain. I still have not moved. One of the cops says, "Are you okay?" I have no response. I look up at them through the little snowflakes, tears rolling down my cheeks. Suddenly, I can feel the cold. Lifting my head up enough to look at my left leg, I see it's at an odd angle from my knee and my foot is hanging limply off to the left. This is not how a foot is supposed to hang. The second cop apparently notices this at the same time I do. My pain is punctuated by the absolute horror that something is seriously, seriously wrong with my left leg. Starting to cry harder, I hear the other cop say, "Oh, shit. Look at his foot."

On the way to the hospital in the ambulance, I call my boyfriend on my cell phone. He seems to think it's ridiculous that I am in an ambulance for a "broken leg." I don't bother to explain. Asshole. I ask him to meet me at the hospital. To compound the misery, the paramedic starts to cut my Calvin Klein Slim Fit jeans from ankle to pelvis. My favorite pair. My "good butt" jeans, as Lisa calls them. This is how crazy the pain is. The agony goes from horror to concern about my jeans, to being able to use my cell phone, and back to agony again. I do not, at the moment, realize the utter absurdity of being concerned about my clothes. I can hear the siren as we barrel down Eighth Avenue to St. Vincent Hospital in the Village.

My naked leg is black and blue from the knee to the ankle and something is pressing the skin outward. Blood is pooling there. I realize it's the bone. Mine. Practically popping out of my leg. I almost faint and beg the paramedic to help me. She tells me we'll be at the hospital soon.

In the hospital I lie on a gurney, crying. What is going to happen? When is the pain going to stop? The hospital is noisy. Nurses and doctors rush around, pagers beep, and medical machines compete for airspace with patients' yells and moans. The pain sears through my brain, obliviating all but the most primitive thought: "I hurt. Save me."

Brent shows up and holds my hand, but I can feel him thinking I'm being too dramatic over a "broken leg." The gurney starts moving and I am taken into a small room. Not the usual curtained-off area of an emergency room, but

an actual small room. A
very tall, very large doctor
is looking at my leg. This
giant is going to help my
little crushed leg? He has
yet to know exactly what
happened to me, what the
bones look like inside my
very swollen leg. He only
knows that both bones are
broken and I am writhing
around on the gurney in
pain. The doctor clears the
room of three nurses and the

Brent and Jack

orderly. Even Brent is asked to leave, but I see his face peering thorough the wire
mesh of the tiny window in the door. I have absolutely no idea what is going
on and why everyone except the doctor and one nurse were asked to leave, but
I know it can't be good.

They help me onto a higher table and roll me over onto my stomach. I am
half on and half off the table. The nurse is holding my shattered leg and I am
crazed with fear that she will drop it and let it dangle. The doctor tells me he
is going to try to realign the bones and that it might hurt. Hurt? More? Surely
you jest. Before I can complete my one sarcastic thought, he is holding my
leg in both of his huge hands and rubbing it up and down as though to push
the bones back into place. The agony is unbearable and I scream. The kind of
screams you hear on television, which I always thought were dramatically fake.
My scream is completely unplanned, uncontrollable—the only possible reaction to what is being done to me. I beg through my tears and screaming for
him to stop. Literally beg out loud. When he does stop, I am left sobbing on
my stomach, face down on the table's white paper that is soaked with my tears.

I see the nurse's face for just a second. She is young and beautiful and her
big, brown eyes are wet as she looks at my leg. What on earth must it take
for a nurse to get tears after seeing what they see every day? Suddenly I know
something is even worse than I had thought. I know, instinctively, that this

doctor did something to me that he didn't need to do. I wish him great and grievous bodily harm.

Finally, I am cognizant enough to wish and beg, specifically, for a pain shot.

This is a lovely way to start 1998.

An hour later I am in the hallway on a gurney and have been given a shot of Demerol. I am instantly in love with this drug. If my leg still hurts, I no longer care. I think I am lying on a little cloud instead of the gurney. I smile at people as they walk by. I am so pleasant. I feel lovely. I'm amused that this has happened.

In the strangest of strange moments, my Auntie Lanie calls. Somehow she gets through to the hospital and through to the emergency room and they find me and move me and my little cloud toward the telephone. Auntie Lanie isn't really my aunt, but any relation who is older than you as a child becomes an aunt or uncle. She is my father's first cousin and has always been a part of my life. I have always known I could call her if I needed to talk, although me calling someone for help would be as likely as me growing a second head. She wants to know what happened. I tell her I tripped on a subway grate and fell. "And you're in the hospital for that?" I have yet to realize this exact response will continue to play like a broken record. She tells me she loves me. She tells me she'll call everyone. I tell her I'm okay. I'm Jack. I'm always okay.

Orderlies come and take me to get x-rays. Four hours later I'm in a room with my leg propped up, begging for another Demerol shot. The pleasure of the situation is wearing off. The pain is returning and I am both frightened and irritable. Brent is sitting in a chair next to me. In walks the gigantic doctor who hurt me earlier. I look at him thinking, "Give me Demerol or get the fuck out." Instead, I stay silent. Not smart to be rude to the doctors who have control over my comfort, or, as it were, the lack thereof at the moment. This lesson of learning to be nice and charming to doctors and nurses will serve me very, very well later.

He starts to tell me what the x-rays showed. Apparently I shattered both bones—called a spiral fracture. It's as though someone put one hand on my knee and one hand on my ankle and twisted in opposite directions, like wringing out a washcloth. He asks again exactly what happened. I can tell, already, he thinks there is more to the story. I tell him I was walking and got my toe stuck in a grate and fell, twisting backward while my toe was still in the grate. "Were you running?"

I want to kill this man. "No," I say.

"Were you drunk?"

If only. "It was 9 a.m.!"

Mom has always said that I operate in first gear or overdrive and nothing in between. God forbid I simply break my leg. No. I have to shatter it. I am told I will have to have an operation to put it back together with metal plates and screws. Lovely.

Despite another Demerol shot, the pain is getting worse. If I move even an inch, it is agony. I still cannot believe that I am in this much pain. Suddenly, in walks Nicholas, my brother. He's four years younger than I am and a student at the University of Toronto. When he heard what happened, he immediately got on a plane in Toronto, flew

Nick and Jack

into JFK, and took a cab directly to the hospital. I am stunned. Not because this is out of character. Quite the opposite, actually. I am stunned, though, that this is bad enough to get people on airplanes. I try to be nice and talk like a normal human being, but the pain is too much and he and Brent go into the hallway. I am very irritable. I am in pain. And I am scared.

Later that afternoon, the huge doctor comes back. Nicholas and Brent stand next to me. The huge doctor is at the end of my bed and he begins to cut off the cast they had put on in the emergency room. Intense pain instantly shoots from my leg to my brain. I bite hard to stop from crying. It feels like my leg is a bag of bones and skin and nerve endings, which are on fire. Oh, wait, I think, my leg *is* a bag of bones and skin and nerve endings on fire. He peels back the cast and starts to manipulate my leg. That's it. I start crying and moaning for him to stop. The pain is unbelievable. I lift my head and look at my black-and-blue leg. It has blown up to twice its normal size. I can no longer see the bone pressing against the skin because the swelling is so bad. I keep begging for him to stop. I don't know what he is doing, but I think it cannot be necessary. Tears are rolling down my cheek as I lay my head down and stare at the ceiling, giving up, crying and begging in a whimper for him to stop. Then I look at Nicholas; he is crying and leaves the room. This moment sears its way into my memory. He has watched me be in such pain that he can't even stand watching. Oh. My. God. It's that bad.

That night, I am given morphine and I have some kind of allergic reaction. The morphine immediately throws my heart into tachycardia. It is beating fast and irregularly. I have dealt with this for ten years. When I was seventeen, I was jogging after school. Our house in Santa Fe, New Mexico, is at the base of the mountains and I loved to jog after school. One time, I came back home after jogging and my heart would not stop beating fast. It refused to slow down. I lay down on the tiles in the bathroom and tried to breathe slowly and deeply, to no avail. Then I pressed against my heart with my hands and took a deep breath. Suddenly, it stopped. It didn't simply slow down. My heart actually stopped for a moment and then began to beat normally again.

An hour later, Mom took me to the cardiologist, who told me I had something called Paroxysmal Atrial Tachycardia. P.A.T. Normally, the electrical system of the heart shoots little charges through the heart to keep it beating correctly. The charge goes through the heart, stops, then starts again. In my heart, however, the electrical charge somehow gets stuck in the atrium of the heart. It goes in a circle, so the heart begins to beat irregularly and fast to try to correct itself.

He told me there were various ways to stop it when these "attacks" happened. All lovely. I could shove my face into a huge bowl of icy water. I could take deep breaths and push them out very fast. Or, my favorite, the "valsalva" maneuver. I could take a breath and push down as though I were trying to poop. He told me I couldn't have caffeine or antihistamines. He told me there were drugs for this, but that I wouldn't need them until I was around 50. He also told me that there was a deformity in my heart—a bicuspid aortic valve— that I had been born with. Normal valves are tricuspid, with three little flaps at the end of the valve that open and close like a flower to regulate the flow of blood. I have only two flaps, so the valve leaks. The cardiologist told me that I might need medicine for this as well, but again, not until I was much older. He also told me that surgery might be needed, but not "until you're at least sixty, if at all, I would think."

Brent has gone home and I am alone with my tachycardia and shattered leg. I press the button repeatedly for a nurse and she finally comes. I tell her what is happening and she doesn't seem to believe me. I tell her that I can't get it to stop. She tells me that I must calm down and that this happens to patients with severe injuries. I try to explain to her and she tells me, again, to calm down, and she leaves the room. I am furious with her and feel like she is taking advantage of my helplessness. Not like I can jump out of bed and smack her. I start crying because I cannot stop it this time. Doing valsalva is horrifyingly painful on my leg. Besides, it's not working. And, strangely, there doesn't seem to be a bucket of ice water nearby.

Half an hour later, I buzz the nurse again. This time it's someone different and she immediately calls a doctor. The doctor freaks out and puts me on a machine. It beeps loudly in accordance with my heartbeat. The noise agitates me and that is bad when I am trying to stop the tachycardia. He listens to my heart and looks shocked. He leaves. I have no idea what is happening, but I am terrified beyond words. He comes back and tells me he is going to shoot something into my IV called Adenosine that will stop my heart for a moment. Charming. And it does. It is the strangest sensation. No movement in my body for a few seconds. Nothing. My body has shut down for a second and I just lie there. It seems like five minutes. Then, my heart starts to beat again and it's normal. The obnoxious beeping machine is quiet.

He asks me if I know what I have. I tell him yes. He tells me it's pretty bad. I tell him I have gotten tachycardia "moments" for ten years. He seems stunned, but accepts the fact that I say I know what's up with my heart. He discontinues morphine. I ask for Demerol. I instantly know this is a mistake. Ask for a certain narcotic and that is a sure way to make sure you don't get it. Once they figure out you like a drug too much, they won't give it to you anymore. He gives me something called Dilaudid instead. I remember this drug. My mom took it after her mastectomy when I was sixteen years old. It was a new drug back then and we could only get a few pills at a time from the pharmacy; they were very expensive on the street. It is, I remember, the only painkiller stronger than morphine. It terrifies me that I need it. An hour later, I'm terrified that it barely takes the edge off the pain. The nurse gives me a sleeping pill and I fall blessedly asleep.

Nicholas and Brent show up mid-morning. I am still in agony. The pain has not gotten better and the leg is still too swollen to operate. If they operate now, the skin on the leg will just peel back away from the muscle. This does not seem desirable. I tell them what happened during the night. Neither is shocked since they have both been around me for many, many tachycardia "attacks." When I have them, I lie down wherever I am. I have no shame about this. I have lain down in the middle of a dance club, in the middle of Broadway performances, in the middle of a grocery store, and on top of the Eiffel tower. That is the strangest claim to glamour I have ever had. "My heart freaked out and, oh, yes, I was on top of the Eiffel tower. It was delightful."

People who are close to me know all about this and know not to freak and to let me be quiet. Sometimes it will stop in three minutes. Sometimes it will stop in 20. The longest has been about 40. But I have never been taken to the hospital. I always figured I could fix it myself. I'm Jack. I'm always okay.

Nicholas and Brent stay there all day and I am extraordinarily irritable and rude. I am so unhappy. I am in so much pain. I am scared. Unfortunately, I make them the recipients of all my irritation. I snap at Brent and I lecture Nick. I know I am doing it, but I can't stop. Later, much later, I realize that Dilaudid makes my snapping and lecturing worse than normal. The phone rings. Brent answers it and immediately hands it to me. It's Eric.

"Took you long enough to call me," I say irritably.

"I see," he says. "So, are you being a total bitch or a complete asshole during this extravaganza?"

"Depends on the medication," I reply. "I think I'm being an asshole at the moment."

"I hope they're giving you Valium and Demerol," he shrills.

"I think everyone else hopes that, too, but they aren't."

"Jack, I cannot believe that you did the same thing to your leg as I did to mine three years ago. It's ridiculous. Things like this do not happen to normal people!"

"Exactly."

"Yes. Amazing. The same thing," he says almost wistfully, as though it is bringing us closer together, which isn't possible.

"Yes, dear, but I did it falling for no reason and ended up on my ass on a sidewalk on Eighth Avenue all by myself. You decided to slip on a piece of ice in front of Bergdorf's and have five face-lifted women immediately throw their fur coats on you."

He laughs. "Of course, dear! I AM fabulous in all respects, you know!"

"Yes, keep telling yourself that while you put the Preparation H on your eye bags in the morning."

"Bitch."

"No, I already told you. Today, I'm being an asshole, not a bitch."

By this time, Nicholas and Brent have left the room because no matter the circumstance, there is really no point in being around Eric and I when we're together. We've been extraordinarily close and have developed a very complex relationship over the past two years.

There are certain people you meet in life who you befriend and care about and even love. Then there are certain people you meet in life who change you. Mold you. People who you can look back and say, "I would probably be a different person if I hadn't known him." Eric is like that for me. A fortuitous moment. A fortuitous mood. Two people who needed each other and that need turned into a friendship bordering on a couple. Eric and I were very much like a couple who didn't have sex and didn't live together. In other words, a happy couple.

Jack and Eric

I met Eric in the Fall of 1995, when it was getting chilly in NYC. I wore my new, forest green, Donna Karan sweater that I had no business buying since I was living mostly on student loans. But it was gorgeous and soft and big and felt like fall in Manhattan. I put on my faded Gap slim-fit jeans and my five-year-old black leather jacket. I planned to read through my Advanced Corporate Tax Problems materials for tomorrow one more time while drinking a vodka cranberry. I walked into my little kitchen, like something from a doll's house. It's an oversized wet bar with a mini-oven. Perfect, since the only thing I know how to make in a kitchen is a phone call to order out, or a drink. I love it.

After filling one of the thick glasses I bought at a tiny store in the Village with ice, I pour it half full of Stoli and half cranberry juice. Very strong. I sit on my bed with the books strewn all over the place and the window wide open to the fire escape. It's very cold outside, but I have discovered, much to my horror, that the heat in older buildings in Manhattan is controlled by the landlord. This past week it has been running full blast and slowly roasting me. I take a gigantic sip of the drink. I do not think it strange in the least that I am going over one of the most difficult law courses with the IRS tax code in one hand and a vodka cranberry in the other.

After five minutes, I decide that it is hopeless. I am going to Splash. Stepping out of my apartment building at night, I am right on Fifth Avenue between 16th and 17th streets; I can see the Empire State Building lit all in white and glowing in the mist. When I look downtown, I see the majestic twin towers. I fit here. It's home. When I rented the apartment, I had absolutely no idea that it was less than a block from what was then the trendiest gay bar in town. This was before Rome, before G, before XL. Splash is fun, friendly, and has periodic shows where male strippers get into a shower above the bar and, well, shower and strip. It's hot. It's exciting. I've never seen anything like this. The exuberance of L.A. can't hold a candle to the outrageousness of NYC. And I love it.

Tonight it's cold and I am the tiniest bit tipsy from my vodka cranberry. There is nothing like Manhattan at night when you're slightly drunk. Everything is possible. I can literally feel the millions of attitudes, places, happenings, events, all over Manhattan. I feel that all of them are accessible for me. Soon they will be. My life will be consumed with the variety and disparity and insanity that is Manhattan.

There is a line at Splash, but I smile at the bouncer and he recognizes me from the other night and lets me in. As I walk into the very crowded and smoky bar, the first song I hear is Madonna singing "Holiday" and I love that the stereotype is so alive without embarrassment. When you buy a drink at Splash on certain nights, you get back a wooden nickel that can be used to buy another drink. I happen to have a wooden nickel. I insert myself in between two people at the bar and order a vodka cranberry and pay with my wooden nickel. A very tall man sitting on a barstool next to me leers and shrieks, very dramatic, "What is that? A wooden nickel? You can't afford one drink?"

I am utterly astonished, but I seem to have my wits about me and I respond fast, "If you're that concerned, you can buy me the next one." We both stare at each other a moment and then he laughs—a sort of high cackle that reminds me of something. Oh, yeah . . . me.

He is very tall, even sitting on the stool. He has wide, brown eyes and dark hair pulled back into a small pony tail. To my horror, I notice a fur coat draped over his shoulders, long and trailing on the floor. "Your fur is on the floor of the bar. It's kind of gross down there," I say, very droll.

He leans towards me and says, voice low and snotty, "I have others."

"You can't possibly be for real."

He laughs and his voice goes higher, "I'm not! I'm completely fake! A total phony! Aren't I fabulous?"

"You're definitely something," I say, and add, "Who is that boy?" There is a blonde boy, my age, on the other side of him watching our whole exchange and taking no part of it. He is sipping a martini and is very, very cute.

"He's an accoutrement," he says with a wave of his hand.

I almost spit out my drink from laughing. The boy doesn't seem offended; instead, he tells the man he needs another drink. The man pulls out a gigantic wad of crinkled hundred dollar bills from the inside pocket of the fur coat and puts it on the counter without even looking at it. He turns to the boy and says very politely, "Get a drink for yourself." Then he points to me and offers me a drink as well.

"No thanks." I ask the bartender, whose name is Matt (I have never met a Matt that I do not have a crush on; I've been completely enamored with this one for weeks) for a straight vodka on ice. I no longer feel like diluting it with anything pink. "You can buy your accoutrement drinks. If I were him, I'd probably need to be very drunk to tolerate you, as well."

Again, we stare at each other. Suddenly he gets a delighted smile on his face and says gently, "I'm Eric. It's a pleasure to meet you."

I am astonished by the sudden change in his demeanor. "I'm Jack. The pleasure is all yours." And we are fast friends from that moment on.

Eric ran in the high echelons of Manhattan society. I ran . . . in the average echelons of baby-lawyer-who-happened-to-know-connected-people. I was 25. Everybody else at the dinner party we attended soon after we met, wasn't. I was directed to sit next to an elderly blonde woman who wore black clothes and dark sunglasses. Eric was across from me. I looked at him to catch his eye and he ignored me, which meant he was punishing me for being late.

A few minutes into the first course, the elderly blonde asked me, "So, who are you and why are you here?" I know that it sounds awful, but she actually asked it in a way that was sweet and curious. I told her that I was invited as Eric's guest, to which she said, "Magnificent! Eric is wonderful!"

Her name was Holly Solomon. She had been close friends with Andy Warhol (who had used her as a model for a portrait done in that famous bright-colored style of his), owned a beyond-amazing-and-trendy gallery in Soho, and, for whatever reason, decided that I was worth talking to. She had an interest in Southwest Art and, due to the fact that I grew up in Santa Fe, I knew something about this subject. She was hysterical and delightful. We both remained hysterical and delightful as the martinis kept being served throughout dinner.

Towards the end of the dinner, Holly turned to me and said, "You'll meet me at the gallery in Soho tomorrow at 6 and then we'll go have drinks afterwards." It wasn't a question or an invitation. It was a solid declarative statement. (I'm relatively sure that if I had said something, it would have been like that scene in *Devil Wears Prada* and she would have interrupted me to say, "No, no, it wasn't a request. You'll be there.")

I owned only two good suits—one in dark taupe and one dark charcoal. I also owned one charcoal herringbone blazer. My apartment, on lower Fifth Avenue, still wasn't furnished (in fact, it never, ever was furnished except for a bed, but that's another story) and I had no full-length mirror. I put on the charcoal suit with a grey shirt and teetered on the edge of the tub to see my full reflection in the mirror over the sink. Then I did the same with the dark taupe suit. Then again with charcoal suit. Each time teetering on the edge of the tub to try and see myself full length in the sink mirror. I finally decided on the dark charcoal suit as I gave one last gaze into the mirror, and promptly fell backwards into the tub and covered the suit with leftover bubbles and soapy water that hadn't quite yet drained out. I'm sure the fact that I was already on my second martini had no part in the fall.

Just as I was done dressing in the dark taupe suit pants, grey shirt, and herringbone blazer, the phone rang.

"Jack, it's Holly."

"Holly! Just getting ready to leave for the gallery."

"Meet me at Three Degrees North, instead. Is now okay?"

"Sure. See you there."

"Yes," she declared, and hung up.

I loved that: "Yes." As in, "You will be where I tell you to be at the time I tell you to be there."

The thing about being insecure, but still being able to "look the part," is that nobody knows you're insecure. What I've learned as I've gotten older is that this is a function of youth. I knew I could look the part and speak the language, but there was always a little part of me that wondered if someone was going to "find me out" for the poseur I thought I was. Looking back, I really didn't pretend to be anything other than a 25-year-old kid, reasonably good-looking, newly-lawyered, living in Manhattan and a little star-struck. The people I met through Eric were definitely powerful and well-known, moving silently in very high but very quiet circles. You had to know people to know people who would know them. I skipped a lot of levels by being with Eric.

I cabbed down to Three Degrees North, parked myself at the bar and ordered two martinis. As the bartender put them in front of me, in walked Holly. She saw me immediately and sat down and didn't even comment on the martini I had ordered for her, as though to say, "Well, of course, dear. You are well-mannered to have ordered a drink for me. That's the baseline of class, not the ceiling."

Holly launched into story after magnificent story of her life in the art scene. Warhol-this and Warhol-that. Names of famous artists dripped off her tongue. She was, all at once, completely fabulous and untouchable while being totally down-to-earth and accessible. There didn't seem to be a false bone in her body, nor a snotty one. She was just . . . her.

At some point Richard Picasso came over and said, "Jack! It's wonderful to see you! How are you, my friend?"

"Richard! I'm great! How are you? This is my friend, Holly . . ."

Richard turned to Holly, interrupting me to say, "Holly. Magnificent to see you. How are you?" He kissed her hand.

Stupid me thinking an introduction would be required between these two.

We chatted a little with Richard and then he walked off. Holly said to me, eyebrows raised, "Sooooo, you know Richard?" Richard Picasso, as in Pablo Picasso's grandson. I gave Holly a knowing look and said, "Yes, through Eric."

For the next hour or so Holly regaled me with this story and that story of the art world and famous artists. At one point I had to ask who an artist she mentioned was; she laughed and said, "I love that you admit to not knowing.

Most people are so full of shit they have to pretend to know everything." I loved her.

As she gathered her things to go, I said, "I don't know why you're so interested in me. I'm an absolute nobody."

She looked at me, laughing, put her hand on mine and said, "No, dear, you're an absolute somebody! You're just not old enough to have figured out who yet!"

Two weeks after meeting Eric, I leave for a three-day trip to Paris after final exams. Eric gives me a few hundred francs as a Christmas gift. I give him an inscribed copy of *Portrait of a Lady* by Henry James.

CHAPTER 2

Metal and Screws

PARIS HAS ALWAYS BEEN ONE of my favorite places in the world. It also led to my relationship with John—a supremely marvelous human being. Spring of 1994. I had just spent a week in Paris with Carol, someone I've known since I was 11. She and I met in Santa Fe, where both of our families belonged to the same synagogue. We grew apart during high school. She got wild. I didn't. Carol planned to stay in Paris for a year since she was majoring in French. I decided to visit her.

After a fabulous week of total debauchery (I danced shirtless on the stage at Le Palace and Carol crouched down in a gutter to pee, both of us stark, raving drunk), I am on my way home, flying coach on an American Airlines 767, on a flight that goes through Dallas. I have a window seat and a nice French lady sits next to me, but I don't speak French (yet). I have taken off my beige, flannel, very plain, Calvin Klein, oxford-style shirt because I'm completely overheated. I do not know why the woman next to me is wearing a rather heavy sweater and seems fine. Underneath, I'm wearing a charcoal Calvin Klein t-shirt. I'm not built by any means, but I have nice arms and, even though they are small, they form little biceps when I'm holding my book. I'm a bit self-conscious, since the t-shirt makes me look little. Having always been called "little" and "skinny" and, worst of all, "wimp," while growing up, I'm very sensitive about it, and probably always will be. At least until years later when I get completely addicted to working out. Among other things.

I hear, near me, "What's your name?" I don't look up at first because it doesn't register that someone would be talking to me. Then I hear, "You.

With the biceps." Everyone three rows forward and three rows back looks up because he is talking in a normal voice. He's looking directly at me, waiting for me to respond. He's about 6 feet tall, a little overweight, maybe 35 years old and far along in his balding. Startled, I answer, "Uh, Jack."

"Okay, come with me so we can talk in the back," he says in a nice, calm voice. Not lascivious or anything.

I get up and follow him to the back of the plane. He pulls a jump seat out of the wall for me and one, across from me, for him. He's very nice. Very sweet. We talk about Paris, life in general, his apparently very hot boyfriend, and what it's like to be a flight attendant. Sounds very exciting and glamorous to me, but most things would since I spend my time sitting in law school classes discussing the difference between first and second degree murder and reading casebooks in a café slurping as many iced coffees as I can. So, four hours and five Kahlua-minis later, we're about to land in Dallas. I get up to go back to my seat and he tells me to stay. We're literally about to land. He picks up the air phone and dials it and I hear one side of the following conversation:

"John, it's Steve. No, I'm in the office on the way back from Paris . . . need you to come to the airport. Yes, now. I want you to meet someone. No, I mean it. John, do you trust me? Okay, then. Bye."

He looks at me and says, "There's someone you need to meet and he's coming to the airport."

I laugh. "Steve, I'm in law school. I have no time for a boyfriend. Let alone someone who lives in Dallas."

He ignores me and says, "Look for me when you come out of customs."

When I come out of customs, Steve is standing there. Thank goodness he's alone. The absolute last thing I want to do is meet someone after a flight from Paris, in coach! I look frightening and I'm exhausted. I really would rather go to my gate and catch my flight home.

We chit-chat more about his life as a flight attendant. Apparently, he works only international flights. Mostly Europe. Some South America. His trips are generally three days, then he has three to four days off. Or he can juggle his schedule around and trade trips with other flight attendants. If he wants a Paris trip instead of a London trip, he can trade with someone. If he wants to do two trips back-to-back, he can trade with someone and then have a week off. He can work the maximum hours to earn more money, but still end up with about ten days a month off. He also flies free (well, he pays a small service charge), in first class, anywhere in the world, as long as there is a seat open. Sounds like a good gig to me.

I'm standing on the curb looking at a very crystal-clear Dallas sky. Gorgeous weather. Spring. Slight breeze. Lots of open space. Such a dramatic difference from Paris. Everything here looks so, so new. I'm considering his job and what it would be like to fly all over the world and trade trips with people and have so much time off and meet so many people, when this red pick-up pulls around in front of us and I hear, "Okay, what are you doin'?"

Jack and John

Steve tells me to get in and he gets in after me. John is going to drive me to the other terminal. I am now in a car with one person I've only known for five hours and another person I don't know at all. They could kidnap me and use me as their own personal boy toy! I consider this for a moment and contrast it with reading case-books for the next year and a half.

I find myself sitting next to a very handsome, boyishly-cute guy with thick dark hair, intense blue eyes, and the most innocent and open smile I have ever seen. As with anyone I'm actually attracted to, I have no clue what to say. John asks me what I was in Paris for, how law school is, etc. Nothing of consequence. He asks me if I have an email account and I tell him that I think I have one at the law school, but that I never use it. He gives me his email address, not his phone number. He is farther along in the email/AOL world than most people at the moment.

Two days later when I check my email for the first time ever (after an hour figuring out how to log onto the law school email system and failing time after time), there is an email from John. We begin exchanging emails. Now I check it constantly. We are sarcastic and sly and witty and he makes me laugh. We start talking on the phone. When I'm in Santa Fe for the weekend, we fax each other. Fax after fax. Sometimes one word, sometimes two, sometimes a letter, sometimes lewd pictures. I am completely enthralled. He is, too.

He visits me for a weekend. Then he starts flying to come visit me on all his days off, sometimes flying back to Dallas barely in time to get on a work trip to London or Tokyo or Buenos Aires or whatever fabulous place he's going to next. I am so jealous of his life, even though he tells me it's just work. It's all he's ever done. An office life is completely foreign to him. In my life as a lawyer, taking a break will probably mean going out to dinner instead of writing memos about breach of contract. In John's life, taking a break means a weekend in some faraway place, either alone or with other airline buddies equally able to travel with only a moment's notice. Again, I'm jealous. I'm also really falling for him. He's sweet and hysterical and sincere and smart and doesn't take himself too seriously. He's naïve, but not innocent, although he loves to come off that way.

We are together until Fall of 1995 when, four months into my LL.M. program in NYC, I break up with him. We'd been having a hard time for a few months. An hour after I break up with him, sitting in my little apartment on Fifth Avenue and 17th Street, Steve calls me and tells me that I've made the biggest mistake of my life and that John will find someone to spend his life with much faster than I ever will. I'm stunned and hurt and can't believe Steve would say this to me. At least he's a loyal friend to John, but what a fucking asshole.

When I take my first semester final exams for the LL.M. degree, John sends me rice crispy treats that he made. This makes me cry, but all I can do is write him an email (from my now very techno-savvy AOL account) and merely say how surprised I am and touched. I also tell him that it says amazing things that after I've hurt him he would still be sweet to me. It's a typical John thing to do; he cares about me and isn't trying to somehow get back together.

Two months from then, he'll be angry and stop speaking to me and I won't blame him. Two years from then we start to keep in touch very sporadically, almost tentatively. By the time I am about to have my heart surgery, we have "bursts" of email and phone conversations about four times a year. He tells me he will come stay with me after my heart surgery if I need him. Again, I know that it comes from his sincerity and not because, even so many years later, he wants to be back together. It is just the way John is. He's a sweet, loving man. I will never figure out why he isn't for me. Twelve years later, we will have one phone call. Very random. Just chatting. It is the same connection we had when we first met. Exactly the same feeling, but neither of us does anything about it.

Unfortunately, when I shatter my leg, we are still in the stage of not speaking.

Nick leaves in the afternoon to go back to Toronto because he can't miss any more classes. I am told that they will operate that night. For some reason, this scares me. I figure the surgeons will have been operating all day and then, at night, on me. What if they are exhausted and not paying attention? Surgery absolutely terrifies me. I almost want to lie there and hope the bones mend themselves after a while. The surgeon tries to reassure me that this is not a complicated operation and that all will go well. "Hello! You're cutting into my body and inserting metal objects! How is that not complicated?"

I am also terrified of anesthesia. What if I never wake up? What if I end up as a vegetable? What if I am actually awake during the surgery and they can't tell and I can feel them cutting into me? I am told that they will only be giving me an epidural and some combination of Versed and Valium. An epidural, I am told, is when they stick a needle into my back, near the spinal column, blocking the nerves from my leg to my brain. The Valium and Versed will keep me asleep. Despite being assured that I won't feel anything, I insist that they give me enough drugs to put me to sleep.

Brent reassures me that I won't feel anything and that it will go okay, but it only irritates me more. One would think that having a boyfriend who is a doctor would be comforting, but when Brent goes into "doctor mode," he is clinical and not very sympathetic. Although I am smart enough to know that, to some extent, doctors have to be this way to get through all they have to get through with patients, and pain, and injuries, and illness, I still hate it. I'd rather he hold my hand, but he doesn't realize that something that simple can be reassuring.

Two doctors are at either end of me while I lie on the operating table. I am way, way too aware of what is going on. One doctor holds my feet. The other holds my arms. They are pulling me into a tight fetal position on top of the operating table. This is in order to curve the back as severely as possibly while they push the epidural into my spine. I can feel pressure, but I don't feel pain. I am still terrified of waking up or being awake. Thinking about the epidural, I have visions of them hitting my spinal cord and paralyzing me. Basically, I'm scared of everything now. They put me on my back and ask if I can feel them touching my leg. I cannot.

I am in ecstasy. I am in heaven. I am in nirvana. The pain is completely and utterly gone. I have fallen in love with everyone in the operating room. They are angels, hovering around me. No people have ever been so kind.

Of course, now that I am pain free, I can coherently beg for as much medication as is necessary to put me to sleep. I tell them I have a very high tolerance for drugs (not mentioning that I know this because it takes 4 mg of Xanax to put me to sleep even though it only takes .25 mg for most people). I am worried they will run out if they don't have enough ready and waiting. They reassure me they have enough, that I will be asleep the whole time. I am not, however, reassured. I have convinced myself that despite their instant angelic status since cutting off my pain, that they still won't keep me asleep and that I'll wake up to hear them sawing the bone or watch the metal plate being pushed inside.

The last thing I remember is that the operating room is very crowded. This surprises me. I always thought of operating rooms as practically empty except for the table, the patient, and a few buckets to put organs into. There are shelves full of things. There are fluorescent lights in addition to the expected bright-as-the-sun operating light directly above me. I wonder if everything in here is sterile.

I begin to wake up in the operating room. I am shivering, but feeling very warmed. It's lovely to be swaddled in these blankets. My drug-soaked brain tells me this whole experience is lovely. I feel heavenly. Extremely happy and relaxed. On the way through the hallway, I tell my doctors, "That was the best operation I ever had. Thank you so much. I am so grateful. You did an amazing job." I babble on and on and on. Later, I feel like an absolute idiot.

I would imagine, however, they must be used to it. Besides, at the moment, I really do feel lovely. No pain and lots of Valium is an astonishing feeling after utter agony for three days. I hope I get to have it again! Little did I know.

I wake up in ICU. My leg is starting to hurt. My whole body aches. The operating room doctors have quickly gone from angels to devils. The nerve of them to let my cloud of comfort drift back into pain. Brent is sitting next to me in the ICU. I know he wants to say something to comfort me, but in this setting, his clinical self takes over and he's just not capable. Suddenly, a gaggle of doctors come into my ICU room. They start listening to my heart and one says, "Wow. Very interesting." Another says, "Very loud."

I want to scream, "Get the fuck out of here! I'm in agony! Get the hell away from my interesting sounding heart!" It mystifies me that they think this is appropriate. I am, in their eyes, just a piece of meat, albeit apparently an interesting one.

I get more and more cranky. The pain is back full blast. I am absolutely positive that my leg is about to swell and split open inside the cast and nobody will know it. And the Dilaudid seems to be doing nothing. It does, however, enhance my cranky mood. A nurse comes in and tells me I have to urinate into a bottle. Mortified, I try. Nothing. How the hell am I supposed to pee? And why the hell does she care? I haven't been allowed to drink anything for 12 hours. Peeing lying down? Surely you jest. She tells me that if I don't pee soon, that she will put a catheter in me. The idea of having a tube shoved up my penis is revolting. The penis is an exit-only organ. She comes back in an hour. I have not peed. Granted, I have not tried again. I have convinced myself that it is simply not possible. I am cranky beyond belief. She tells me that she is going to have a catheter put in me and I completely freak out and yell at her, "If you touch me, I will sue you! I'm a lawyer and touching me without my permission in an offensive way is assault and battery!"

She rolls her eyes and says, "Fine."

I look at Brent. He is hanging his head in his hands. I have been triumphant! I shall pee on my own, as I please. An hour later, I manage to pee lying down and into a bottle, somehow manipulating my penis, which I am sure will be completely useless for the rest of my life, to get the pee only in the bottle.

I am staring up into the yellow fluorescent lights of an elevator. I am on the gurney being wheeled back from ICU into a regular room. The antiseptic hospital smell is overwhelming in this little space. An orderly is with me. Brent is with me. A doctor is with me. He tells me, "You know, your heart is going to need to be fixed. That valve is really loud. A lot of our students never heard anything like it."

I think to myself, Oh yes, this is really what I need to be considering after my leg has just been filled with metal. I tell him, "Yes, I know. I've been told I might need that some day."

The next 30 seconds happen in slow motion. The doctor opens his mouth as the elevator doors open. The orderly has pushed my gurney halfway out of the elevator. Brent is still in the elevator. The doctor is next to me, easing himself out with the gurney. As I continue to stare up at the fluorescent lights, annoyed that he thinks he has to mention my heart crap right now, he says, "You're going to need open heart surgery for a valve replacement in about three years."

Quite suddenly, everything stops. I am so stunned, I can't even ask him questions. I have just been told, in the most nonchalant way, that I will need open heart surgery in three years. And for a long time, despite the agonizing pain and the fear of my leg and the surgery and having to pee lying down, this is the only moment I remember with any clarity. There is no way I can sort through what I have been told. It doesn't make sense.

"Are you sure?"

He doesn't even look down at me as I am being wheeled to a new room. "Yes. Absolutely."

I don't even cry. The idea of open heart surgery so soon is so terrifying and so unreal that I can't get past my shock into being afraid. Yet.

Two days later I am allowed to leave the hospital. I have an enormous cast. The old-fashioned plaster kind that probably weighs more than I do. I have crutches, but I am in a wheelchair.

Brent manages to get me into the back of a cab. Every movement is excruciating. I go butt first into the cab, backing myself up against the opposite door, my leg stretched out in front of me. I feel like I'm wearing heavy metal on my leg, instead of in it. Every bump the cabbie hits on the way uptown hurts. I ask the cabbie to slow down and drive carefully. I can't tell if he does. When we get to our building, Brent sets up the wheelchair. While moving from the cab to wheelchair, I am terrified that I will fall or hit my leg. Nonetheless, it will be so nice to be home. Brent wheels me up the wheelchair ramp. The only time I've ever used the wheelchair ramp before was to bring packages inside on the bellman's cart. Never did I think I'd need the wheelchair ramp for a wheelchair!

I maneuver myself from the wheelchair to the sofa and immediately begin taking pain pills. Brent leaves to fill the prescription since I only have a few left from the hospital. I am staring at the wall and decide that I'd rather stare outside. We live on the 15th floor and can see the East River. This will be the first in a long, long string of efforts to learn how to move around with my leg in pain and the huge cast. I am terrified of accidentally hitting my leg against something, as I'm sure the cast won't protect it if I step down hard on my leg. Later, much to my dismay, I find out this is true.

I swing the cast off the edge of the sofa, holding it in midair with every ounce of strength in my body. I lift my head up and push up with my hands and basically pivot on my butt. I feel like a gymnast—without the strength, the body, or the audience. Once my left leg is safely turned the other way on the sofa, I put my right leg onto the ground and help maneuver myself into something resembling a comfortable position. Now, instead of staring at the wall, I stare out the floor-to-ceiling windows, high above the city and the river. The sky is crystal clear and very blue and I get a tiny little smile on my face because I feel like a human being again, kind of. I sigh, realizing this is the beginning of a very long road to getting my leg working again.

Just as I am somewhat comfortable on the sofa and absolutely drop-dead exhausted, the concierge buzzes the apartment. Oh my god! There is no way I'm going to be able to get from the sofa into the wheelchair and over to the little telephone that connects me to the concierge. The concierge saw me in my wheelchair and saw Brent leave, so she'll probably ask whomever it is to wait. I manage to get to the door in my wheelchair ten minutes later and at that very moment someone rings the bell. Jesus Christ! I reach out to unlock it and say "Come in," really not caring who it is. Much to my shock, in walks my mother.

When my mother is in caretaker mode, there is nobody better. She is loving, understanding, and incredibly efficient in every way. However, I never thought that at 27 years old I'd be happy to have my mother taking care of me for a week. Brent is most likely thrilled, since it means he won't have to do it himself full-time. I'm not exactly pleasant to be around right now. I'm trying. I force myself to make little jokes, but it's just a mask. Inside, I'm bitter that I have to go through this and I'm still in a lot of pain and still scared something will go wrong. I don't trust that the surgery worked. In my head, every pulse of pain means that something is going wrong and nobody will believe me. So, I don't say anything. I am

Mom and Jack

completely helpless, which is beyond upsetting for a control freak.

I had no idea mom was coming this soon, as in 30 minutes after I got home. I have absolutely no strength right now, so I can't even back away from the door to let her in. I tell her this and she pushes me backward, grabs her suitcase, and lets the door slam behind her. She leans over to give me a hug and I say, scared at someone getting this physically close to me right now, "Don't! Careful! Don't touch my leg!" The words shoot out of me like a machine-gun and we are both startled. I see tears forming in her eyes as she looks down at me and she quickly walks past me into the living room. She thinks I didn't notice. She should know better. I notice everything. Always. About everyone and everything.

A moment later, she is pulling my wheelchair from behind and asks me where I want to be. I tell her that I have to make the journey from wheelchair to sofa again. This time I have help, although I am absolutely insistent that she not touch my leg. I don't notice, however, that she has put one hand underneath my leg as I try to lift it to the sofa. My moment of strength ceases and my leg almost falls to the floor. I yelp. She supports it with the one hand she held there—just in case—and lifts it carefully onto the sofa. I stare at her for a moment. She smiles softly at me. I completely lose it and start bawling. She tucks herself onto the sofa next to me and holds my head in her lap. I feel like I'm 10 years old. Even through the pain and fear, I love this feeling. It only took that one gentle moment—the simple act of knowing that she might have to catch my leg even though I insisted that I would do it myself—to make all the fear go away and all the emotion rush to the surface. I am weak. I am small. I am in pain. I am scared. But my mom's here.

In half an hour, she has called somewhere to rent me a wheelchair since the one I have has to go back to the hospital in the morning. She has made a list of groceries to get. Strange, since my mother does not cook. She's an excellent cook; she just hates it. Besides, who buys groceries in Manhattan?

That night my mom sleeps on the sofa bed and Brent and I sleep together in our bedroom for the first time in a week. Brent has a tendency to move around when he sleeps. He generally starts way over on his side of the bed and by the middle of the night he has spread himself out to take up most of the bed. Sometimes I push him over since he sleeps so soundly. Other times I don't do anything because I feel guilty that I have such a hard time sleeping. My sleep psychosis is not his fault. Nonetheless, I am very scared that he will kick my leg. There is no way in hell I'm going to get to sleep. I cannot sleep on my back. I cannot sleep without being able to toss and turn. How on earth am I going to sleep with this pain?

It takes us half an hour to maneuver my leg into a position on four pillows, but it doesn't work. My leg is too precarious up there and moves from side to side, which is agonizing. We try three. Same thing. Then we try three and add two underneath my knee. I think I can stay that way. Even the slightest movement is agonizing. Brent is silent the whole time. I am irritated because he has been gone all day, but I also know that this cannot be easy on him. I tell myself to shut up, which is a rare thing for me to do. Brent crawls into bed and curls up as close to the edge of his side of the bed as he can without falling off. He doesn't say goodnight.

I reach carefully over to the nightstand and open the bottle of Vicodin. I pour one into my hand. I look at the white oval horse pill. Then I add another. The hell with it: I take four. If one is good, four must be better. I pick up my book, Judith Krantz's *Scruples.* I need something completely brainless and fun. I usually read a few books at one time, depending on my mood. Along with the Krantz novel on my nightstand is Plato's *Republic*. I love that I am a contradiction in terms. Makes me feel very superior, even with my bag of bones and metal as a leg.

I don't sleep all night. I am drowsy and light-headed because of the Vicodin. I read. I lie back to doze off. I read again. I take four more Vicodin. I look at the label. "Take one every 3-4 hours for pain, not to exceed four pills in a 12-hour period." Well, how nice that the pharmacy gods think that'll do it. I've just exceeded my 12-hour allotment in 5 hours. I really don't give a shit. I love my pills. They are my happiness right now. I am very frustrated that I can't sleep; several times I almost cry from frustration—the kind of crying that means some kind of emotion needs to come out that can't be expressed in words. If I wake Brent to talk and tell him how upset I am, will I feel better? I don't because I know I won't.

An hour later, after finally getting into my novel, after taking eight Vicodin (which still doesn't put me to sleep), I have to go pee. I picture having to get out of bed, using my crutches instead of the wheelchair, making it to the bathroom, and somehow hovering over the toilet to pee. This will be impossible without help. But there are some indignities that I have to draw the line at. I flash back to peeing into the bottle in the hospital, but there is no bottle to be found. I manage to get onto my crutches and stand next to the bed. My side of the bed is by the windows; Brent's is against the wall of mirrored closets on the other side of the room. I like to wake up looking out onto the city. The downside of this choice/demand is that, due to my sleep neurosis, I wear a sleep mask to cut out even the smallest amount of light. I've yet to find a sleep mask that can cut the reflection of the morning sun off the East River, and I've yet to find anyone who has any sympathy for my plight in this regard.

By the time I have slithered out of bed and climbed up onto my crutches, terrified that my leg might actually touch the ground, I am out of breath. I then maneuver quietly and carefully around the foot of the bed to the other side of the room to the door to the hallway. Brent murmurs, "Are you okay?"

"Oh sure," I think. "I'm high as a kite and still hurting and am sure they did something wrong in the surgery and despite not having drunk anything my tiny bladder seems to require emptying and the last time I had to consider how to use the bathroom was probably twenty-two years ago." I don't say anything out loud. He falls blissfully back asleep. Brent sleeps like a log. How on earth do people simply end their day calmly, go to bed, drift off to sleep and wake up refreshed in the morning? I sincerely cannot comprehend that happening to me. At some point, people will realize that insomnia is the new sleep. They just haven't caught up to the trend.

I manage to make it into the bathroom and shut the door. It's a damn good thing this is a normal size bathroom and not the usual Manhattan apartment-size bathroom in which there would be room for maybe my huge cast and that's about it. I end up semi-straddling the toilet. I am standing directly over it, hovering on my crutches. I have managed to lift my bad leg and wedge it in between the toilet bowl and the crutch. I am using all my strength to make sure it stays there. The leg is completely unstable since it is still just bones and metal. If I drop the leg onto the floor, I will need another surgery. So, while trying to make sure the bad leg is in place, I lift up my other foot and put it directly on the rim of the toilet. Now, I am completely balanced, hovering above the toilet. And I am exhausted. And high. And really irri-fucking-tated.

With the hand that isn't holding the crutch against the wedged cast, I push down my sweatpants. Then, with one hand, I try both to maneuver my penis out of the sweatpants and hold the elastic back. If I'm not careful, I will not only pee on the rim of the toilet seat, but I will also pee on my sweatpants. I'd be laughing my ass off if this was happening to someone else. There is only one other thing for which I will expend this much effort at maneuvering my penis and this is about as far from that as you can get.

I end up peeing in the bowl, not on myself. I also end up not smashing my leg on anything while steering my way back to bed. I lie back, take two Vicodin, decide to drink a lot less water no matter how many people tell me I need to "hydrate" because it is not worth it. Before I drift off a little, I decide that tomorrow I'm going to ask someone to buy me some Depends.

CHAPTER 3

Babba and the Phantom

MOM HAS BEEN GONE FOR two days. Strangely, I miss her. I don't think you're supposed to want your mom around for more than three days anytime after you're 22. Guess it takes shattering a leg to be more patient. I'm lying in bed, reading another Judith Krantz novel, and the sun is streaming through the floor-to-ceiling windows in my bedroom. The last thing I need is to be sweating inside my cast. The second last thing I need, however, is to get out of bed and turn the air conditioning on. This is the poor design of the apartment. It's probably 40 degrees outside, but because of the sun and the windows, it is roasting in here.

The other reason I don't want to move is because I switched from Vicodin to Tylenol this morning, thinking I could handle it.

Babba and Jack

Apparently, I can't. My leg has gone from its usual severe ache to an ache with shooting pains that make it feel like it's going to pop the cast open and swell up. It's almost unbearable and I am so frustrated. Not only can I not move around, but I can't tolerate this pain without tons of narcotics. Maybe I need something stronger than Vicodin. Too bad I'm one of the few freakish people who have never ever done street drugs. At least then I'd have a source. I could call some high class drug dealer to the apartment, give him my ATM card and code, and get whatever I'd want. Instead, I get to lie here in this heat feeling frustrated. At least if I could move around, I could handle this with a little more elegance. At least the Vicodin bottle and some water are on the nightstand next to me. I take three at once and decide to deal with the heat until the pain subsides. The doctor told me to always stay ahead of the pain. Guess this is what he meant.

Babba arrives this evening. At 80 years old, she has told me she will fly here from California for a week and look after me. I am thrilled. The idea of having my grandmother here delights me. She won't fawn, but she'll cook a lot of food and she'll make me laugh. I need to laugh. And she'll insulate me from Brent's coolness. I know he isn't cold. I know he cares. It's just the clinical thing about being a doctor. He doesn't leave it at work. Sometimes I feel like being babied. I'm embarrassed to actually say what I need out loud. In fact, I'm embarrassed that I need anything at all. I'm Jack. I'm always fine.

Brent is getting his coat and scarf on, getting ready to go pick up Babba at the airport. "Wait, I'm not ready," I say. He looks at me like I've grown an additional head.

"You can't go."

"I'm going."

He rolls his eyes at me and says, "You're in pain and you can only travel by wheelchair."

"I'm going."

He relents, knowing there is absolutely no point in fighting with me when it comes to Babba.

Forty-five minutes and six Vicodin later (albeit with a glass of milk, since I've decided I want to keep my stomach lining), we're in the car. The wheelchair has been folded up and put in the trunk and I'm sitting in the backseat with my back against one door and my leg flat in front of me. Driving as fast as possible in the Lincoln Tunnel, Brent asks me which airport. I'm a little woozy from the Vicodin, but it was the only way I could get my ass into the car, and there was no way my Babba, at 80, was traveling 3,000 miles and not have me meet her at the airport.

I notice that we are on our way to La Guardia. She isn't coming into La Guardia. She's coming into JFK. I tell this to Brent, frantically, since we are already going to barely make it in time for her flight to arrive and I don't want her sitting alone in the terminal.

"Jack. I asked you and you said La Guardia."

"I did not."

"Yes, you did."

"I did not. I said JFK."

He laughs. "Jack, you are so high on Vicodin that you don't remember."

I find no humor in this situation and his amusement annoys me even more. "I know I said JFK!" I snap.

He doesn't reply. Instead, he drives faster and we end up passing La Guardia on the way. In silence, I consider that maybe I did make a mistake and tell him La Guardia. It's possible. This morning after I managed to turn on the air conditioning, I called the doorman and asked him to bring me a bagel. Twice. I don't say anything to Brent to admit that maybe I made a mistake because I think he'll be smug. I don't like smug. Especially when it's aimed at me. And especially when it comes from Brent, who is really fabulously good at it.

I gave very, very specific instructions to Babba about where to go to get my prescription refill for Vicodin and where to get my bagel and iced coffee. Life support, at the moment. The sun is streaming through the window and I've propped myself up on the sofa and the sun is directly on my cast, making my leg sweat inside. I can only imagine the smell. Fetid skin held together by the cast and stitches. Gross. But I'm too tired to move and I ran out of Vicodin, so it's aching badly. I have a piece of paper and I'm writing directions down and drawing something resembling a map. I'm being as specific as possible because I imagine Babba ending up somewhere in Brooklyn or the Bronx. I don't want her to go out alone in the big, bad city. She insists. She is here to help me. And I need to let her. I also vowed a long, long time ago to treat her like an adult. Funny how we start treating old people like children.

Off Babba goes. I wonder how long it will be until she gets back. As soon as the door shuts, I regret not giving her my cell phone, although she wouldn't know how to use it anyway. I'm feeling self-indulgent for sitting around doing nothing while Babba takes care of me. As I get hungry and more in pain and more sweaty in the sun, I pivot myself to the edge of the sofa and grab my crutches. I hobble into the kitchen and grab the telephone and my wallet. I phone telecharge and get two tickets for this evening's performance of *Phantom of the Opera*. I tell them that I'm in a wheelchair; they have accommodations—a space in the orchestra very close to the stage for my wheelchair with a seat right next to it for Babba. And the tickets are only $15 instead of the usual $105. I get the tickets and feel desperately guilty. What if I am taking the seat away from someone who really needs it? I know I'm in a wheelchair, but for me it's only temporary. What about all the people for which it's a permanent state of living? What if someone out there wanted to see *Phantom* tonight and I took the handicapped seat? But the guilt doesn't stop me from getting the seats. I'm in a wheelchair. My grandmother is here from L.A. I want to do this for her.

I am always like this. I never feel like the little stuff is good enough to say thanks. A small part of me knows she doesn't need or want thanks. She doesn't like expressions of gratitude. Does she feel, for some reason, she *owes* the goodness she gives? I could just as well get her a nice card and write something heartfelt and thoughtful on it. But that's not how I think; I think in grand terms. Only the big stuff is happy.

An hour later, I am frantic. Duane Reade is only a block away. The bagel place is only a block away from that. And they are both on Third Avenue! She hasn't called. I made her keep a piece of paper in her pocket with the address and phone number. I told her to grab a cab and say "32nd and 3rd" if she gets lost. She's not only stubborn, she's independent to a fault. Guess It's genetic. I pivot off the sofa and start settling up my wheelchair and just as I and my now-really-hurting leg hop into the chair, the door opens and Babba comes in . . . with grocery bags? She went to D'Agostino's? She tells me I'm nuts when I tell her I was about to go find her. She points out that I'd just be wheeling myself up and down the street. I point out that she was probably wandering around and I'd see her or she would see me. A 27-year-old in a wheelchair with a cast as big as my waist is hard to miss.

When I tell her I got *Phantom of the Opera* tickets for tonight, she tells me she doesn't want to go with Brent and leave me home alone. Oops. When I tell her it's me she is going with, she looks at me like I have two heads. "How on earth are you supposed to go to a theatre?"

"Babba, people in wheelchairs do get to leave the house!"

"It is snowing outside and it's freezing!" I ask her to give me my Vicodin. I dig into the plastic bag full of my accoutrements to get a bottle of water and take four tablets. Followed by my huge iced coffee. Twenty minutes later I have a very nice buzz going and the idea of going to the theatre is even more appealing. *Phantom* is such a lavish musical. Babba will love the spectacle. I am telling myself that I am doing this for her, but I know that I'm also doing it to prove that my life is still my life.

When Brent comes home, he doesn't seem enthusiastic about us going to the theater. I tell him I didn't get him tickets because I know he doesn't like *Phantom*. He agrees and makes negative comments about it in front of Babba, which I find totally unnecessary. I would like him to be excited for us that we're going and that I actually want to venture out, but Brent rarely shows any excitement even when he is excited. Somewhere inside I know that this is not unusual behavior for me—to do something that nobody else in my "condition" would do.

The show is at 8. By 7 p.m., I am in my wheelchair, wearing huge baggy sweatpants that are cut off at the knee above the cast on my left leg. I wear my huge ratty NYU Law School sweatshirt with the hood and one dirty white tennis shoe on my right foot. I am the epitome of style. I usually wouldn't walk down the street like this, let alone go to the theatre. I do not wear sweatpants, except as jammies when I'm curled up on the couch. But I am not staying home tonight and my couch curling days are probably months and months away. We try to stretch a sock over my exposed toes. The circulation in that foot is still shitty and my toes are cold even at home, let alone out in the freezing night air. I have popped four Vicodin with a glass of milk. I hate milk. I also stick eight more Vicodin in the pocket of my sweatshirt.

Once we are downstairs, Babba holds the umbrella over me and hails a cab. It takes us ten minutes to get into the cab: five to get me off the wheelchair and spread out in the backseat, four for the cabbie to fold down the wheelchair, and one for Babba to get situated into the front seat. It doesn't seem right that anyone should ride in the front seat of the cab. I tell the cabbie where we're going and he pauses. He looks back at me, then to Babba, an 80-year-old woman with gigantic hair, and squints his eyes. He probably thinks we're insane.

Being handicapped in the theatre definitely has its advantages. We do not wait in line. The crowd spreads out as I wheel my way into the theatre. I am hoping my arms are going to get muscled from all this wheeling around. My shoulders especially need some work. Even I roll my eyes at myself for being so concerned with my muscles while one leg is withering away in a cast. Our seats, or rather Babba's seat and my space, are, I am delighted to see, about six rows from the stage. This is spectacular because the musical is so visual. I am thrilled for Babba. I have already seen *Phantom* about seven times since everyone who comes to visit wants to see either this or *Les Miserables*. In my self-adulated congratulations, plus two more Vicodin, that I have gotten myself out of the house in a wheelchair a mere three weeks after having metal inserted into my shattered leg, I'm pretty thrilled to be here. I know Babba will love it. The lights dim. Everyone quiets down to a silence that still shocks me when there are a thousand people in one place. The curtain goes up. I look at Babba. She is already entranced. Her dark eyes are gleaming, reflecting the light coming off the stage. This, for me, is the first feeling of peace since my surgery. Love will do that.

At intermission, she gets up and I figure she wants to go to the bathroom or get a drink or something. I, of course, stay where I am. There is no way in hell I'm wheeling myself through a crowd again, no matter how quickly they make a path. "Jackie, that was amazing! I had no idea!"

I am, again, thrilled. She stays standing. "Are you going to get a drink or go to the bathroom?" I ask.

"Aren't we leaving?"

I start to laugh. "Babba, it's intermission! There's almost two more hours!"

She huffs and says, "Well! I thought it ended kind of strangely!" To which we have a huge, hysterical laugh—the kind of laugh Babba and I have had as long as I can remember. At ourselves. At each other. The best kind. Our own little world of silliness and I love it. Again the lights dim and her eyes gleam and I am thrilled. I also take two more Vicodin.

We are outside and it is snowing. I do not know what I was thinking. Of course, there are no cabs to be found. They are all out in Times Square and everyone right in front of the theater is taking town cars from a car service. They were smart. Not even handicapped. I used to run and find a cab, which is clearly not possible at the moment. My toes are freezing. People are coming by and commenting. They try to get cabs. Babba tells me she will walk a block to Times Square. I absolutely forbid her from doing this. I'd rather have my cast soaked and my toes frostbitten than have her running around Times Square at 11:30 at night. Eventually I give up and call a car service. Twenty minutes later we're in a town car, on our way home. I am absolutely exhausted. Every muscle in my body aches despite my vast consumption of Vicodin and I want to crawl into bed and fall asleep. Babba is thrilled that we went, however, so that keeps me going.

In bed, Brent is already asleep. I try to arrange my leg up on the pillows and finally give up. There is no way I can do it alone and I don't feel like waking him up and dealing with his frustration at how long it takes to get me comfortable. I pick up my copy of *Scruples* and figure I'll read until the four more Vicodin I took begin to make me drowsy.

I am still in my wheelchair, yet insistent that I can maneuver the streets of Manhattan myself. Brent is at work. Mom is gone. Babba is gone. It's actually a pretty nice day. Despite the fact that my leg aches, I can't move around very well, and I hardly slept, as usual, but I feel okay. I call the doorman and ask if he'll go down the street and get me a toasted poppy seed bagel with cream cheese and a large iced coffee. He asks, "Ice?" I reply, "Yes."

Pause. "Mr. Freedman, it's about 40 degrees outside."

"I know. I just can't drink hot drinks."

Thirty minutes later he rings the doorbell outside the apartment. I shout to the door, "Do you have your master key?" Seconds later he is in my kitchen, putting the bags on my counter. "Sorry I can't get up. Would you please take $20 out of my wallet? It's on the table in the entryway." He obliges without saying anything. That's the strange thing about disabilities or sickness: the nicest, kindest people suddenly become mute. Since they don't know what to say, they say nothing at all. Being ill is very lonely. Actually, being ill is fine. It's the getting better, that middle-ground, that is lonely.

After "I love Lucy," after a rerun of "Oprah," after my bagel and cream cheese and halfway through my iced coffee, the phone rings. The handset is next to me. It's Lisa. Lisa is the attorney who was hired about two weeks before I decided to smash my leg to smithereens. I saw all the people who interviewed for the job. She was the most attractive and I knew she would be hired. That's how the senior partner in charge of entertainment was: he hired only attractive people. Afterwards, I saw her resume and realized she went to better schools than I did, had a more impressive major, lived in France for a year, etc. She had the brains and the experience to match the looks. Brilliant, poised, smart, and hysterical. Still, Steven wouldn't have hired her if she wasn't attractive.

End of December, beginning of January is a very busy time for independent films. Mostly because the Toronto Film Festival is at that time. Everybody flocks there to try to find the next *Crying Game* or *Sling Blade* or *Pulp Fiction*. If there is a very desirable film, a bidding war starts that drives up the price of acquisition of the film. The film ends up getting acquired for a large, up-front fee. The buyer first recoups the up-front fee and then the profits, if any, start getting paid to the filmmaker. It's very hectic. Lots of screenings. Lots of ego. Lots of competition. Lots of alcohol. Lots of debauchery. I was not invited to go. Neither was Lisa. The idea was that Lisa and I would be left behind to take care of existing clients—their deals, their legal issues, their movies, etc. Instead, because of my leg, Lisa, two weeks into the job and without any entertainment experience, was left totally alone, and the senior partner expected her to function perfectly well.

"Hi. Are you okay?" she asks slowly.

"Well, yes, aside from the agony, fear that metal will fly out of my leg, being in a wheelchair, and having the bad hair day of all bad hair days, I'm fabulous," I say friendly and sarcastic all at once.

She laughs. Thank goodness. Sympathy laughter is the best kind.

"Well, I hate to tell you this, but Steven wants you to come in."

"Come in where?" I say, already knowing the answer.

"Here. To the office."

I am not even stunned because this is how it is with lawyers in NYC. Absolutely nothing is supposed to get in the way of doing work and billing hours. Aside from death.

"Does he know I'm in a wheelchair and eating Vicodin like it's candy?"

"I don't think he cares. They bought a movie in Toronto and I can't do the deal by myself and he says you need to come in." She pauses. "I'm really sorry."

"No, it's okay. I'll manage." I hate him, but I want to help her. It's not her fault he's an ass.

It takes me an hour to get showered since I have to wrap the cast in saran wrap and hold it outside of the shower while I sit on an upside down plastic garbage can. The cast cannot get wet. I don't even deal with my hair. It is sticking up everywhere and not the way I like with gel. I have the worst hair. It's course and kind of wavy and puffy. It's a testament to my vanity that I'm in a wheelchair popping Vicodin and I actually care about my hair. I struggle into my sweatpants and put on a sweatshirt and my black leather jacket. I wear one black Doc Marten on the good foot. My left foot with the cast has my toes sticking out. Just barely. Little piggies going to hell. I try to stick a sock on them, but I have to bend straight over from my waist and I am not that limber. I don't, apparently, have enough sex. I decide to leave them bare. By now, I am sweating like a pig, completely uncomfortable and absolutely desperate to get outside. I manage to open the door and do a "1, 2, 3!" to get over the doorjamb and take huge, gasping breaths all the way into the elevator. I'm already exhausted.

The concierge and doorman seemed surprised to see me, but they smile and ask if they can help, can they get a cab. I tell them I'm going to get there myself. The office is on Park Avenue, two blocks away. It's January in NYC and I'm going to wheel myself to work. This is your brain. This is your brain on Vicodin.

I am wheeling myself to work down Park Avenue and people are staring at me. I get across streets. Across grates. Around people. I am crossing a street and I get to the other side. The sidewalk ramp is steep and I start to roll up it and begin to fall backwards. I am about to fall directly backwards onto my head and a little old lady catches me. I thank her profusely as she walks away without a word. A little old lady just saved me. Life is getting stranger by the moment.

I am wheeling myself into the hallway, saying nothing to anyone because I am in the darkest mood possible. I will have to kill anyone who comes near me. Death by wheelchair. I pass Lisa's office and pause, looking in. She looks really, really guilty.

"It's not your fault. Don't worry about it," I say.

I continue to wheel toward my office, which is right next to hers. We share a common wall. I hear her say, as I'm wheeling away, "How are you?"

"Constipated," I shout as loudly as possible, hoping to mortify absolutely everyone in the office. "How are you?" I yell.

"Bloated!" she yells back, since I'm in my office by now.

I love her at once.

Later, she's in my office and we're going over some things. She's drinking huge amounts of coffee and I'm popping huge amounts of Vicodin. We are very *Valley of the Dolls*. It's amazing my stomach lining exists after three weeks of this. I'm already convinced I have no liver. Just something like a coffee filter down there.

"So, you know I'm gay, right?"

"Yes."

"Obvious?" Not that I really care after seven years of being out of the closet and two years into a relationship with Brent.

"Not especially, but to me, yes."

"How so?"

"Because you told me you liked the periwinkle suit I wore on my interview."

"So?"

"Straight guys don't say periwinkle."

I laugh. Hard. For the first time all week.

CHAPTER 4

The Heart Thing

It seems that every now and then I am suddenly reminded of what I have come to call the "Heart Thing." I can't seem to call it a "heart problem." Just, the "Thing."

Brent and I have gotten tickets to see a new production by William Finn called *A New Brain*. In the taxi on the way to Lincoln Center, I ask Brent if he knows what it's about. He doesn't. Neither do I. We assume we'll like it because we like William Finn's other stuff. We have also heard good things about one of the actresses in the show, Kristin Chenoweth. This is before she won her Tony for *Charlie Brown*, before *Wicked* and before "West Wing." When the lights dim and then go to black, I feel like I am all alone. Not in a bad way, more like I am suddenly in my own little world and it never matters whom I'm with or if I've actually come alone.

Some of the music is really good. Most of it is average. Like other William Finn stuff, in my opinion. All the actors are reasonably good, but nobody stunning, except Kristin Chenoweth, who is really good; there is something very unique about her. Later, when she becomes well known, I am pleased that I could notice the difference between talent and star power.

The story is about a gay couple, and one has a stroke. They fear death. He has to choose to have an operation on his brain; he may or may not live, become a vegetable, get worse, or be cured. While all this is happening, the songs are about hope and the broader meaning of life and how things change very fast when you are least expecting it. I am in silent tears almost the whole time. I feel like I am looking at a story about myself and am amazed at the similarities. When the lights go on and the applause are over and people get up to leave the theater, I am still sitting in my seat. Brent asks if I'm okay and I say, "That hit a little close to home." I am trying to hold back the tears. I tell myself I'm being dramatic about the whole "heart thing." It's a lot easier to tell myself I'm being dramatic than to tell myself I'm legitimately scared. I'm 27 and a half. There are two and a half years until I'm 30. An eternity, right? I'm sure that my fear has nothing to do with my impending cardiologist appointment next week.

Two nights later, Eric and I are having dinner together. Eighteenth & Eighth is very, very crowded tonight. It's a tiny restaurant in the heart of Chelsea. Very gay. The whole place is the size of a medium living room. Maybe 15 tables and a few banquettes against the walls. It's warm and soft and louder than you'd assume given that it's such a small space. But the boys are packed in here every night because it's a "place to be" and the food is really yummy.

When I was at NYU, I used to walk here in the evenings and have dinner by myself. I'd write in my journal and have a chicken Caesar salad or pasta and a vodka cranberry. I loved the feeling of walking the few blocks from 5th and 17th to 18th and 8th in the freezing winter cold. Watching the lights on in all the buildings, wondering who lived there and what the apartments looked like inside. I had these Jack-boots that made me feel so tough. A thick green sweater I wore constantly with a black turtleneck. My black leather jacket that wasn't nearly warm enough for the cold Manhattan winter, a light grey, very thick, wool scarf that I'd wind around my throat and pull up over my mouth, and very unfashionable ski gloves. By the time I'd get to Eighteenth & Eighth, I would be absolutely freezing. I'd open the door and step inside to laughter and warmth. I loved everything about it. I loved that I ate alone. That I was walking around Manhattan at night in winter. That I lived in my own little world that didn't feel the least bit lonely.

That's the thing about Manhattan: It lets you be totally alone without making you think that you're supposed to feel lonely.

Years later, I've traded my vodka cranberries for vodka martinis. I've traded my I'm-so-innocent look for I'm-pretending-I-don't-know-you're-looking-at me look. I have not, however, traded Eric for anything. I am wearing my "boot" since my leg is in the last stages of healing. It's bulky and unfashionable and gets me a lot of sympathetic attention. Of course, I love it. When I walk through the door, Steve rushes over to hug me. Steve is the host. He has caramel skin and bright green eyes and I find him gorgeous, although I have never done anything about it and I don't think he is attracted to me. I can usually tell.

I've known Steve since he used to be so nice to me when I'd come in by myself to write in my journal, have my drink, and eat my dinner by myself. Pre-Eric. Pre-Brent. Pre-Leg Surgery. As it turns out, Eric has known Steve since he was a waiter at one of the uppity restaurants on the Upper East Side. Ed, who owns Eighteenth & Eighth, is also friends with Eric, although I never could figure out how. Ed was also a waiter at one of the restaurants Eric probably loved/terrorized/supported. Ed is a very attractive Asian man and Eric and I have a constant game of guessing his age. It's impossible to tell. I thought he was 30 and Eric says he's at least 45. Not plastic surgery. Just genetics, I guess. The other mainstay in this restaurant is Yvonne. Yvonne is quite a force. She is Caribbean and speaks with an island accent that is both frightening and alluring at the same time. You want her to wrap you up in her voice. I think she used to own the restaurant on the Upper East Side that Ed and Steve used to work at, but as usual with Eric's stories, I'm never quite clear. Eric tells stories of her having cash fly out of her handbag and lunches with Oprah and Cicely Tyson. And now, according to Eric, "She is just down-and-out girl!" She cooks the most delicious food.

Steve gives me the best table, which is actually a corner banquette. Eric isn't here yet, so I order three martinis. One for me. Two for Eric. He likes to have a liquid appetizer to his liquid. When I started coming here with Eric, I knew that Ed, Steve, and Yvonne thought I was some random sugar boy. Not that they were fake. I could just see it in their faces. Eric always has a cute young boy, and it didn't help that Eric always paid. I would offer and he would refuse. Every time. Eric and I had a talk about this a few weeks after we met. I told him I was uncomfortable with it. He told me that he wasn't going to change the kinds of things he liked to do and the kinds of places he liked to go and knew that I didn't have the money for them. So we agreed that as long as we were doing something together, he could pay. But he was never allowed to buy me a present. Too many people were around him for his money; I didn't want to be in the same category. The second night we had dinner, here at Eighteenth & Eighth actually, he told me, "That leather coat is too old and not warm enough. Why are you wearing it?"

"Well, it's all I have right now." Eric immediately offered to take me to Bergdorf's in the morning and buy me a winter coat. I refused immediately. Adamantly. There was, though, a part of me that wanted to do just that. Go to Bergdorf's, try on extraordinarily expensive winter clothes, and have them bought for me simply because I smile nicely. But the other part of me wanted Eric's genuine friendship. We both liked to tell the "winter coat" story in later years.

Two hot guys at the table next to me smirk when Steve brings me three martinis. I look at them and say, droll, "Sometimes you just can't be drunk fast enough." They laugh. The front door opens and Eric walks through the door, pulling apart the dark purple velvet curtains protecting the restaurant from the wind outside. He likes to give people a moment to take him in. He cultivates the fact that he is quite a vision. At 6' 2" tall, with thick black hair and a full-length black sable coat, he's hard to miss. He has that look of, "Who is that?" He knows it. And he loves it. And he teaches it to me very well. I'll get to be an expert shortly.

Steve hugs him, takes his sable, and points me out. I see people looking at him. It's hard to miss a 6' 2" man in a sable coat in a small restaurant. He ignores the looks, comes over to sit next to me, kisses me on the cheek and says, "Thank GOD you ordered me a drink. I haven't had a thing to drink since I left my apartment! I'm parched!"

"When did you leave the apartment?"

In between his first and second gulp, he says, "At least 20 minutes ago, dear!"

We banter about everything and everybody and eat half of our dinners and each have four or five martinis and are stunningly still not too much more than very tipsy. I put down my last glass. One of the hot Latin busboys takes our dishes away and Steve drops by and tells us that he'd like to "buy" us dessert. We're charmed even though we're used to it. Then, I decide to tell Eric about my "heart thing."

"Eric, I have to talk to you about something."

"The answers are, 'Yes, but we still have work to do' and 'No, absolutely not!'" he says instantly.

I laugh. "Okay, then, what are the questions?" Playing along.

"Your first question was 'Eric, am I fabulous?' and your second question was 'Eric, should I hit on the busboy?'"

He takes a sip and I just keep laughing.

"And why shouldn't I hit on the busboy? *Quel* snob!"

"Jackie-sue, I am not a snob. I don't care if somebody is a ditch digger as long as they're nice and interesting."

"Then, not that I want to, why shouldn't I hit on the busboy?"

"Because he's wearing a ring." Eric gives me his withering over-the-edge-of-the-martini-glass look.

"Eric, seriously, I have to talk to you about something. I found something out in the hospital."

He puts down his glass. Even when he and I are being serious, which is more often than people suspect, we don't let ourselves sound serious.

"I have to have an operation on my heart sometime in the next few years," I say.

Once I hear myself say the words out loud, in public, I'm not sure which of us is more stunned.

He doesn't pick up his glass. He doesn't look around the restaurant. He doesn't sit back in his chair. He doesn't move a muscle and he doesn't take his eyes off me. But his lips disappear. When Eric is really pissed about something, his lips disappear.

Very slowly he says, "What. The. Fuck. Does that mean?"

"Well, you know all my tachycardia attacks . . ." I start. My last one was three weeks ago. We were having brunch at Le Relais high on Madison Avenue and I had one, so I had to lie down next to our table. Eric, never embarrassed by anything, said, "This is Jack! He's having a heart thing, but he's fine! He actually admits to having one, unlike myself!" The room laughed. I was amused and shot him a look pretending I wasn't, as usual.

I continue, "One of the valves is bad and it's getting worse and they are going to have to replace it."

"When?" His lips are still gone.

"Probably about three years from now."

His lips reappear. But he still hasn't moved and he still hasn't taken his eyes off me. And, more telling, he still hasn't reached for what remains of his martini.

"When did you find out?"

"In the hospital just after my leg surgery."

He doesn't ask why I didn't tell him. He has a way of knowing exactly what matters. And that doesn't. "Open heart surgery?" He asks just to make sure.

"Yes."

Now he takes a sip. Looks around the room. Takes another sip. His lips disappear again.

"We are going to get you the best fuckin' doctors in the world. I don't care if we have to build you a hospital. We're going to . . ."

I cut him off, softly, "Eric, stop."

And he does. He gets up and goes back toward the bathrooms, looking straight ahead above everyone's heads, brushing by Steve.

Steve comes over, "Are you two okay?"

"Uh, yes. Why?"

"Well, you looked like you were fighting," he says.

"Oh. That. No, we aren't fighting. I promise."

Steve looks reassured. He asks, smiling, "Okay then, for dessert?"

"*Hmmmm*, I think we'll share that chocolate-pudding-mousse-cake-brownie thing we usually get."

Ten minutes later, Eric comes out of the bathroom and does the I'm-not-seeing-any-of-you thing and sits down. His eyes are bloodshot and the skin around them is red. He's been crying and rubbing his eyes in the bathroom. I don't say anything because there's nothing really to say, and Eric and I only waste words when we're bantering. Not when we're being serious. He looks up at me. I still haven't moved. His eyes look up for a second and his brows squish together and he looks to the side and then back at me and says, "Jack, I can't lose you."

"You're not going to. I'm going to be fine."

But that's not how I feel. Not at all. Unfortunately, this is not where I begin to slowly accept the heart thing. It's where I begin to slowly start to deny that it will affect me.

CHAPTER 5

Laughing with Lisa

THE MOMENT I WALK INTO work, there are five messages, all from the same producer, and my boss wants to see me. I take a peek into Lisa's office and tell her, "Coffee needing." She looks up and nods her head. Five minutes later we're at the deli up Park Avenue South getting the usual disgusting burned coffee that is all over Manhattan at all the little delis. God knows why we drink it when there seems to be a Starbucks on every block.

"Let's ditch work this afternoon," I say.

She laughs, "Oh, like we're in high school."

Lisa and Jack

"No, if this were high school, I would be ditching the whole day going skiing."

"Fine, where?" she says without a moment's hesitation. We're both alarmingly decisive when figuring out ways to avoid the law firm.

"Balthazar for a late lunch and then let's roam around Soho and buy clothes and things we can't afford and don't need."

"Oh," she laughs, "you mean be our usual fabulous selves acting like trust fund babies."

"Yes, I'm sure we were supposed to be trust fund babies. Something must have gone horribly awry when we were born. We're lawyers because we want to pretend like we're part of the working class."

"Without the work part."

"Exactly. We frown upon work."

"We spit upon it."

I laugh.

"When this afternoon?" she asks.

"Two. I have a cardiology appointment at one."

We both pause, look at each other, and then down into our cups of coffee. Even though she knows that something is going on with me and my heart, we're not really close enough yet to discuss much more than how fabulous we are.

At 1:15, I am at the cardiologist's office on Park Avenue. I am lying on my left side with my shirt off and my right arm over my head. The doctor has spread some gel on my chest and is doing an echocardiogram to take a little look at my heart. I can't see the screen, but I can hear the sounds—a rhythmic whooshing. Almost like breathy windshield wipers. Back and forth, but slower. *Whoosh* in. *Whoosh* out. I am told to breathe normally. Then I am told to take a deep breath and hold it in. Then I am told to breathe normally again. Then I am told to breathe out forcefully and hold. By the time we are done, I am completely out of breath. He wipes the goo off my chest and attaches electrodes to take an EKG.

In a way, I feel good that I'm having this done because it's worse to sit at home and be scared. I don't know if it's worse to be scared of what *is* or what *might be.* Later in this game, I'll find out that what "is" is, in fact, pretty scary. I don't realize at the time that this is the beginning of three years' worth of cardiologist visits, each of which will get worse and worse. And with each, I will go more and more into denial. I will either be totally in denial or suddenly in quiet tears with little in between. Wrecked or fabulous. Balance has never ever been my strong point.

The cardiologist is a stereotype of the doctor with no bedside manner. He tells me that my valve is leaking and the electrical system in my heart is fucked; he says this as if he's telling me I have a cold. He tells me the valve will need to be replaced and he thinks that the surgeon who did my leg—the one who told me that my heart surgery will have to happen by the time I'm 30—is probably right. He writes me a prescription for Propranolol, a beta blocker, to help with my tachycardia. He also tells me that they will make me relaxed. I look the beta blocker up on the Internet and it doesn't say anything about relaxed. It says, "lethargic." It also says there is a slight chance of suicidal tendencies. Oh, good. This just gets better and better. I see nothing odd in the fact that I begin to consume massive amounts of espresso to counteract the feeling of lethargy. I also see nothing odd in the fact that I now cannot sleep without Xanax.

In the cab back down to the law firm on Park Ave South, I call Lisa and tell her, "I'm done. Balthazar. Food. Soho. Fabulousness. On my way back."

She responds, without missing a beat, "Hungry. Caffeine needing. Merlot needing. Christian Leboutin shoes needing."

I rush upstairs and outside Lisa's office, without stopping, say, "Ready to go!" She says, "Must pee first." Despite the fact that we are just now becoming close, we are already able to discuss various bodily functions with absolutely no embarrassment whatsoever. I'm delighted. As we leave, I tell Jeremiah, the assistant I share with Lisa, "We're going for a long lunch. Try to avoid telling anyone. Call us on our cells if something comes up." He looks at us and smiles sarcastically and says, "The kind of long lunch where you are back a little later or the kind of long lunch where you aren't back until tomorrow morning?"

We stand on the curb waiting for a cab. Both dressed in black. Both very trendy. Both very attractive and knowing it. Both feeling very superior for being so rebellious. We have serious superiority complexes. In the cab, Lisa looks at me and says, "How was your cardiology appointment?" I know she is asking because, already, she cares and really wants to know.

I focus on taking my scarf off and don't look at her and say, "Oh, it was fine." Then I look at her and say, with a flourish, even though I know how fake I sound, "I got to take off my shirt, but he wasn't even cute! It was frightening!" And we immediately go back to being embroiled in our fabulousness.

Lisa gets her shoes. I buy a Fabergé egg clock for a ridiculous amount of money. We eat at Balthazar because I know the unlisted, unprinted, private number for reservations. Privilege. Empty, but still privileged.

This morning I have to call a senior business affairs executive at CAA. CAA is supposed to be the most powerful talent agency in Hollywood. Although it is, of course, in Beverly Hills. All the big "Hollywood" agencies are in Beverly Hills. Any "Hollywood" agency that is actually located in Hollywood is rather unimportant, at least until one of their unknown clients makes it big and they get a moment in the sun. Until said previously unknown client moves immediately to one of the Beverly Hills' agencies. Then the unknown agent who actually did all the work to help the unknown client become known goes back to being nothing again. Seriously, this is a lovely industry. Anyway, this morning I have to call this woman back about an issue that came up yesterday. My firm is representing two well-known and prestigious producers of independent films. They have won Oscars. They are very experienced. In other words, they are completely out of my league and I have no business representing them. It wasn't my choice. They are clients of the firm and the senior partner basically said, "Here's a movie. Here are the clients. Go do it."

The thing about independent films is that they are shot with very small budgets. Therefore, the actors in them are either total unknowns who will work for almost no money so that they can, ahem, become known. Or the actors have been in one or two mainstream things and want to do something more arty to show their range, and will work for almost no money. Or the actors are very well-known and want to work in what may end up being a very successful and/or very prestigious (the two rarely go together) film, and are willing to work for almost no money. The actress with whom I'm negotiating a deal to work on this movie with two prestigious producers is of the latter variety. She is well-known and generally paid extraordinarily well. She is being paid un-extraordinarily well for this picture.

My negotiation with the senior CAA business affairs executive goes like this:

"Jack, let's talk about consultation rights. She needs to have consultation on all wardrobe, hairstyles, and script changes."

"Okay regarding wardrobe and hairstyle as long as the producer's final decision rules. Consultation on minor script changes only."

"*Hmmmm*, okay. Once production is over, she really should get a pro-rata amount of her total acting fee for extra time."

"Well, the deal really has to be that she only gets SAG [the union that represents film actors] minimum because there's nothing else in the budget."

"Honestly, Jack, I think that's really offensive. Don't you?"

"I think it's more offensive to me that her salary for two months of work is still more than my student loans, which will take me 20 years to repay."

She giggles. "That's why I love negotiating with you, Jack. You make it at least playful."

I say, "Honesty is like that sometime. So, anyway, what do you think?"

"Okay, I'll see how she feels. She needs to have her name above the title."

"Okay."

"In first position."

"No," I say very fast.

"No? Why?"

"Because I said so." Pause. "Just kidding. Because the lead actor already has first position, but she can have second position."

"That may be a problem."

"The lead actor has more prestige."

"Jack, I think that would offend my client."

"Well, then don't tell her." Pause. "I'm kidding again. Look, it's already negotiated, so she can have second position."

"Okay, I'll check with her. One more issue is that you need to give her a cell phone while on location."

"Not a problem," I say.

"It needs to be digital."

"What?" I have no idea what she's talking about.

"We need that contractual. That the cell phone will be digital."

"Uh, am I missing something? Aren't all cell phones digital?"

"No, Jack. Some cell phones are analog. Digital cell phones have better reception. Isn't yours digital?"

"*Ummmm*, I dunno."

"You don't?" she says, sounding somewhat horrified.

"Sorry, I didn't mean to scare you. Look, I'll tell our clients to try, but I'm not making it contractual."

"Can you at least put that you'll use best efforts."

"No, but I'll put that we'll use good faith efforts as long as our failure to get her a digital cell phone isn't a breach of contract," I say, as though I'm speaking English.

"Well, if that's the best you can do . . ."

"It is. I haven't had enough coffee or sugar today to do better."

"Well, I'll see if my client can live with that. Wonderful talking with you, as always, Jack."

I picture her as my height, with shoulder length straight brown hair with a shampoo-commercial sheen. Her nails are French manicured. She wears Armani clothes with short skirts and sensible pumps. In general, very sophisticated. I later find out, from a friend who works at the agency, that she is, in fact, short, somewhat overweight, with very long, talon-like nails, has a very tight, frizzy perm and wears pants suits, and shouldn't. I am horrified at how delighted I am when I find this out.

I walk into Lisa's office and perch on her desk.

"I just got off the phone with Senior CAA Business Affairs executive negotiating Big Hollywood Star's contract."

Lisa responds, "I talked to her about Upcoming Production That Turns Out To Be A Total Flop last week."

"She is just so Hollywood fake, but somehow sweet."

"She hated me," Lisa says matter-of-factly.

"Why?" I ask.

Pause. "Because she could tell I was cute over the phone."

I go back to my office and hear her shout, "Hey! Your butt looks really cute in those jeans, by the way. Good butt jeans!"

I can't quite figure out why I'm so distracted at work today. Other than this phone call, I have done nothing but walk around and chit-chat, ask a few of the assistants if my butt looks good in these jeans, or look up the prices of fabulous vacations I probably can't afford. Surely the distraction can't possibly be because I have an appointment with my cardiologist for yet another monthly EKG and echocardiogram. I'm sure he'll have the same delightful bedside manner. And I'm sure I'll keep my smartass mouth shut since I know better than to annoy doctors.

I also have to remember to look up the difference between an analog and digital cell phone. If a digital one is, in fact, better and more prestigious, I must buy one at once.

At some point, Lisa and I come to our senses and realize that living a life where you have to keep track of every six minutes of your time, no how much money you can make, is not a life. She decides to quit and gets a job working for a firm that informs big law firms about how to admit computer forensics into evidence.

I decide to be a flight attendant.

To everybody who doesn't matter, they think it's absurd and that I'm ridiculous. To everybody who does matter, they are proud of me that I can be so absurd and ridiculous. Maybe I'm fucking up my life, but I know that it'll be fucked up if I stay at the law firm. At least this way I have a 50/50 chance. Besides, if I fuck it up, only I can put it back together again. I also have to prove that I mean what I have always said: That my ego is not stuck in being a lawyer.

Lisa and I have agreed to take the high road and quit thirty days apart from each other. Since we are the only two lawyers who pretty much run the production attorney department, it would be too hard on the clients we like. Besides, we also want to make the petty point to Steven that we behave better than he does and, although he doesn't deserve it, we'll stagger our departures. We're just so honorable. There is no end to the ways we find to feel superior to the rest of humanity.

During the 10:30 weekly conference, I barely pay attention. We go around the table giving the status of our various cases and clients. I hate it. I have hated it for two years. I am elated that I'm leaving. The head of the music department plays a demo reel of some young girl's attempt at a song and Lisa and I look at each other like, "She'll never be anyone. Her voice is horrid." A year later, turns out it was Britney Spears. Good thing we weren't in the music department.

I've already sent in my application to be a flight attendant, but I haven't heard from the airline yet. Maybe they'll think that a lawyer is over-qualified and won't be interested. Maybe I'll be quitting and have nothing to do. I've never been so terrified of something so positive: Limitless possibilities because I have no definite plan.

During the meeting, while Lisa and I are giving our status reports, Lisa comments on a very difficult client—one of the 25-year-old trust fund babies who wants to be a producer. He's obnoxious and arrogant and Lisa handles him expertly, but warns Steven that he may be getting angry phone calls. She does not say this to complain in the least. She does this out of professional courtesy so he isn't caught off guard. Steven pauses for a moment and says, "He may respond better to a guy. Jack, you deal with him." Again, silence. This, I think, stuns even the people who are used to Steven's antics. Even people who are sometimes on his side. I look at Lisa; the expression on her face remains totally neutral. I'm horrified and say nothing because Steven immediately ends the meeting before I can even respond that he's a sexist asshole (which would have probably come out more like, "I think Lisa can handle it").

As everyone is meandering out of the conference room, grabbing the last bagel or piece of fruit or whatever is left in the middle of the conference table, I ask Steven to stay. We sit down at the end of the conference table.

I say, without preface, and while trying to keep all aspects of glee and victory out of my voice, "Steven, I need to give you notice. I'm going to be leaving the firm in thirty days."

I can see the immediate distress in his face. He knows he's fucked without me right now. We're too busy and he's been too cheap to hire any production attorneys other than Lisa and me. If Lisa had help, she could do the job without me. She's that good, that fast. Steven hasn't seemed to acknowledge this and, besides, he doesn't know she's going to be leaving, too.

"Jack, I asked you a month ago if you were looking for another job."

"I haven't been looking for another job. I don't have another job." Which is true, other than sending in the flight attendant application.

"I can't believe this. You have to give me more than thirty days notice."

"Steven, that's four weeks. It's not unreasonable."

There's a big pause and we both stare for a moment out the conference room glass walls to the reception area and say nothing. Then, he says, "Look, if this is about money, we can talk about raising your salary and giving you a bonus."

"It's not about money."

He looks at me and smirks, as though he's talking to a small child, "Jack, it's always about money."

I look at him and smirk, as though he's a complete moron. "That attitude is one of the main reasons I don't want this job anymore."

Then I see Lisa hovering outside the conference room. She raises her eyebrows at me. I have not a clue what she's doing since we planned that she isn't giving her notice until the day I leave.

Steven tries to give me a withering look and I give him the "oh well" look and do a little shoulder shrug. Lisa is still hovering.

Steven and I are both getting out of our seats when Lisa walks in and says, "Steven, I need to talk to you." She's pissed. That kind of "I don't give a fuck" pissed. Not the kind of "I'm pissed, but will be professional."

Steven looks from me to her and my face is completely neutral. I continue to get up to leave. Lisa doesn't sit down, but says, "Jack, please stay."

Oh dear.

"Steven, I'm leaving in thirty days," Lisa says.

I try desperately to keep the huge, surprised grin off my face and succeed only by not opening my mouth and biting my lower lip. It's so much better to do it this way, because it makes it so much more snide.

He looks from her to me and back to her and says, really angry, "You two planned this."

Lisa says, "No, actually we didn't. We planned that Jack would leave in thirty days and then I would leave thirty days after that. We planned to do the right thing and not leave any clients or you in a lurch despite the fact that you don't deserve it." She pauses and there is no smile on her face now. "But, after implying, no, actually after saying in front of the whole firm that Jack can handle a male client better than I can, to make such a sexist remark doesn't really make me want to do the right thing. You've done a lot of offensive things to me, but that is one of the worst. So, I'm leaving in thirty days."

He is speechless.

She gets up and leaves. I get up and follow her. I walk to Lisa's office, shut the door, and give her an enormous hug. "Oh my god, that was fucking fantastic." I'm barely able to get the words out.

"I know. That was the single most enjoyable moment of working here," she says, half elated, half still pissed off.

"He is so fucked now."

"He so is."

"He so deserves it."

"He so does."

We smile at each other and I walk into my office and sit at my desk, which is covered in papers and contracts and yellow legal pads. I cannot wipe the huge grin off my face. I also realize that I don't mind one bit that I'm a little scared of what happens next.

Three weeks later, someone from American Airlines calls and asks if I would fly to Dallas for an interview. I am absolutely elated and run into Lisa's office.

"Oh. My. God. American Airlines called me for an interview! They want to fly me to Dallas next week!"

"Congratulations! I still can't imagine you pushing that little cart."

"Well, me either, but I can imagine myself flying for free all over the world."

She laughs, "Yes, that part I can imagine."

Thirty days later, it is 10 a.m. and I'm sitting in my now almost empty office at the law firm. I spent the weekend carting my stereo, artwork, personal files, and other stuff I used to make my office my "home." Some of it I actually carried while walking from Park to Third because, well, you know, I'm Jack. I can do it all.

I completely ignore any heart restrictions now. The only things I've been told are that I'm not supposed to lift weights over my head, take antihistamines, or drink caffeine—something about blood flow. I think I stopped paying attention to the details a while ago. It occurs to me that carrying three components of a stereo in a box balanced on my shoulder might be against the rules, but these are rules created by my heart, not me. I've already divorced myself from my heart. It's against me. I frown highly upon it. That is, when I think about it at all. Taking my beta blocker is almost a joke now. Since I'm out clubbing and restauranting almost every night with Lisa or Eric, I usually take the pill with a swig of whatever alcohol I happen to be drinking. It was so amusing for a while and now we barely notice it. Which is also what will hold me back from dealing with my fear until the very last minute before my surgery. I'm pretty insightful. I'm also ridiculous enough to not do shit about the insight.

Some of the things have to be taken home by taxi. Since home is only two blocks from Park, several taxi drivers turn me down until I offer one $20 for the three-minute trip. This is one of the best uses of money: convenience. One of the things is a huge movie poster for *Far and Away*, a Tom Cruise and Nicole Kidman movie that Ron Howard directed and released in the summer of 1992. It flopped. Too historical. Most people don't go to the movies to be taught, even if the acting and directing are good. Most people go to the movies for escapism. I know this because I'm very competent at escapism. Even now. Soon, however, I'll be a total expert and I'll be very proud and flaunting it everywhere and everyone will love it and be enchanted and excited and love me and then I'll have my chest hacked into and none of it will matter anymore.

The Imagine Team

I got the poster when I worked at Imagine Entertainment during my last two years of undergrad. I'd go to class as a normal college student and then go to work at what was then one of the most successful production companies in "Hollywood." *Parenthood, My Girl, Backdraft.* Everything was a huge hit. I was the youngest person in the company. Driving my beige Honda Accord into Century City every day to work at the company co-owned by Ron Howard. Feeling pretty proud of myself. When I first started, I didn't even know how to work the fax machine. By the time I left, I was really good at my job.

My boss, Linda, and I worked well together. She taught me so much. One of the most important was, "If your name is on it, it has to be perfect. Absolutely perfect." She also taught me that Rolaids are relatively necessary when your boss is anal-retentive. The day I left, she said, "One day you'll look back on this and realize you had it really good."

I replied, "Oh yeah, I'll think I had an ulcer, but I had it really good." To which we, of course, cackled.

On the last day I worked at Imagine, they had a party for me in the big, glass-walled conference room. Since *Far and Away* was about to be released, everybody had signed the poster for me. I was 21. I was leaving Imagine. Unbeknownst to me, I was also about to come out of the closet. Obviously, there was a lot that was unbeknownst to me back then. Sometimes it's better not to know.

I took a lot of pride in that poster. It ended up, however, going from my office to the taxi to the storage space in the basement of my apartment building. What was I going to do? Put an old movie poster in my living room? I never hung it up anywhere again, but I carted it around with me for years before being able to throw it away.

CHAPTER 6

Barbie Boot Camp

FOR THE INTERVIEW IN DALLAS, I wear a really nice grey/brown glen plaid Perry Ellis suit, with a shirt that has alternating light and dark mint-green stripes and a grey tie with little green paisleys on it. I match. I look conservative without being boring. I hate, however, wearing the tie. I part my hair on the side and sweep it conservatively over my forehead instead of doing the gelled/messy/spiked thing.

I'm given a seat in the very back on a full flight from La Guardia to Dallas. The two flight attendants in back are a young guy and a young girl. Both cute. Both nice. Both amusing. I think to myself, oh ya, I could totally do this.

The guy, smashing a bag of ice on the floor to break it, looks up and says, "Going for an interview?"

I laugh, "Is it that obvious?"

He smiles. "You'll see. When you're a flight attendant you'll be able to read most people like a book."

Well, I usually already can, so this should be a piece of cake.

A tram picks me up at DFW with a few other interviewees. We make nervous small talk for the ten-minute ride to American Airline headquarters. I really, really cannot believe I am doing this. When I am sitting in a room with about 50 other interviewees waiting for my name to be called, I really, really cannot believe I'm this nervous. I have three degrees, have passed two bar exams, worked at a law firm, and I'm nervous about interviewing as a flight attendant because this is unlike anything I've ever done before.

My name is called by a woman who is wearing a flight attendant uniform. She has dark hair to her shoulders, lots of make-up, red lipstick, is very sweet looking and put together. She looks like the perfect flight attendant. She explains, "The interview is actually three parts. We put you together with three other interviewees. The first part is making sure you are tall enough to reach into an overhead bin to grab a fire extinguisher from the back. The second is a little role playing with your fellow interviewees. The third is a private interview between you and two of our employees."

I flash her a big smile and say, "Great. I'm excited to be here." I have already figured out the game. I need to be a people person. I need to be calm, but amusing. Professional, but subservient. And I need to smile. A lot.

My private interview takes place in a small, square, windowless room with typical corporate fluorescent lights. There is a photograph of an airplane flying into the sunset on the wall. There are three chairs—two against one wall, one in a corner—those plastic chairs that I remember from grade school. Instead of being orange and brown, they are all navy blue. I sit in the corner chair. I'm nervous. I could reach into the overhead bin. I did my role playing with the other interviewees. But I don't really know what to expect for the interview. I have, however, rehearsed a ton of different answers and have made an effort to remind myself to make sure they don't sound rehearsed, which basically consists of making a lot of pauses and moving my eyes around a little while I'm talking to give the illusion that I'm coming up with stuff right on the spot.

In walk a woman and a man, also in flight attendant uniforms, both perfectly conservative, nice looking, white, friendly and, of course, with large smiles. Both very American looking. In fact, the woman looks like a clone of the woman with whom I checked in moments ago. We shake hands. They are very nice and try to make me feel relaxed.

The woman says, "So, you're a lawyer who wants to be a flight attendant?" She says it in a funny way.

I laugh and say, "Yes, a little unexpected, right?" We all laugh some more. It's very corny, but still friendly.

He says, "Why? Why this? It's such a drastic change."

I was ready for this one "It's not as drastic as it seems. As a lawyer I had to deal with clients and handle their moods and needs and pacify them. They were from different backgrounds with different agendas and I needed to learn to adapt to all of them to be able to function. I had to be a people person." I know I am using too many words. I'm trying to convince them, and that's generally a losing strategy in an interview.

I add, "I also think that going from one profession where people want to rip your head off sometimes to another profession where people want to rip your head off sometimes is something I could handle."

We all laugh a lot at this. I am oh-so-amusing.

She says, "We have a few what-would-you-do-if questions. There aren't necessarily any exact correct answers, so just answer with what comes to you."

He says, "What would you do if there was a passenger with his shoes off and the woman sitting in front of him complained that his feet smelled badly."

I say, after thinking for a second, "I'd see if there was an empty seat on the airplane and offer it to her."

She says, "Okay, that would be a great solution, but what if the flight is full and there are no empty seats."

I think again and ask, "There isn't a rule that passengers must wear shoes while in flight, is there?"

She says, "No." Then she looks at the guy and says, "But there should be."

We both laugh a lot at this although I'm not sure I get what's so funny. My point of view is still from the side of being a passenger who would want to be able to take his shoes off, not that of a flight attendant who is trying to deal with someone's smelly feet. It's also from the viewpoint of being a deal negotiator from Manhattan who would tell the guy quietly that his feet smell and that he should put his shoes on. I don't, however, think this is the answer.

My law school training kicks in and I say, "Well, the issue is being able to keep the female passenger happy and help her to have a good flight while finding a way not to offend the male passenger."

They both smile.

I continue, "While I'd really want to ask the guy to put his shoes on, I think I'd try to sincerely apologize to the woman and explain that it is a full flight, that I'd move her if I could, and ask her if there is anything I could do to make the rest of her flight better."

I smile. They smile. She says, "That's great. It could work. I'm pleased that you saw where the concerns are. Actually, there is an air freshener on the airplane and you could walk by and discretely spray it near the floor."

We all laugh. I say, "I suppose I couldn't simply spray it directly onto his feet."

We all laugh some more. My face is starting to hurt.

"Okay," he says, "What would you do with a passenger who is afraid of flying?"

I say, pretty fast, "I don't think there'd really be much I could do. I'd ask him if there was anything at all I could do to make him more comfortable. Get him a different seat, a blanket, a drink, etc. and I'd tell him I'll come by a lot."

They smile and don't say anything.

I add, "I'd also tell him that, although I am not sure if it will help, for what it's worth, I feel very comfortable on this flight and I know the captain is excellent—even if I don't really know the captain."

He says, "Well, that would be good, although it's not a good idea to ever lie to passengers." They both smile at me as though they have to say that. I feel like they are silently telling me that a harmless fib would be okay.

They ask a few more questions and I get the feeling that they are more wanting to see how I react to them than to the questions. I smile a lot. I make sarcastic but amusing comments. I act a little nervous. Oh, and I sit up straight in my chair. Both of them are so erect.

Fifteen minutes later I'm in the room alone and the woman I met in the front pops her head in and asks, "Could you stay until this afternoon and go over to medical to run through a few tests?"

"Of course," I say. Smiling. My face feels like it's going to fall off. My smile is going to rebel, jump off, and run away in fright.

Medical is the one area I've been worried about. I may have to tell them about my leg. They may hear the murmur in my heart. A blood test may show that I've been taking Xanax to get to sleep, although I stopped taking it six weeks ago after learning on the internet that this is about the time it takes to get totally out of your system. I've also gotten a doctor's letter saying that my heart thing is a non-issue. Which, on a personal level, even if it is true regarding the job, is a massive understatement.

A woman makes me pee in a cup instead of taking a blood test. She checks my heartbeat and hears the murmur and I show her the letter and she puts it in a file. I tell her about my leg because a form has asked me to mention all medical issues and I am going to be honest. This is the part at which she hesitates. I explain that I have no restrictions. That I run, skip, and walk all over Manhattan. I have no pain whatsoever. That it is simply a permanent part of me now. She takes my word for it. I didn't lie.

On the plane back to NYC, I am absolutely exhausted and sleep the whole way. I figure, however, that I must have the job. Why would they run medical tests on me the same day if they didn't want to offer me the job? This is the obvious answer, but I can already feel the veil of secretiveness regarding the airline. I have already been instilled with the "You are being watched at all times and don't ever take something for granted" feeling. It was there the whole day. I felt like every move was being watched and every word was being analyzed. For one of the first times in a very long time, I felt that I had very little control over the situation. Maybe this is why I slept so well on the way back to NYC.

I'm back in Dallas. I'm wearing my black cap-toe Kenneth Cole shoes, grey glen-plaid Perry Ellis pants from a suit I bought in law school in 1994, a mint-green striped Perry Ellis snap-collar shirt, and a tie that is making me feel stuffy and uncomfortable. I hate this tie. It's a solid grey Armani and makes me feel like a waiter. People are called one at a time to go to the front of the class, which is amphitheater style. Each one has to get up and walk down several levels to stand below the class, with all of us peering down at them. We are told to say our name, where we're from, and something personal about ourselves. We are also told, not too gently, that we are to follow instructions to the letter, without question. I suppose that means we cannot give a monologue about ourselves.

I hate this kind of thing. It makes me feel very self-conscious, as though everyone is judging every word, every movement, every piece of clothing, my hairstyle, and my eye color. People from very diverse backgrounds range in age from 20 to 60. They are all different shapes and sizes. There is a girl who dropped out of law school to do this. There is an older woman whose husband died a few months ago. There is a 20-year-old girl who had never been out of her small town in Oregon and who had been home-schooled. What I did notice was that the class was predominantly white and predominantly attractive. Nobody was downright ugly. There were, however, a few overweight people. Women outnumbered men about 3 to 1. As far as I could tell, not all the men were gay.

My name is called and I sit there for a moment and put on my serene, professional face and walk toward the classroom. I'm going to say my name and that I'm from NYC and I've done many different things in life, but that I really want to work with people and be able to travel. A standard response that won't make me stand out.

"Hi, I'm Jack Freedman. I'm from New York City. And, uh, I'm an attorney and . . . you can imagine how thrilled my parents are about this."

Huge laughs and surprised faces. I couldn't help myself. It slipped out. Not only that I'm a lawyer, but my charming little comment about my parents. I did exactly what I meant not to do: I made myself stand out and charmed them all at once. Besides, my parents were, in fact, very supportive. It just sounded more charming to say otherwise. As I went to sit down, I caught the eye of a guy in the class. Young. Dark hair. Greenish eyes. Staring at me. I stared back for a second and then avoided his glance.

We were given the ground rules for the next six-and-a-half weeks of our lives. We all had to dress business-professional at all times, except when we were at our hotel. We only spoke after raising our hands. We could take bathroom breaks during class as long as we did so as quietly as possible. We could not eat or drink while standing

Jack as Flight Attendant

up anywhere on campus. We were not allowed, ever, to use a straw with any drinks. We had to conduct ourselves as we would see ourselves on the airplane, which meant smiling at everyone in the hallways and saying hello. We were always to be on time for class. We were to have good posture. We were always to be prepared. We were always to do exactly as we were told without question. However, questions, after the fact, were fine. Within two days we called it "Barbie Boot Camp." And we called the campus of classrooms and airline simulators "The Charm Farm."

The Charm Farm was very cliquish. I quickly developed a clique with Matthew, Samantha, and Kelly. Unfortunately, Kelly didn't make it. We never knew why. But, like others in our class, she simply disappeared. They had a way of secreting someone away. Rumor had it that if you were terminated, they'd find you when you were alone, take you back to your hotel, ask you to pack, and then drive you to DFW to fly home. The thought that this had happened to Kelly made the rest of us very sad. There were others we were friendly with and had fun with, but now it was basically Matt, Sammy, and me.

I figured out immediately that I had to behave flawlessly during training or I'd get kicked out. This meant no arrogance. No talking about myself. No alcohol. I was in boot camp. Barbie Boot Camp. Instead of vomiting myself up as usual, I was quiet and said little unless I was with the few people I was close to. We had to learn commands to get people out of a plane as quickly as possible. We had to learn every emergency procedure for every aircraft for any possible situation. We had to learn to use almost every piece of equipment on board. Oh, and we had to learn to serve coke 30,000 feet in the air. You could fail once, then re-do it; if you failed again, you usually disappeared. I only failed once at the very end. I harassed one of our instructors to tell me if I was going to get kicked out and he finally said, quietly, "Shut up. You're fine."

I had no idea that I'd actually not be terminated given my usual manner of being hello-I'm-me-fuck-yourself. I thought that maybe renting a car to go clubbing in the city might have done it. Or paying for my own room rather than share someone else's once my roommate disappeared. I was scared, the way everyone else was, but I rented cars and we all snuck into Dallas to go out. Sammy and I pretended to be brother and sister, making Matthew jealous. Matthew and I were sneaking back into my room. His roommate was not part of our "crowd," so we never figured out what he thought when Matthew didn't show up. In any case, I gathered up a group and taught them to exercise a slight amount of caution so they wouldn't get kicked out.

I don't know what I felt for Matt. Everybody said we were joined at the hip. I loved having sex with him. We did it in first class of the 767 simulator, thereafter calling it the 767 stimulator. He, however, annoyed the hell out of me sometimes and could never, ever admit he was wrong about anything. Which meant that I was wrong about things, and I can't abide not being right about all things. Despite this, I couldn't seem to stop this little affair we were having. We were together basically 24 hours a day, since I had my own room. Apparently you were not supposed to have affairs with fellow classmates. Rumor (again) had it that two guys messed around in the class behind us and got kicked out. How Matt and I were not kicked out is unbelievable. People knew. "Oh, puleeeez. Of course they're together! They bought tanning packages together!"

We were never told anything in advance unless it was about a test, which we had weekly. Most of them were on a computer. I passed on the first try each time and everybody knew. How everybody knew everything about everyone else was so bizarre. Apparently we had forgotten that we lived together and studied together and went to classes together 24/7. People started to revere me. They knew just enough to make me interesting, I suppose. Since I didn't talk, the mystery grew.

Matt said to Sammy, "Everyone loves Jack." Matt said these things. He didn't hold his flattery in, and it was hard to resist. Besides, his eyes were gorgeous. You could stay in those eyes forever. I think he made me a little insecure, being so young. I was all of 27 and he had turned 21 the week we all started training. The difference between 21 and 27 is vast—different worlds—whereas 31 and 27 would make little difference. The older you get, the more age is irrelevant. When you're young, you don't really think about it except that "being older" means that nobody can ground you or make you do your homework. When you're middle age, you start to realize you aren't 21 anymore. It isn't that you want the actual youth back. It's that you want the looks and the attention back. And the naivetéé of thinking you didn't really care about it. Innocence is a luxury.

Anyway . . .

One day in class, we walked into the room where we had had to show we could open the doors of every aircraft for which we were certified to fly. The bigger planes, of course, have electric doors. But the older, smaller planes— the earlier 727s, 737s, 757s, etc.— are manual. The room was filled with balloons flying around with peoples' names on them. We realized they were about to tell us where we would be based. After training, we would fly directly to the base and set up house. Most people made arrangements in advance with each other or other flight attendants who were already at the bases.

The exception, however, was NYC, which is so expensive that they would let you choose if you wanted to be there. Obviously I made this choice since I already lived in New York. Because of me, Matt did the same. Sammy got based in Chicago. Once training was over and I was home, and Matt was setting up house with other flight attendants in Queens, we faded. Admittedly, I "left" our little affair without a lot of notice to him. Brent knew about him and accepted it, had even discussed it with me while I was in Dallas, but I didn't want to live with one person and sleep with two. Neither of us did. Whenever Matt and I would see each other at a club or work a trip together, we weren't very nice to each other. It was sad. Matt ended up being in and out of my life for many years. He visited me in L.A. twice. We flew to Argentina for a weekend once. We kept in touch, but it was very peripheral.

Once I was back in NYC as a Flight Attendant, I begin to fly all over the world. I met amazing people. I began to spend obscene amounts of money. I ran far and fast from anything that even remotely connected me to the fear of the Heart Thing.

CHAPTER 7

The Frantic Skies

4/19/99 5:31 a.m. Bonaventure Hotel, Los Angeles

THE ADVENTURE OF MY LIFE continues. I enjoy flying tremendously, although it is more exhausting than I would have imagined. It was warm yesterday and I sat outside for a bit, rented a car, went to Weho and had dinner at Cobalt Cantina with Eric. We had such a nice time. I look at him sometimes and see such a lush, such sadness, while others see this colorful, accepting, wise, and tremendously fun friend. I called my former boss Linda and she tried to speak with her mouth full of sores from radiation and chemo, but ended our conversation quickly. What does one say to a friend in agony? For someone who always wants to fix everyone's lives, this feeling of helplessness is most frustrating. And to hear her sound so weak, so defeated, so completely unlike the Linda I know—it suspends time. As though I am holding my breath until it is over for her.

4/20/99 10:35 a.m. Big Cup, New York

It seems a contradiction of moments to sit here reading Camus' *The Plague* while ABBA is on the stereo. Of course, I am consistently intrigued by contradictions of all varieties. They seem so very honest. It is a difficult book to read. Not due so much to Camus' style of writing, but more because it is full of observations. It reveals the characters' emotions, and the narrator also reveals grandiose views on life and the way people handle it. The reader is told what he should absorb from the story; what to look at from a broader stroke. "Ah yes, that is true for me also," I say as I read.

I sat in the cockpit when we landed in L.A. the other day. It was absolutely exhilarating! I knew it would be interesting, but the thrill of it, the amazement at seeing the earth from 40,000 feet rising up to meet this enormous 767 was nothing I could have predicted. I sat silently watching everything and, before I knew it, I had an ear-to-ear smile pasted across my face. The unexpected thrill had rendered me a little boy again. Not only was it a new experience, but how long had it been since I'd been so unexpectedly and quickly thrilled and amazed like that? Adults, unlike children, predict and imagine—perhaps envision is a better choice of words—their own amazement. They say, "I can't wait to do X; it'll be so thrilling." They enjoy the experience, but aren't amazed at their own thrill. Anyhow, it was rather spectacular.

4/26/99 10:36 a.m. Café Espresso, San Francisco
It is chilly this morning and I found this little French café—a true replica of cafés I've entered in Paris where people stand at a marble-and-wood bar sipping espresso from tiny cups, chattering loudly. I half expected to need 35 francs for coffee. Of course, there wasn't the cloud of cigarette smoke one finds in places such as this on Parisian mornings, as much due to social ordinance as cultural differences.

Sometimes I feel as though I should simply surrender to my sadness. As though my moments of exhilaration and serenity are simply aberrations. It isn't sadness for any specific reason, such as a loved one's death or rejection or financial problems. It's truly the only sadness I'm familiar with. I used to think it stemmed from frustration at not finding my "path." This morning it dawned on me: I'm lonely. Like any depression, it gets metastasized: I am a loser, I'm not successful, my relationship is bad, etc. Somewhere, somehow, I am not getting sustenance from the various elements of my life, although I don't always feel this way.

5/2/99 12:08 p.m. Deidrich's Café, Laguna Beach
Was out with Eric and my cousin Moriah at Rage the other night and I recognized a guy from years ago, the "Roy Days" in 1992. I remembered we were at the ATM at BofA and he screamed, "You're the love of my life. Come back!"

Jack and Moriah

Roy and I had just returned from Laguna in the Beemer. A beautiful, top-down, sun-tanning, Evian-drinking, palm tree-swaying day. I was wearing flip-flops, cut-off jeans, and my black tank top that I still have, now ripped and grey. That was the night I met the drop-dead gorgeous Jordan at Studio, had sex with him all night, then flew to Berlin the next morning.

The time I met that lady therapist from Taos on an airplane going to L.A., she said she could tell instantly that I am a "pleaser." A kind of chameleon for people. She told me we are all like disco balls. One or two mirrors shining at a time while the rest are dim, waiting to be in the light for a moment again.

I saw Linda yesterday. I brought her some boxer shorts from Banana Republic and wrote, on the card, "Linda, I always wanted to buy you something for your crotch." She laughed a lot at that. I also saw the flowers I had sent to her. They were huge! She was in good spirits and will have no more radiation or chemo treatments. She looks haggard and aged. She wore a turban, although she showed me a bit of her scalp—pale, with wisps of hair matted against it. She seemed softer, somehow. More gentle. Not surprising, considering what she's gone through. It has broken her so completely. She even said she would never go through it again. As has my mom. Perhaps all those things are what made me cry a little when I left. It was all too similar to mom so many years ago. Yet, she will be fine. She still made jokes and did seem like "Linda."

5/12/99 9:07 a.m., Bubala's Café, Provincetown
Brent had planned on being here all week alone, but I elected to take the bus yesterday. I've never taken a bus trip in place of an airplane. It was actually quite relaxing.

It's absolutely gorgeous today. A bright and sunny New England spring morning. The water ripples with sprinkles of light and the sky is the color of blue that looks painted. Brent and I have had such turmoil in our relationship lately. Worse than ever. We've lost our friendship, although you'd never know it to look at us. Handsome, well-mannered, sitting here in the sun, discussing Kosovo and jobs and our finances. Him reading today's paper and me writing with one hand, coffee in the other.

I was out the other night with Lisa, Isabel, and Isabel's boyfriend, Jose, who used to work at Moomba when it was the height of trendy and difficult-to-get-in. I met Lisa at her little one-room apartment on Jane Street in the village. She detests its size and I think it's a quaint place. Candles in the fireplace. Music on the CD player. We sat sipping wine from crystal goblets, speaking of people and fears and hopes and laughing at lots of silly phrases and empty stories. And ourselves. She wore her translucent Bebe shirt and black stretch pants. Later, we all met at Bar Six and had fun. I kept saying, through tipsy giggling, "Feel my pants. Feel my pants." They were the crushed velvet jeans Mom made me buy in Paris. I was getting lots of attention from girls, which always surprises me for some reason.

On the subway on my way to Soho the other day, I saw myself in the blurred reflection of the subway car window as we sped along underground. It made me feel lonely for some reason.

5/19/99 2:14 p.m., Barnes and Noble, Union Square, New York
I have been thinking of suicide lately. Not in any sense that I am ready for it now. When I think that I may never find my path, that I am destined always to be searching, it feels good to think I have a way out. Perhaps that's pathetic. I always say the path's end isn't exciting and that, as they say, it's the journey that counts. My journey, for all its craziness and confusion, is pretty neat.

Written on the bathroom wall above the urinal, of all places: "What is love?" Underneath, someone answered, "A brick in bed with an eel." I love that. They can do nothing for each other; there is no reason or logic. There is simply love. I always say, if you're looking for a way to define it, you probably aren't in it.

6/9/99 6:12 a.m., Sheraton, San Diego
I spoke to David and got a shock. Roy was put in jail again and David left him there for a week. Apparently, it scared Roy so much that he got clean for

Roy and David

80 days and is now in a three-month rehab program. David says he's also on protease inhibitors again. In fact, David says he is back to the Roy we all knew six years ago.

David wants me to be in L.A. when Roy returns from rehab. It's odd to realize what a grasp he has on my life. It's as though everything stops during the moments I think of him and our friendship. After all the ups and downs and feeling abandoned when he was so into drugs for those years, well, you'd think I'd be hesitant about getting close again, but I'll jump in with both feet the very second he's back in my life. Roy made me feel better about myself than anyone ever has because he didn't ask me to be anything I wasn't. How can you not continually risk hurt to have that again?

6/10/99 1:40 p.m., Jamba Juice, Hillcrest, San Diego
Flew back to NYC and had dinner with Brent at Sotto Cinque. We had a pleasant, yet cordial time. Kind of like being with a relative whom you're tied to only by blood and history and little else. It saddens me so much. When we tried to discuss issues, we found ourselves arguing and getting testy instead.

Lisa, Isabel, and I went to Rose's Turn in the Village It's in an ancient townhouse about half a story below street level. You walk down cracked cement stairs to go inside. A dark place with odd light fixtures, small round tables, merely functional. The kind of place that is nothing without its occupants. The ambience comes from the contrast between the dark "nothing" space and the laughter and music that filter up to the street every night. Lisa and I kept saying, through tipsy amazement, "Only in NYC."

These people get a chance to be stars, even if only for a moment. An enormous Miss Piggy-like woman, blonde wig out to "here," slinky red dress encasing slabs of fat, got up and belted out a tune that had us all in hysterics and wonderment. The nerve! The confidence! We loved her at once! Another girl, whom Lisa and Isabel and I kept rolling our eyes at, put us into tears by singing a song her friend had written. I remember the chorus: "Give me the stars and the moon and the silver sky . . ." This totally unknown woman, unknown song (at least to us), in a dingy half-underground bar in the Village with the elements simply coming together. The contrast. Isabel and I danced in front of everyone when a girl sang "Someone To Watch Over Me," and dirty danced when she sped it up in a way I have never heard before. Such camaraderie. Such support. Even the older woman with the thick Long Island accent and horrible wig got big applause because she tried! It was an inspiring night.

6/15/99 10:25 a.m., Big Cup Café, Manhattan
After three and a half years of living here, Brent and I are finally having the windows cleaned. I have to make sure I'm home at noon. It's a gorgeous day. Not too humid since it rained a bit last night. I do not know how I handle the humidity, having grown up in New Mexico where it is so dry. Yet summer after summer here, I do.

Lisa and Isabel and I went to Tonic, an intimate restaurant/bar on 18th and 6th Ave. Got drunk, since I hadn't eaten anything on the plane. We laughed, giggled, and shared. It seems like most times I go out, I find myself an observer—it's as though I am out of my body watching the three of us, or whomever I'm with. Which is good because then I get to record it. Brent almost went out with us, but didn't. Big shock. God forbid he actually come out to play. Lisa and I walked down 8th Avenue after Isabel went home. Danny came running out of Eighteenth & Eighth as Lisa said, "I wonder if Danny is working?" I hugged him a second too long. It made me want to be close to him. Not lust. Just comfort. A tingle. That feeling where you can barely fathom being near someone without touching.

Left a message for Lisa apologizing for not walking her home last night. She called back and said, "Enough with your chivalry!" We laughed.

6/22/99 10:55 a.m., on plane NYC to DFW
On my way to Progressions Class in Dallas. This plane is full of people who were in Flight Attendant training with me and little groups and gossip have already begun. Yet everyone is pleasant to each other, fulfilling our stereotypes as perky FAs. Thoughts of seeing Matt annoy me. I wish I could ignore him completely. Brent and I have been getting along better. Not only civil, but even tender at moments. It will never be the stars and the moon with us, but

perhaps stability is more enduring. I don't know. When I return from Dallas tomorrow, we are driving up to Cape Cod for four days in Provincetown.

6/25/99 9:55 a.m., Bubala's, Provincetown
We sat in our place last night and watched *Peggy Sue Got Married*, which was wonderful. Nicholas Cage, scared to settle down and give up even one dream, says, "I'm just scared the world won't like me when I'm not exciting." I drew a sharp audible breath and tears sprang to my eyes.

Progressions wasn't quite the horror I had predicted. I stayed on my cell phone most of the time, which I'm sure prompted comments of elitism. I simply didn't want to make small talk. Matt was odd. Not so much cold, but not a person who handles awkward situations with grace. After the reception, he brought Tori to the hotel. I wanted to take the high road and not make Matt feel uncomfortable. The next day he followed me around while I was on my cell. He even followed me into the bathroom. Finally, he interrupted my cell phone escapism, asking if we could talk when I "had a moment." I avoided it. Matt is annoying and immature, yet you see his potential and kindness. His innocent curiosity about everything. You can't quite ignore him no matter how much you want to.

I kissed Lance when we were all out at Moby's. I told Brent later and he didn't care. Of course, my FA instructors watched with little grins of amusement. My eyes were closed, but Victoria saw all and told me Rene was pointing and laughing. Good kisser. Lance offered to give me a ride back to the hotel. I declined. That could have been dangerous. At one point, Sara and Victoria were up on a little stage dancing to some song from *Grease*. It was hysterical. I got a really cute guy to kiss Sara. I told him she needed a self-esteem boost. He told Lance and me we looked "yummy like toast" and he'd be the baloney. I burst out laughing, having never heard a cornier line. Of course, I wanted to remove my head from my body the next morning, but it was a fun night.

6/30/99 8:30 a.m., Downtown Subscription, Santa Fe
On a whim I flew to Albuquerque yesterday. Rented a car and zipped right up to Santa Fe. Took Mom to a fabulous dinner at Geronimo and had $160

worth of drinks. We were tiiiiiiiipsy. It was grand. Everyone thought Mom was the cutest thing on earth. We had cosmos and chocolate martinis. Lots of chocolate martinis. With Pellegrino to try to avoid hangovers. Which didn't work.

7/3/99 10:15 a.m., Radisson Inn, Jacksonville, Florida
Crew Schedule stuck me with an icky three-day trip—position two on the MD-80, which I loath. I really only like transcons on the 767. I always bid for the "senior mamas" vacations in order to get those trips, since I'm not senior enough. On reserve, I have little choice.

The van driver last night was quite a character. An older black man with bits of white hair and an accent like Morgan Freeman's in *Driving Miss Daisy*. His answers of "Yessuh" and "Yes'um" seemed right out of another time, but they were, I realized, merely from the South. He said he's been so lucky to have never been out of a job in 41 years. I thought to myself: how different his perspective is from mine. I never even consider the possibility of being out of work. For me, and all those I know, it's the type of work and salary that's the challenge. Yet many of us aren't even half as content as this older black man driving a van.

7/7/99 12:36 p.m., Café Bari, Soho, Manhattan
Billie Holiday croons. White marble café tables. Trendy people in trendy clothes sipping trendy coffees. The humidity has finally lifted. Not a cloud in the sky. I'm meeting Lisa at Balthazar for lunch today. I mistakenly showed up an hour early, which was a nice mistake because it has given me time to write, sitting here in the window of the café watching people. Feeling that "things are good."

Brent and I are going to L.A. to see Babba and Aunt Mil, Babba's sister, in a week. We had a pretty awful fight yesterday and discussed separation. Then he heard me discussing apartment costs with Lisa on the phone. I wasn't trying to hide anything. At one point in our argument, he said something about my devotion to friends and how I "take on their burdens" as my own. It brought instant emotion to the surface, which I hid. I often think he sees only a caricature of who I am, and that hurts. It shocked me to see how much it meant that he noticed. He obviously did not mean it as a compliment, but as I value it in myself, I was glad to hear him say it.

7/31/99 11:02 a.m., Café Barthillon, Paris

Yesterday afternoon I got the bug to be here in Paris. I packed the leather backpack Eric got me so long ago from Barneys. New black jeans, my grey Polo shirt, a black Calvin Klein t-shirt, and undies. And, of course, my journal. I'll go home tomorrow. If I'm going to serve coke 30,000 feet in the air, I might as well be pampered and have the utterly ridiculous jet-setting privilege of spending only a day in Paris.

There is no way to describe how I feel the moment I step from the Metro to see the sun hit ancient stone buildings and high narrow-paned windows with their frames a beautifully contrasting white against stones of beige and taupe and grey. Window boxes of pink and red geraniums. Little tiny attic windows that cause one to fantasize as to what adorable rooms lie beyond or what treasures might be hidden in a dusty attic. I am lucky because it is gorgeous today. A slight breeze, a tad cool, and a hazy sky shielding the sun a bit. It's peaceful this morning as I sit at a café, close at the south point of Île Saint-Louis with a view of the Seine, Île de la Cité, and the back corner of Notre Dame.

Jack in Paris

I ordered, in French, *un café* and a croissant. I was served a tiny pitcher of espresso, a little china cup, wrapped cubes of sugar, and

a demitasse spoon, as well as a small carafe *d'eau*, a wine glass, and two chocolates on a doily-covered plate. Divine. I went directly to my favorite hotel in
the Marais and they had a room. *C'est charmant.* A sloped ceiling in a tiny
room, a skylight, rough dark wood exposed beams, an armoire that looks like
an antique, and a bed that many would deem too soft, but I will adore later
tonight. I don't think anything could be more perfect. A spontaneous first
class flight, wonderful balmy weather, a quaint hotel room, practicing my
French every chance I have, and the most divine mid-morning espresso at a
café overlooking the Seine.

Same day 12:41 p.m., Musee de Orsay, Paris
The Musee de Orsay is often my first stop after the café when visiting Paris.
I immediately climb the many steps to the fourth floor, disregarding the
masterpieces on other floors. I have noticed another Degas today: "*Madame
Jeanfaud au Miroir.*" A woman sits viewing herself in the mirror. She has pure
skin with rosy cheeks and fresh eyes, but the vision in the mirror is darker,
drawn, older. I cannot help but wonder if the reflection is meant to be her true
self and the woman sitting before the mirror views herself as more full, more
attractive, and younger than she really is. Degas' characters appear to be in the
middle of movement. About to go on to something different. As though he
has caught them on a precipice of sorts and we are left to our own predictions
as to where they are off to next.

There is also the famous painting by James Whistler, "*La Mere de
L'Artiste,*" of the woman sitting, watching a lovely patterned black curtain.
In contrast to Degas' characters, there is no movement here. This woman
contemplates nothing further than merely sitting and watching quietly. It is
simply about existence as opposed to any sort of progression. Unfortunately,
I do not find my favorite of all paintings: "*Café de l'absinthe,*" also by Degas.
It must be on loan to some other museum. Yet, I did see my favorite van
Gogh: "*L'Aglise d'Auvers.*" A farmhouse. I once had an enormous poster of
it over my futon. It must have been 8 x 6 feet, at least. Funny. Others had
Nagel and cars and bodies and I had Van Gogh and didn't even know I was
weird.

Same day 8:40 p.m., Café Rive Droit, Paris

I have sat here countless times before. With Carol, alone, with Brent, alone, with Mom, alone. It is so French. The corner of the Fountain Les Halles, the diversity of the people who walk by, and a glimpse of the most beautiful orange sunset off to my right. I walked through the Tuileries garden a bit and went to L'Orangerie. Mostly, I found Toulouse Lautrec interesting. Degas with an edge. His figures appear, if not merely mischievous, then altogether bad. A man with a fierce scowl. A woman with an impure, teasing look in her face—eyebrows raised, head to the side. I felt teary as I walked up the Champs. The museums move me to such a great extent this visit. Their value is solely because they exist. Because they are inspiring in the most pure manner possible: they create perspective. One steps away feeling refreshed, alive. And to think one person can create something like that. Someone placed oil on fabric and, due to their vision, hand, and talent, millions treasure the result and are moved by it.

I had a monumental experience in Paris. I almost wish it hadn't happened. I met Joseph and we danced hard at Le Queen. We talked, tipsy, at 4 a.m. in the moonlight on the Champs. He said, "I thought I might die on this trip. Now I realize it was just that part of me that had given up and assumed I'd never meet someone for my soul." I remember it almost word for word. Although it may sound trite or sappy on paper, the circumstances—Paris, Le Queen, vodka, 4 a.m., the moon, the Champs, and the lights—all took my breath away. We talked about relationships. About life. About friends. About aspirations. We went inside and danced again. At 6 a.m., we left, came back to my hotel, and I said goodbye before going inside. We kissed, but just barely. I tore up his address and email, because it scared me to have them. And I didn't tell Brent because that scared me, too.

I know I must be romanticizing it, but the mere fact that it matters so tremendously to me says something, doesn't it? The exchanged glances, the knowing smiles, to feel understood and valued so instantly, even if it was just the circumstances. You meet someone and talk and share glances and wonder if they're The One. You feel silly for wondering, but you wonder nonetheless because you still have hope. Maybe the last vestige of innocence from childhood. Often you connect and walk away anyway because you are trained not to take chances. Anyone who puts aside their fears of the moment, their concerns of the day, in order to make another feel better, that is someone to fall in love with.

CHAPTER 8

The Height of the Ridiculous

I POUR MYSELF OUT OF a cab at 32nd and 3rd at 5:50 p.m. I walk in the door, leave my suitcase in the hall, go into the kitchen, immediately pour myself a glass of white wine, swallow 2 mg of Xanax, take my beta blocker, put George Michael's "Listen Without Prejudice" CD on very loudly, peel off my uniform, and step into a scalding shower, holding my wine glass out of the way of the stream of water while leaning out to take big sips. I have absolutely no idea where Brent is. This is the last day of three back-to-back transcons. New York, L.A., New York, L.A., New York, L.A., New York. Six days in a row, flying across the country each day on full 767s. I'm exhausted and I feel disgusting and I have never, ever liked a job more than I like this one. For me, it's magic. And, thankfully, it is all consuming.

After my shower, I put on my undies and curl up onto the sofa and watch the lights of the city. George is still singing one of the maudlin songs I like so much and I'm on my second glass of wine. I light candles. Between the Xanax and the wine and the music and the candles and the lights of the city, all is just right.

Countess Nora and Jack

Five minutes later, the phone rings and I hear Nora's very excited, very hyper, very British/Russian accent on the line.

"Jack, dahhhling! It's Nora!" she squeals! "Dahhhling, how are you?" I am quietly delighted that she has called.

Countess Nora and I met on an airplane. I was working a trip (as in, I was actually working as opposed to working it, although admittedly I often did both at once) from New York to L.A. I got stuck working a cart in coach. My least favorite position (again, I mean for working). I asked a nice looking blonde woman sitting in a window seat what she would like to drink. She said something that sounded like, "bought a corn."

"Uh, what?" I said.

Louder this time, she said, "wadda horn!"

A look of what-the-fuck-are-you-saying-I-have-four-thousand-other-people-to-serve-a-drink-to crept onto my face and I said, politely as I could, "What on earth are you saying?"

Then, out of this nice looking blonde lady's mouth, came a shriek in the oddest accent, "VODKA ORANGE!" Half the people on the 767 were suddenly quiet and looked directly at her. She smiled at me, waiting for her drink, and did not look the least bit self-conscious.

"$4.00," I said as I reached for the vodka mini.

Again with the shriek, "What? I will not pay it!" Which sounded like a version of, "Vat? I vill nut pee it!"

I was so startled that I spilled the vodka all over the front of my shirt. Nice that it dried clear, but smelling like vodka does not inspire too much confidence in passengers. I said, in my most condescending cart-tart voice, "Well, if you will not pay for it, then you shall not receive it."

She looked at me and I thought she might pop. And she kinda did. She started to shriek again. Mind you, she was in a window seat and she was shrieking at the top of her lungs over the sweet little old lady next to her. I stared at her dumbfounded. All I understood during her five-minute rant was, "London, New York, delay, standby," and then with the most horrible screech of all, "coach!"

I paused. She paused. I took a breath, then said, "What?"

Then two things happened at once. The sweet little old lady looked up at me and, in this heavy New York accent and a gravelly smoker's voice, she said, "Just give her the damn vodka and shut her up." At the same time, the crazy woman started to get up, saying she was going to the cockpit to speak to the captain about this. She was, by this time, in the aisle, two inches shorter than me, oddly still able to look directly into my eyes.

I said, "The captain is busy with safety right now."

She said, eerily calm, "This is about safety." She paused. "Yours!"

I burst out laughing uncontrollably. Then she did, too. We were both almost crying with laughter. What a total, uppity, accented bitch. I adored her immediately. We talked for almost the whole flight. Nora turned out to be a Russian Countess who lives in London. Ergo the horrifying accent. She said she was 33. I knew she lied. So, when she had her 34th birthday party, I gave her a card that said, "Happy second or third 34th birthday, Countess." She shrieked with laughter. Nora either speaks or shrieks. Extremes. Again.

On the phone, Nora says with hyper exuberance, "I'm wonderful! How are you?"

"Exhausted. Just back from L.A. All curled up with my wine."

"Oh! Sounds wonderful, darling! Absolutely marvelous!"

Why is it that everyone I tend to like speaks only in superlatives? "Nora, it's 2 a.m. there. What are you doing?"

"I've just come back from dinner. I'm stuffed!"

"How was the vodka?"

She laughs hysterically. It's like listening to myself. "Dahling, listen! You must come to London."

"I will! Promise!"

"No, dahhhling! Now! Paddy, who is absolutely lovely and fun and one of my dearest friends, has invited me to an underground jazz performance! You must come!"

"What? Now? What do you mean?"

"Jack, I'm going to go to sleep and wake up tomorrow at noon and I want you here by then! You must come with me tomorrow night! Paddy is excited to meet you!"

"Nora, I'm not coming to London right now."

"Jack! Don't be ridiculous!"

"Nora! You want me to get on a flight to London at the drop of a hat and I'm the one who is being ridiculous!" I laugh, astonished.

"Yes," she says with mirth in her voice, "you are!"

"Nora, there is no way I'm getting on an airplane to London right now."

"But dahling, I checked. There is an 11p out of JFK! You have time! You must come!" She is absolutely adamant. There is momentary silence. She says, slowly but excited, "Jack, dahling. What is the point of picking up peoples' dirty trays of food if you're not also going to get on an airplane immediately?"

"I only work galley, premium class, on the 767, Nora. I never touch a dirty tray."

She laughs, "Whatever you work, you still have to wear polyester!"

Hmmm. She makes a good point here. "But, I still look good in my polyester!"

We both laugh.

"I'll come in a few days! I don't have time to pack and get back to JFK, Nora."

"Jack. All your clothes are either black or charcoal. Throw them into a suitcase and come."

Again, she has a point.

I leave a note for Brent telling him I'll be in Europe for a few days. I feel guilty, but I'm going anyway. Our relationship is essentially over, anyway. It is only the fact that we both have this sense of immense commitment that keeps us together. We have learned this from our various older friends who have been together for over 30 years. We want to be them, but we aren't. There are reasons for divorces. We're not there yet, but we should be. It never really gets any better. The more we try, the more we realize that all this "trying" is part of breaking up. We won't figure this out until six months from now, however.

Four hours later I'm sitting in premium class on a 767 heading over the Atlantic for a six-hour flight to Heathrow. I've already decided to stay in London for a few days. In the cab to JFK, I made reservations and booked a corner suite at my favorite London hotel, St Martins Lane. Which is very much the hotel-of-the-moment. I also made reservations to visit Joanna in Warsaw and booked a suite at The Bristol, which, according to Joanna, is the finest and classiest hotel in Eastern Europe. I'll spend two days in London and two days in Poland and then fly back to NYC. Since the notice of my "heart thing," I've become extraordinary at not denying myself anything. Although I fail, at the time, to see the connection.

Joanna and I met in London a few months after I met Nora. I was there for a night or two (this being the time in my life when I was "hopping across the pond" between NYC, London, and Paris a few times a month to feed my inner snob, which was the Jack version of escaping reality. I went to this small gay bar called West Central. It's not there anymore, but it was great. People would dance wherever they stood. It wasn't packed. Nobody got too drunk, although drunk enough since the British, even the gay British, need to liquor up a bit for any sort of casual conversation. At some point each evening, two bartenders would climb onto the bar and do a synchronized dance to some 80s pop song. It was very playful. I like playful. I wore a devastatingly fabulous, hip outfit with my hair (which, unfortunately, I didn't appreciate at the time) spiked. I took notes and had a nice cognac.

I do this. I take notes anywhere, at any moment, in any situation, in front of anybody. I have no embarrassment where this is concerned. I'll write on napkins, menus, matchbooks, or whatever I can find. I especially favor using little tablets from Ian Schrager hotels. They must have been designed by Philip Stark since I've never seen them anywhere but Ian Schrager hotels. They fit in my back pocket perfectly and bend comfortably into the shape of my butt when I sit down. Sometimes I transcribe these notes into my journals. Sometimes I leave them in a drawer. I am convinced that I could die and someone will find something horribly profound I once wrote on a piece of toilet paper. It could happen. I write observations, pieces of conversation, something I say, something someone says to me, a random thought, a moment. Anything. I forget that it's weird to do this.

I'm standing in West Central being a walking contradiction of terms—wearing hip, black clothes while writing in a notepad drinking cognac. As opposed to the gay drunk British, I'm not good at making casual conversation, so I stood in the bar, watching the dancing duo, looking very quiet-fabulous, grinning like an idiot while drinking my alcoholic obsession of the moment. A very attractive girl, a bit younger than I, came up to me with an equally attractive guy. She said, "What on earth are you writing? Is that cognac?" Before I could respond, she says, twinkling with all smiles, "Oh my god. You're fabulous. I must know you."

I burst out laughing. Who was this creature? Joanna explained she was in London for business, grew up in Connecticut with a very well-connected political family, 25 years old, and was living in Warsaw since she spoke fluent Polish; she had a last name with far too many consonants in it. I said, "So you're intellectual, hip, and gorgeous."

She looked at me and said, pointedly, "Yes." Like Countess Nora, I adored her immediately. I dragged them to Light Bar. We had lots of vodka. Joanna said I was "very Bret Easton Ellis." I wondered, for a second, if my Klonopin was falling out of my pocket and then realized what she meant. I leaned over and kissed the hot guy full and sensuously on the mouth. He was a very good kisser. Joanna yelped, delighted! Somewhere during the night, I told her I would come to Warsaw to visit. A month later, I did. A year later we met in Paris for a quick weekend. A year after that she was in Paris with me again for my birthday.

I have a routine when I'm on my flights to and from Europe. I take a Xanax or two (or five) before the flight, while I'm waiting to get my seat announcement. By this time, a small amount of Xanax gives me utter euphoria. Since I already have wine in my system, this euphoria is intensified. Everything is wonderful and serene. I am calm and charming and comfortable with everything and everyone. I know exactly what to say and how to say it. I feel this with every fiber of my alcohol- and Xanax-infested brain.

The plane is not crowded. Only two other people are in premium class, which only seats nine anyway. I settle into my sleeper seat and am immediately offered "champagne, orange juice, or water?" by a very, very cute flight attendant. His hair is dark and short. His eyes are green. He is my height. He looks about my age. And his lips must be made for kissing. It takes a lot for me to be startled out of my oh-so-hip look-how-sophisticated-I-am demeanor, but I take a moment too long and hold eye contact with him for a second. That's how I know he's gay. Straight men do not hold sudden eye contact even for a moment with another man.

I don't reply to his offer of a beverage and say, "Hi, I'm Jack." It doesn't come off as cool and confident and nice. It comes off as awkward. Seriously. It is ridiculous. I can fly around the world, pass two bar exams, and get on every VIP list, but when it comes to flirting with someone I'm actually attracted to, I'm absurdly incompetent. He smiles a winning smile and says, "Hi, I'm Bill." He, on the other hand, comes off as kind and relaxed and low-key. I take a champagne because at the slightest moment of being nervous, I do the obvious: I drink. Well, at the slightest moment of anything, lately. I'm not clueless about my own absurdities. I'm simply amused by them.

I doze (mini-pass out) before we take off and wake up as one of the flight attendants walks toward me. Bill, I notice, is taking dinner orders from the other premium class passengers. I am instantly bitter. It means that I will have to make the effort to get out of my seat and go into the galley when I want to talk to him. The woman taking my order is my age, blonde, perky and very cute. She says, "Good evening, Mr. Freedman. I'm Tami. Have you had a chance to look at our dinner menu?"

I absolutely hate this, although I do the same thing to passengers when I'm working since it's a rule. "Please call me Jack." I look at the dinner menu and it's the usual five course menu that starts with caviar and ends with a make-your-own sundae. "Actually," I say, "I'll just have a glass of red wine. Doesn't matter what kind." I'm not drinking it for the taste anyway. I'm drinking it so I'll talk to Bill. There is very little alcohol I drink for the taste. Which is strange since there is very little alcohol I don't drink. I'm "over it" as far as the meal is concerned. After a while, even a gourmet meal is just a meal. My glass of wine, Evian, a Power bar, and a six-hour nap induced by 5 mg of Xanax will be sufficient for dinner tonight.

I wait until dinner is served, eaten, and picked up, and then head into the galley. Bill and Tami are there and their faces light up. Tami looks at Bill and

Bill avoids her glance; I know this look instantly. It means they were talking about me. There are two things flight attendants talk about on an airplane: passengers and sex. In my case at the moment, it seemed they had combined the two. We talk about where we're based and why I'm on the trip and how long I'll stay; they are delighted with my crazy life. *Hmmmm?* My life is crazy? Silly me, I thought it was glamorous. Won't be the last time I misinterpret other peoples' view of my over-the-top attitude towards life. It also won't be the last time that I don't give a shit.

I go back to my seat and go to sleep. When I wake up, Bill is bringing me coffee, orange juice, and a croissant. The sky outside is murky. I immediately take two Excedrin. Excedrin, absolutely the best for hangovers. I should know. In fact, if you have McDonalds at about 3 a.m. and then take Excedrin when you wake up, you're practically hangoverless. Some people drink a lot of water before going to bed. I fill my stomach up with fat and then take Excedrin. If everybody would do this, nobody would have hangovers. They'd be fat and addicted to the caffeine in the Excedrin, but they wouldn't have hangovers.

Bill slips me a piece of paper with his cell phone number as I step off the plane. I smile and say thank you. He also hands me a bag with champagne and wine from the flight.

At Heathrow, I zip through customs and take the tube into London. I love sitting on the train. People get on and off from and to the outdoor platforms. To and from. To and from. I get off at the Leistecer Square underground station and lug my bag up the stairs to the bustling street above. It is dreary and misty. It's always like this in London, it seems. I like it. Makes me feel comforted somehow. I walk down Charing Cross Alley with its little antique stores, mostly with old books and prints, turn right towards St Martins Lane. As the doormen open the two enormous glass doors for me, I marvel at the fact that I know my way around so well and feel so completely at ease. Between continents. Between hotels. Between cities. Between lives. I'm far too impressed with myself. Which is furthered by the fact that the gorgeous woman, with dark hair cut into a short bob, remembers me so well from two weeks ago that she says, in her sultry French accent, "Welcome back, Jack." She remembers I hate being called Mr. Freedman. Divine!

Ten minutes later I am standing against a wall of floor-to-ceiling glass looking out onto the city. My corner suite is all white except for a clay terra cotta flower pot on the wall with trailing ivy. I head to the mini-bar to see what goodies await my digestive system and open a small bottle of chilled white wine. No sooner have I sat down on the little chaise against the window than the phone rings. Nora.

"My god! Your timing is very good. I just arrived!"

"I know dear! I had the hotel call me!"

"Nora, why would the hotel call a stranger to let her know I'm here?"

She exclaims with glee, "Because I'm me! The Countess! How was your flight?"

"Divine. I flew premium class, ate my caviar, had my wine and Xanax and went to sleep the whole time."

"Marvelous, dahling! Utterly marvelous!"

We play at this conversation for a while. Our joy and amusement come more from the fact that we are mocking ourselves, mocking our privilege, than from the fact that we have it at all. As with most of my friends, we find ourselves endlessly amusing. If we heard this conversation from two other people, we'd be horrified at their snootiness.

"Dahling, I have thousands of things to do! Meet me at the Atlantic Club for dinner at 9 p. From there we'll go meet Lady Paddy at the jazz club and have an absolutely wonderful night!"

"Perfect! I can sleep the whole day then. I'm exhausted. Call me at 8 p to wake me up so I can get ready."

"Okay, I will. It's so lovely that you've come!"

"As if I had any other choice," I say laughing.

"No. You're right. You didn't."

"Nora, I hope I don't horrify your friend tonight. My British upper-crust act isn't exactly very polished lately. I have more of an international-socialite-snob thing going on."

"Dahling! She wears black leather pants!"

"Oh! Say no more. We'll get along famously."

After we've hung up, I realize I have no clue where or what the Atlantic Club is.

The bathroom has beige travertine tile and is heated from below. A heated floor. Love it. I blast the air conditioner because I like to sleep in an icy room. I take a blistering hot shower to scrub off the airplane. I finish my white wine, take 2 mg of Xanax and curl up in the king size platform bed with an enormous billowy down comforter. In seconds, I'm out.

Six hours later I hear a vague electronic pinging sound from somewhere deep in my head. I realize it's the phone.

"Jack! Dahling!" It's Nora, excited as always. "Wake up! Meet me at 9 p. You've got an hour."

"Okay. Where is this place?"

"Off Trafalgar Square, dahling. Must run! Can't wait to see you!"

Click. She's gone.

I get up and pull back the blinds from the windows to see the twinkling lights of London against a seamless corner of two walls of floor-to-ceiling glass. I stand there naked, marveling at the privilege of my life. I do this a lot lately. As though I can't quite believe I'm here. I light candles, dim the lights, put in some kind of trance/dance CD on loud and start to get ready. I have 45 minutes because, even though I don't know where the Atlantic Club is, I assume it will take me fifteen minutes to get there. I order a piece of chocolate cake and two coffees from room service. I need the caffeine/sugar buzz to wake me from my jetlag/wine/Xanax/nap.

I call Brent to tell him I'm in London, am going to Warsaw, and will be back in four days. He isn't home. It's late at night in NYC. I also call Tom and David in Boston to inform them of my Thanksgiving plans two weeks from now. David loves that I am calling from London. "Grand, grand, grand," he says, to my delight. Tom loves that I'm calling from St Martins Lane. Tom is an architect and always knows about any new and different building anywhere in the world.

I shave and brush my teeth in the shower. John taught me about brushing my teeth in the shower back what seems a million years ago. I remember thinking it was the silliest thing, but he thought it was more efficient. I guess it stuck. Makes less mess in the sink, too. I put my Murad Combination Skin Formula on my face and let it soak in. Then a moisturizer. I've been taking good care of my skin since high school. When you live in the desert and ski all winter, you have to. Hard to believe I was vain even then. Especially when I wasn't all that good looking back then. I run a huge amount of gel through my hair, spike it up, spray it down, blow it dry, more gel, spike it up again, blow it out, twist it around in my fingers. "Doing my hairs" as Lisa calls it, is time consuming to say the least and annoys absolutely everyone in my life.

There is a knock at the door and I go to answer it, assuming it's room service. I almost forget I'm completely naked. Wow. I really do need the caffeine! I throw on one of the oversized robes, answer the door, and an impossibly gorgeous room service waiter walks in. Everybody is gorgeous in this hotel. They must hire directly from modeling agencies. Same with the hotel guests. Everybody is always impossibly hip, sophisticated, well-turned-out and attractive. When I'm signing the check, I notice him looking around at the candles and stereo and the fact that my robe is almost coming untied and I catch just a tiny smile as I redo the tie on my robe.

I put on black pants, a black turtleneck, bulky square-toe black shoes, my black leather jacket, black gloves, and a charcoal scarf, and I'm out the door. At the elevator, I realize I've forgotten to bring a notepad and there is no way I'm going out on a night like tonight without a notepad with which to take notes, observations, thoughts, lines from conversations. Often, it feels like someone else is living this over-the-top fabulous life; I'm watching myself in astonishment. I will forever be the kid picked last for the baseball team in grade school, not this impossibly hip person traveling the world, a pampered prince.

Another one of the Beautiful People is at the concierge desk and she shows me on a map where the Atlantic Bar is and offers to get me a car. It looks like it's within walking distance, so I decline the car. I leave the hotel and walk toward Trafalgar Square. It is very cold now—that damp cold that seeps into your bones. I burrow my head into the high neck of my leather jacket and pull my turtleneck as high as it will go and head off into the misty London night.

I find the Atlantic Club fifteen minutes later and find myself in a huge, cavernous, very un-Europe-like restaurant. Restaurants in Europe are not huge and they are not cavernous. The reservation is under my name and I am immediately shown to a large round booth table. Nora is not here yet. So much for rushing to be on time! There is a large round bar in the center of the restaurant where a combination of rather glamorous people and men in suits loiter, smoke, and sip their cocktails. Like most Europeans, their voices are soft, but every now and then I can hear a burst of laughter from a man or a high-pitched I'm-so-fabulous-and-desirable laugh from a woman.

A mirror is against the wall. I wonder, with no shame whatsoever, if the back of my hair looks okay since it is reflected in the mirror. I order a martini, straight-up, no olives. Between the nap, the cold, the Xanax, the sugar and the caffeine, I am pleasantly fabulous again. Part of the Europe crowd. Disdaining the loud, crass, uncultured Americans and feeling oh so superior. I sip my martini. Then I see Nora rushing toward me. Pale skin, deep brown eyes, curly blonde hair falling to rest on the neckline of an enormous fur coat. We are ecstatic to see one another. We hug and hug and I motion the waiter for another martini for Nora even before we have a chance to sit down.

Dinner is filled with banter, shared intimacies, and tons of laughter. Nora is a huge personality. All flailing gestures and boisterous laughter. I never know if she's in London, Romania, China, Russia or Singapore. She travels the world doing her deals, charming everyone with sparkling eyes in the candlelight of long drawn-out dinners. There is nobody more international. It is impossible not to fall in love with her infectious charm and energy. Yet, she is a damaged person. Of course, we all are, but Nora and I are similarly damaged: we've cultivated our masks to such an extent that we barely remember what's beneath them. But Nora sees beneath my mask and I see beneath hers. We flirt with everyone and feel a part of no one. We adore the people we flirt with while making sure to walk away, excluding them from our lives. We find each other endlessly hysterical and are sure that few others would get our sense of humor. We are in love with our own combination of sophistication and don't-take-it-too-seriously-we-are-so-above-all-that attitude. Two hours, four courses, and three martinis later, we are off to meet Lady Paddy at the club.

The club is underneath a building. It's similar to a brownstone in NYC, but not posh. We step down from the street to get into the door. It's very dark and murky and I've never seen this neighborhood before. Seedy. Where the fuck are we? As we enter the door and close it behind us, we find a huge bouncer looming in front of us. He looks menacing. Nora says, brightly, smiling, "Hullo! And who are you?" A huge grin spreads across the bouncer's face. Audacity either breeds alienation or shocked respect. He checks to see that our names are on the list and, of course, they are. There is an old, unkempt iron gate we have to get through to go downstairs and the doorman opens it for us. It creaks on its hinges. This is more of a you-have-to-know-someone-to-be-here place than a velvet rope VIP list place.

We head down another set of very narrow, very steep stairs and I find myself in a small room that is so crowded with people that, once seated at a table, there is really no way to get up again. The walls are covered with murals, so the appearance is of a much bigger place. A small, barely-elevated stage is far enough in front of us for me to look at the crowd. To observe. To examine. To emulate, apparently. Thank goodness I'm a chameleon. I can be anyone! It's fabulous! Makes it so easy to avoid the me that is scared shitless, wondering if I will ever have moments like this again after my heart surgery. I push the thought from my mind. This moment, I sense, is going to be too over-the-top and magnificent for me to concentrate on truths. The me who is scared can have absolutely no part of the me that is fabulous and over-the-top.

Nora and I squeeze past people and suddenly I hear a shriek and see a woman furiously waving at us. Nora exclaims, excited as always, "There she is!"

I look to the woman who is waving and say, "Wow."

The woman who is waving is tan. Her face is narrow and pulled far back against her high cheekbones. Her hair is thin and blonde, pushed softly behind her ears, falling in the back just below her neck. Her smile is bright and her eyes are a gorgeous hazel color. They glimmer in the light from the candles. She is at once rather startling looking and rather beautiful. Her boobs are full and round and curve out from a white blouse that is more like a vest. Along with her vest-blouse, she is wearing tight, black leather pants. I adore her immediately for her audacity. She is clearly fabulous. This place is fabulous. I look around the room with the candles and murals and people stuffed together laughing and drinking and eating small appetizers and I feel divine. Nobody lives a life like I do.

Lady Paddy (Patricia) turns out to be a British aristocrat whose second husband stole all her money. She has impeccable manners. She can manage to say the most shocking things and still sound regal. For example, once at Georges, a posh restaurant on top of the Pompidou Center, after taking a slow drag of her cigarette, she said, "It was rather uncomfortable to have sex with him on the sofa. He had a very large penis and

Lady Paddy and Jack

the insides of my thighs were positively on fire from throwing my legs behind my ears." It sounded like, "Hello, dear. Fancy some tea?"

Picturing Paddy on the verge of a massive orgasm is a vision I do not need to have considering Lady Paddy is somewhere between 40 and death. Quickly, as I begin to know her, I lose interest in trying to figure out her age. We do the double air kiss thing, which comes naturally to me. Left to right. Whenever I get back from Europe, I do this automatically in America, forgetting that it appears affected.

We order wine. I drink it fast and get another glass. The three martinis, Xanax, and the wine I had in my room are apparently not enough to keep fueling my fabulousness. I am warmed by the wine. I am thrilled by the moment. I am entranced with Nora, Paddy, and myself. Especially myself. The image I have is of this fabulous, international, gorgeous guy laughing and flirting with everyone, having everything work out for him.

We drink our wine. The room gets smokier. We are laughing and sarcastic and hysterical. We go from discussing the fact that Paddy's leather pants make her butt look divine to discussing politics and art. I love the combination. Loud fabulousness. Quiet, natural sophistication. The superficial with the intellectual all at once. This is my favorite combination. I'm telling Paddy a story while we sip our wine and our eyes are lit by candlelight and the room is getting more boisterous and loud with laughter and conversations in so many languages. I tell Paddy, "This is magnificent! I could have been in Manhattan tonight being utterly bored!" Lots of laughter at my sarcasm that Manhattan could ever be boring.

Paddy responds, laughing, half telling me and half telling anyone who can hear us, "I love this guy! He's utterly mad!" Lots more laughs and my fabulousness is reinforced times ten. It's hard not to relish being adored. And it's hard not to give people the person they want to see when you know that's what they adore.

Suddenly the sconces dim until it's almost dark. The candlelight throws bizarre shadows around the room. I see the heads in front of me turn to face the stage and the room becomes deathly quiet. A black man steps up from the crowd, moves to the microphone in the center of the little stage, closes his eyes, and out of his mouth comes one of the deepest, most beautiful, liquid voices I have ever heard. It's slow and low and loud and mean. The kind of sound that makes you forget absolutely everything for a moment. A voice that makes your face contort in pleasure. Any pretense or posture or pose becomes instantly disregarded. I literally gape and do not care if anyone sees me.

I watch Nora and Paddy with their eyes lit by the bright light on the stage, their blonde hair in halos around their heads and smiles pasted across their faces. They don't know I'm watching them. I love to see people happy for no reason other than the simply divine moment. I am sure I have never heard a voice like this before, and I know I have never had a time like this before. The observant me makes me smile from ear to ear at the moment. I can't imagine myself having any other kind of life right now. Maybe I'm not the kid picked last for the baseball team anymore.

The man doesn't stop singing for almost an hour. He changes from low and intense and deep to painful to playful and loud and silly. We have more wine. We clap and laugh and dance in the square foot of floor space we each have. Entranced. Hypnotized. Respectful. And this moment makes us all feel so close and so special. The singer stops singing at 3 a.m. Nora and Paddy get their long fur coats, we throw our scarves around our necks, climb the steep steps and head into the very cold, very biting, very, very misty London night.

I am exhausted, serene, divine, and happy. Maybe this is my truth. Maybe the heart thing will be just a small diversion, although I don't really believe that for a second. I don't know what it will be, so I push it from my mind as usual. Which takes very little effort since my brain is swimming in substances and delight. I hug Paddy tightly, do the double kiss, tell her I am ecstatic at meeting her and can't wait to see her again.

She screams, "You're mad! I adore you!" Then, to Nora, "He's hysterical! Bring him everywhere!" I am, apparently, delightful luggage. Paddy heads off to catch a cab even at this hour. Nora and I head to her car. She puts the top down.

"Nora, you're insane! It's freezing!"

"Dahling! Insanity is divinity!"

I laugh. She laughs. She's absurd and I love her for that. Besides, she's also right.

We zip off through the London streets with the sleeve of Nora's fur coat hanging off the side of the door since she has it around her shoulders like a cape. We take the long way to Trafalgar Square, past the Houses of Parliament and Big Ben all lit up in gold on the Thames. I am freezing and delighted and fabulous and cannot keep the smile off my face.

I get out of the car, standing at the base of the London Gallery, on the steps leading up to the gallery and down to Trafalgar Square. As the mist swirls thick and orange in the streetlamps and the wine keeps me warm and the over-the-top, the singular grandness of this moment sears itself into my mind, Nora speeds off into the mist. She shouts, in her unique British-Russian accent, "Jack! Dahling! Life is to live, not merely to exist!"

I walk the ten minutes back to St. Martins Lane, step into the warm lobby of the hotel where soft rock music seeps out from the Light Bar and impossibly gorgeous, hip, sophisticated people wearing black linger here and there. In my room, I call the front desk and ask for twenty tiny white candles in clear glass votives; they are brought to me in ten minutes. I light them all. I open the thick, slick curtains to watch the lights of the city, glowing in the mist. Little halos everywhere. I set the lights behind the bed to a very dim purple. I take a very, very hot, steamy ten-minute shower. I stand there, almost hypnotized by the heat, still smiling.

The body lotion from the hotel is slightly scented with lemongrass and as smooth as silk. I slather it onto my body and look at my chest, wondering what the scar will be like. I think, through my alcohol and Xanax and magnificence, "I won't care. It will be a part of my uniqueness!" It's rather startling to think that the thought comes from the serenity of the moment, the uniqueness of my life, the glamorous people I have spent the evening with. It is entirely unclear to me if I am being hopeful or merely in denial.

I take two Xanax, call the front desk to wake me at 10 a.m., which is five hours from now, and curl up in the enormous, white, down comforter, lying flat, looking at the ceiling just above my bed, which glows with a pale, dim purple from the lights I set. "Life is to live, not merely to exist." This becomes my mantra for the next few years. I think, nobody, absolutely nobody, lives life like I do. At least as long as I might have left. This is my last thought before I pass out.

The facts surrounding the possibility of my death are all too clear. The weak fear of mortality is completely hidden away from me. If it was on the surface, would I be doing all these amazing things? At what point does the freedom one gets from thinking he'll die anyway go from beneficial and freeing to bad and restrictive? Would I want to die in a completely honest way, facing everything and everybody? Or is it better to die as a total rebel, flaunting my fear, flaunting my actions of immortality in the face of mortality, being aggressive with the "I'm here and fuck everyone because I'm going to make it so obvious I'm here that none of you will ever forget me. My last months, weeks, and days will be the stuff of legend." If I had died, they would have been. In fact, they still are.

CHAPTER 9

Up and Down

8/10/99 7:05 a.m., on plane DFW to Santiago, Chile

ONCE AGAIN IN PREMIUM CLASS. I ate my caviar, lobster, and shrimp risotto, drank white wine, then popped 1.25 mg of Xanax and spread out the sleeper seat so it was flat. I slept wonderfully. I have woken to the breathtaking sight of the sun rising over the jagged peaks of the Andes. The snow has lightly dusted what looks like razor sharp edges and one side of the peaks is lit with orange and red glinting off the white snow. The fiery light of dawn goes from a thin line of red to orange to blue. Spectacular. It reminds me a bit of see- ing the Swiss Alps in the bright moonlight on a flight to Italy to play with Linda in Rome years ago. Now I'm excited that I'm going to be in Chile. It's that little thrill that rises from inside and makes you smile and want to dance about a bit.

8/10/99 1:37 p.m., Stephanie's apartment, Santiago, Chile

I arrived at the airport about thirty minutes before Felicia. As is my nature, I simply sat down in the arrivals lounge and watched. Everybody. The people looked almost Italian to me—as dark but with not quite as much flair. Looser. An interesting combination of the sophistication of the Europeans and the more casual attitude of those from more relaxed cultures.

I have seen little of the city so far. Steph's apartment is a small, modern, one bedroom. Very small. European small. As we walked down the street in what feels like crisp, dry fall weather, we all felt as though we could be in Santa Monica. Palm trees. Modern and old apartment buildings. Well-kept grassy areas. Providencia, the main street, is somewhat indistinctive. The metros feel exactly like those of Paris. The people are well-dressed, more innovative than the U.S. but less innovative than Europe. Stylish. I can already tell that people "dress" for nights out. Yes, definitely a combo of the U.S. and Europe. The Andes are remarkable. Jagged, snow-capped peaks surround the city. Their height is astonishing. I have an urge to go skiing.

8/11/99 8:13 a.m., Steph's apartment, Santiago, Chile
I slept well on the futon in the tiny living room while Felicia slept in the bedroom and Steph stayed at her fiancée's. We giggled and laughed like little kids till midnight. We fell silent just before a car alarm went off below the window and scared the wits out of us. More laughter. Felicia was silly cuz of the codeine for her cough. I was silly cuz of the Valium I got at the Farnacia. Around 12:30 a.m., we finally fell silent. It's sunny again today and the three of us are going to take a bus trip to Valparaiso, a beach town on the Pacific coast. My flight back to Dallas leaves late tonight.

Steph, Felicia, and Jack

8/11/99 9.36 p.m., Santiago Airport, Chile

We sat in a sidewalk café this morning and had espresso that almost equaled that of Paris. Surprisingly, fewer people smoke here. Not surprisingly, they are less in a rush. After our espresso, sipped slowly in the brisk morning air, we bought bread at a nearby grocery store. Fresh and sweet. Warm. On our way to the metro, Felicia said, "I want your straight twin."

We took a 45-minute bus ride to the Pacific coast. A Riviera of sorts. The terrain reminded me of rural Southern California, sprinkled occasionally with vineyards. There were several tunnels and each time we emerged, we found ourselves in different weather. One time fog, one time sunlight, another time gray and windy.

At Valparaiso we took a cab up to Vena Del Mar, which had high-rise condos, a casino filled with marble and sanded, shiny wood, sidewalk cafes on the ocean. Gorgeous. Old-world classy. We decided to head out to a restaurant on the beach to have Chilean sea bass, driving along one of the most spectacular coasts I've ever seen. The rocks were dark, large and sharp. Rising from the ocean, they appeared almost volcanic. The water was rough and waves sprayed into a fine frothy shower as they hit the rocks. We kept stopping to take photos. Of us, the ocean, the coast and hillsides of Valparaiso and Vena Del Mar dotted with homes and cottages. I simply could not get over the grandeur of the coast. So brutal and unrelenting.

We ended up stopping near these Chilean Navy boys. Anywhere from 18-20, I imagine, they paid attention to the girls in a shy way. Big grins and stares, but no ogling. Nothing disrespectful. We got them to play their flutes on the beach for us and to let me take pictures of them with Felicia and Steph. A spontaneous wonderful moment. Navy boys playing flutes on the Chilean coast. The sun low in the sky and sparkling as the water crashed just a few feet away. The natural beauty combined with the unexpected moment to make the trip that much more personal.

Back in Santiago, I bought two bottles of Chilean Reisling for myself, a lapis penguin for Brent for his collection, a lapis clock for me for my collection, and a bottle of orange liqueur for Lisa.

Last night, we had dinner at Steph's fiancée's parents' house. At some point, I walked into the hallway and heard Eddie's mother telling him her legacy to him, what she was going to pass on to him as he got married. I paraphrase: "I pass to you, my son, all that love and heart and joy, good and bad times, that you watched your father and I share as we grew up." I cried softly a bit. It was heart-wrenchingly beautiful. The farfel and chicken and candlelight and speaking English, Spanish, and French in such a cozy feel-at-home house with such a family, all the gracious and impeccable, yet casual, manners—my heart was truly warmed. My perspective, so often in the sky, returned for a moment to earth.

8/13/99 10:15 a.m., Eighteenth & Eighth, Manhattan
The flight from Santiago to Dallas was heaven. Met another flight attendant, Christian, on the flight back home to NYC. Beautiful guy. We exchanged numbers. Harmless since he could look me up in the system if he wanted. He knows I live with someone. I don't want to turn down the possibility of a friendship. You never know when someone could pop into your life and become part of it from then on.

Came home, ordered tons of sushi, did laundry and unpacked. Checked email and there was one from Joseph. He managed to find me after all. I suppose he remembered my last name. I told Brent the story. He didn't seem to be upset by it since I didn't do anything wrong, but I'm sure it must have bothered him and I'm not sure why he didn't say so.

I'm flying to Paris in three days. Chile, New York, France. Life is too amazing to stay in one place. Of course, I'm not blind. I know I'm running. I want experience, and I want to share all that with my friends. I want my life to have been of consequence if I die.

I have essentially spent the past two days since I got back from South America being depressed. Spent most of today shopping in Soho. I wore my ratty NYU Law sweatshirt and faded blue Gap slim-fit blue jeans and my *New Yorker Magazine* baseball cap that Barney gave me when I spent a weekend on Fire Island when I was 23. Personally, I felt I looked very college-cute, despite being annoyed that I am getting further and further away from college itself.

However, I was not looking like my usual fabulous self because the sales boys and girls did not jump to cater to my every whim and smile at my charming and sparkling personality. Rather irritating how depression influences my ability to charm. Which, of course, makes me more depressed. It's like I'm in a hole and I can't climb out. It's pretty hard to flaunt how fabulous my life is one moment and expect people to care that I am depressed the next.

In Soho, I hit Balthazar first. It's crowded and fabulous and smoky at the bar and I'm rather out of place in my sweatshirt and jeans. I have an espresso and a Courvoisier and leave being rather amused at the bartender's horror of what I drank in the course of two minutes. I walk in and out of shops rather aimlessly and nobody pays any attention to me, except the occasional guy who notices that I am, in fact, cute and college-like.

Eventually I end up in French Connection. I can almost never tell which clothes are for boys and which are for girls in that store. They are all mixed up all over the store. I spot a very simple pair of black (*quel* shock) flat-front pants and decide they are something I need because, you know, I don't have enough black flat-front pants already. There is a dressing room Nazi waiting for me.

"I'd like to try these on," I say, smiling very innocently and oh-we're-both-in-the-cool-club-aren't-we look.

"Are you sure?" she says with a smile and the oh-I-am-so-in-the-know-and-you're-not look.

"Uh, yes!" I say very "Friends"-like.

She looks at me, cocks her rather severely-cropped dyed blue-black hair and says, in the most condescending voice I have ever heard, very fake-sweet, "They're for girls."

"They can't be. They are black flat-front pants." I am a little manic-nervous.

"Girls wear those, too. In fact," she says, pointedly, "specifically those." She points her eyes at the pants.

Her self-righteous and condescending attitude does not please me. I can't tolerate it when people embarrass me with the fact that they are right.

"We'll see. Just open a dressing room, " I say, with a very fake smile plastered across my face

Thirty seconds later I am standing in a small white dressing room. There is a very bright overhead halogen light and a huge mirror against the wall. The designer of this dressing room must have been absolutely drop-dead gorgeous so as not to care about the shocking white and never flattering overhead lighting. I definitely feel that I have won the battle with the dressing room Nazi. I continue to feel this way for two minutes while I stand here doing nothing, since there is no point in trying on women's pants. I leave the pants in the room and pass by the Nazi on the way out and say, very snotty, "Cheap fabric."

She gives me a snotty look and rolls her eyes at me behind my back. I just know it.

I immediately go back to Balthazar and hit the bathroom first. I take my baseball cap off and run a little bit of water through my hair and pull at the ends of it, kind of curling it around to one side of my forehead. Then, I take a tiny amount of liquid soap and run it through, being very careful not to make it bubble. Unbubbled liquid hand soap makes an excellent hair product when you're on the run. But you have to be very careful. You're only a drop of water away from messy-wet-cool to bubblehead. The smell is something to watch out for, too. Older places have soap that smells really soapy and perfumed. Newer places like Balthazar have trendy soap, which is more citrus flavored. I find it perfectly acceptable to have citrus hand soap in my hair. Luckily, I have used just the right amount of trendy citrus hand soap.

I'm going to have a glass of wine so I won't care what I look like quite as much. After one glass of wine, I'll decide I'm strong enough not to be influenced by the judgmental world around me and, thus, not care if I'm in a sweatshirt and jeans. It takes at least three glasses to get to the don't-care point.

The sky is plunging into a steely-blue outside and Balthazar is all yellowy bright, playful lights and candles, and very Parisian-like fake-antique walls. Everybody is wearing black. Everybody is fabulous. Everybody feels they are barely too cool to be here as opposed to feeling, like me at the moment, not quite cool enough.

I squeeze myself in between a very tall woman and a very tall man. They both smile at me. That oh-we're-all-in-the-club smile. I order a glass of Syrah and a small glass of ice. I love to horrify people by putting an ice cube in my red wine. I like to fit in, but I like to fit in so much that I'm allowed to be shocking, too. That is when you know you're really in the club, after all.

I get my wine, look at the huge assortment of liquor behind the bar, which is very, very long, put an ice cube in my glass and drink the whole thing in two sips. The bartender looks down at the glass, up at me, down at the glass and says, "Would you like another?"

"Would I have drunk that one so fast if I didn't?" He laughs. I have another. This time I drink half in one sip right away. A few moments later I take the other sip. I put thirty dollars on the bar and leave without seeing how much it really was.

I take a cab home. Me and my depression and memories of the dressing room Nazi. I immediately go to the freezer, put ice cubes in a glass, and pour a full glass of vodka. I grab the phone, take my vodka and go sit on the couch, looking out at the lights of the city that are twinkling in the wind. The vodka tastes disgusting after the nice soft wine at Balthazar. Naturally, I take a gigantic slug to finish it faster.

I decide to call Linda. "I'm depressed."

"Why?"

"I'm not sure."

"Well, you definitely have so much to be depressed about. Flying all over the world, just back from Chile, forced to stay home for two days before you go to, uh, where are you going next and when?"

She doesn't really know if I'm going anywhere. She just assumes. And it makes me more sullen that she's right. "Paris. Tomorrow."

She laughs maniacally. "Amazing," she says, very droll.

I say in my pouty-boy voice, which is embarrassingly unintentional, "So, does this mean I'm not getting any sympathy from you for my depression?"

"None at all," she says without a beat.

What is the point of depression if you can't get people to feel sorry for you? Highly frustrating. I call my mother.

"Hi, honey," she says very sweet and mother-like, which makes me instantly suspicious.

"What's wrong, Mom?"

"Nothing. How are you?"

"Depressed."

"Why?"

"Well, I'm not sure. I don't really have a reason to be. I just got back from a great trip to Chile. I'm going to Paris day after tomorrow."

She pauses. "It's the end of the month," she says very gently.

"Uh, right, okay, and?" I am suddenly irritated with myself that I even called her. "What does that have to do with it?"

"Did you refill your Propranolol prescription in the last few days?"

"Yes, yesterday. You're keeping track of this," I say half irritated and half shocked.

"I keep track of all your heart stuff now and I know you only have a thirty day prescription at a time. I remember that you got your first prescription about four weeks ago."

I'm pretty shocked.

She continues, "So, honey, when did you get the prescription?

"Yesterday morning."

"And when did you start feeling depressed?"

Oh. Now I see. "Yesterday afternoon."

A side effect of the beta-blocker can be depression. I forgot. For now, it's just a side effect. A few years from now, my whole life will be gone and replaced, completely, by side effects of one kind or another. Clearly, I don't face this at the moment. We talk a little while longer and I hang up after finishing my vodka. At least now I know the reason I'm depressed. I'm not used to the Heart Thing yet. I don't want to be used to it, so I re-fill my glass and call Eric.

"How are you?" he asks.

"Well, I'm depressed."

"Start drinking immediately!" he shrieks!

I laugh. "I already have! Wine at Balthazar and vodka here at home."

"That's not enough. You need to get drunk enough to not care if you're depressed. Then, drunk enough to have a fabulously fun time somewhere.

Then, drunk enough to go home and have a complete and proper black out." He pauses and I hear ice clinking in a glass while he takes a sip of whatever-it-is that he's drinking, and continues, "There's a natural order to these things, Jack. Haven't I taught you anything in life?"

"See! My depression even makes me forget how to drink my problems away! It's awful!" I whine.

"How was Chile?"

"It has the most beautiful coast line I have ever seen and I had Chilean sea bass in a tiny resort town by the ocean."

"Fabulous. Did you meet any cute Chilean boys?"

"Not really, but I did get hit on by a nice German one on the flight back. His name was Christian and he had cute blonde hair and blue eyes and looked like a proper Nazi boy."

"You should have dated him!"

"Eric, I'm still with Brent!"

"Not for too much longer, I imagine," he says very snidely. "So dear, did you at least flirt with him?"

"Of course," I say without hesitation. "I'm allowed to look and flirt."

"Trust me, dear. Nobody would ever try to stop you. It'd be like stopping the Concorde with butterfly wings."

"I hate when you know me."

"But, I do!" he says triumphantly.

"Okay, I feel better. Meet me out somewhere," I say.

"LaGuloue at 10 p and then we'll go to G," he says without even a second of hesitation.

I figure out which of my black pants to wear, which of my black shirts to wear, which of my black leather jackets to wear, and which of my square-toed black shoes to wear. It's always an agonizing decision.

About six months later, Christian and I hang out at the Mondrian, the hotel-of-the-moment in L.A., for a weekend. Two months after that, he will get caught in a huge international drug bust on a layover overseas. As they break into his room (I am told through a mutual friend), Christian jumps off the balcony from the 31st floor and kills himself. I had no clue. Not the slightest. I figured he was a trust fund baby, and I have been raised not to talk about money. Lisa will tell me, afterwards, as she always has, "Jack, there are things in life that only happen to you and this is another one of them." I will be amused/sickened/sad all at once.

CHAPTER 10

Birthday Wishes

11/22/99 9:44 p.m., on plane from NYC to London

I HAVE ELECTED TO SPEND my birthday in London at the *tres nouveau* Ian Schrager hotel, St. Martins Lane. In fact, I made this decision a few weeks ago when I was in London to see Nora and then on my way to Warsaw to visit Joanna. I'm in premium class, as usual, and Lisa teased me about the ironic image of me doing the laundry in the basement this afternoon, walking to Grand Central, and taking a bus to JFK using my $5 coupons.

When I had been in Warsaw, Joanna, Marta, Brent M. and I went out to a bar that could have been in any hip city around the world. Joanna and I are all hysterical laughs and quips. Marta is brilliant and the most well-read person I have ever met. Brent M. is more quiet and introspective. Almost mysterious. I have always said that one of my favorite quotes is Shakespeare: "To thine own self be true . . ." I have also said that I will fall for any guy who knows the rest of the quote. After a few drinks I mentioned this and Marta

Joanna and Jack

instantly knew the rest of the quote: ". . . and then it must follow as night to day that thou canst not be false to any man." Marta also said one of her favorite quotes was from Myrna Loy: "Tame things have no immensity."

When Joanna and I walked back to the Bristol, we saw the eternal flame and Joanna said, "See. It's kind of like you." We laughed, in hysterics, our breath misting up in the freezing cold night air. We then sat in the Bristol Bar, elegant with flowers and wood and damask sofas. Candles and high paneled ceilings. A piano played somewhere behind one of the palm trees reaching high to the vaulted ceiling. Gorgeous rugs everywhere. We quoted Frost and Shakespeare and Joanna said, "I label people."

To which I replied, "Yes, but I have many labels, don't I?"

She looked at me thoughtfully for a minute. Her lips curling to a sweet smile and she said, "Actually, you do. It's not easy to put you into a nice, neat box." Which pleased me to no end.

She tried to teach me some Polish words. I failed miserably to pronounce them correctly. I told her Oscar Wilde said, "It's only shallow people who don't judge by appearances." And we talked about how it doesn't mean what it sounds like on the surface. He probably meant that you can judge the appearance of someone, not their outside appearance, but who they allow themselves to appear to be. Perhaps he meant that sometimes whatever you see is who they are. Maybe you don't need to look too deep. On the other hand, maybe we were reading too much into it. In any case, it was fun to sit there in Warsaw trading all of our vast literary knowledge. Two very loud Russians sat in a sofa near us and Joanna leaned over to me and said, over her Cognac snifter, "What fresh hell is this?" Oh, she knew Dorothy Parker! I told her I need a boy-Joanna and she said, with a mischievous smile, "Well, talk to Brent M. some more." Oh, dear.

11/23/99 5:50 p.m., St. Martins Lane, London
My flight was lovely, as usual. I slept on and off and was woken up for my breakfast just prior to landing at Heathrow. Took the tube in from LHR, checked in and tried to charm my way into an upgraded room with a woman

who was not too receptive. Where's my usual reservation clerk? This one was nice, but was sticking to the rules. When I saw my room, the view of a rooftop did not suit me. Called the front desk and told them I would like a different room and told them why. I was very polite and almost made fun of myself. The gentlemen said he'd give me another room. In fact, he's given me a deluxe suite, with huge floor-to-ceiling windows and a view of the British National Opera and the top of the obelisk in Trafalgar Square on the other side of the British National Museum, all lit up in spotlights in the already black sky. I sit with candles lit, the "mood lighting" over the bed turned to an orange-red. I write at a table lit from within and painted to look like glowing marble. The gentlemen at the desk, with an Irish accent, said quietly, as he handed me the key, "I've given you a double upgrade. Keep it a secret."

After a two-hour nap, went to Soho and bought a few minis of absinthe, which is banned everywhere else in Europe and in the U.S. It always seemed a core part of the "lore" of the artistic geniuses, painters and writers of the Latin Quarter and St. Germain in Paris. Of course, it reminds me of "my Degas" at the Orsay. I have had one mini and see no hallucinations. Just as well. Real life is strange enough.

So I'm out and about in London hitting a few pubs. Ended up in a conversation with a very nice, handsome British guy and after a few drinks he made it clear he's looking for "the one" (as people are apt to reveal after a few drinks, right?). By this point he knows I'm American and only here for a few days. At some point the conversation turns to this:

Me: "Are you flirting with me? Because I'm relatively hopeless at figuring that out."

Him: "Yes."

Me: "But you're looking for a big romance and I'm only here for a few days."

Him: "Oh, I am, but I'm also a narcissistic overgrown kid who can't commit and you're flying back to LA soon, which means we can have a mini-romance and I can avoid having to face my issues."

Me: speechless as mouth falls open. "Hold on just a second because I need to write that down."

11/24/99 10:40 a.m., Costa Café, London

My 29th birthday! On a foggy, cozy morning at this now-familiar café in London. Some woman sings torch songs in French on the stereo and the double espresso is already coursing its way through my system. Nora rang this morning and told me she and Paddy have an evening planned for my birthday.

Nobody in the States knows how to contact me today. I didn't want to spend my birthday in the U.S. trying to get people from both coasts together. I also didn't want to deal with Thanksgiving with my parents. I always feel so guilty when choosing who to spend the majority of the day with. I don't want anyone to be hurt. So, the escape to Europe is perfect.

I'm off to the Tate Gallery, a moment at Westminster Abbey, a walk along the Thames, and then back here to take a nap and get ready for the evening. I'm meeting Paddy and Nora at the Atlantic Club at 9 p.m. I wonder what the twelve months leading to my 30th birthday will bring? My instinct tells me there are big changes in store, but I'm not sure what.

11/27/99 4:17 p.m., Union Square, San Francisco

On Thanksgiving day, I flew to London from Warsaw (where I had been to visit Joanna again for a day), had lunch with Paddy at a quaint little restaurant on the Thames up near the London Bridge, then a flight from London to Boston in time to have Thanksgiving dinner with Brent at Tom and David's. We had a terrific time. Five cities, two coasts, and three continents in two days. That's a record even for me.

Today is cloudy and cozy. Two young violin players play Christmas songs nearby. I love violin music. And to sit here on this bench on this cozy day with crowds of people dressed warmly, while listening to sweet music played by cherub-faced kids, so soothing after the craziness.

11/29/99 10:15 a.m., Starbucks, 2nd Ave, Manhattan

My London trip was fantastic. Paddy and Nora, the mad women of London, took me to the Atlantic Club. We had a marvelous time eating, drinking, discussing everything. It was terribly fun. We exchanged photos from my prior visit when we went to Club 606 to listen to jazz. Paddy "insists" that I return for December 5ᵗʰ to go to a party of hers. "It will be very international," said Nora. After dinner went to the premiere discothèque in London called "China White." A gigantic crowd of people outside clamoring to get in. Paddy was on the list, so we jumped right through the crowd. I had absinthe immediately.

It was dark with low ceilings and a combination of Moroccan and Indian décor. Lots of huge pillows and alcoves with a dance floor and smaller rooms seemingly everywhere. It was huge without really feeling that way. And my god, I have never seen so many utterly gorgeous people in one place in my life. Simply eye-catching. Men. Women. Sexuality was absolutely irrelevant. All ages. And the clothes! Everything from the beautiful boy with cargo pants and a sleeveless t-shirt to the girl in the amazing black outfit and spiked Gucci heels and hair out to "here." Total diversity, which is the atmosphere in which I am most comfortable. Nora and I drew tons of looks while we danced and, of course, pretended not to notice.

Thanksgiving dinner with Tom, David, and Brent in Boston was warm and relaxing. A balance for the whimsy of my birthday in London. And this is quite the point: My joy at sitting on the windowsill overlooking the Common, the lone ice skater on the frozen pond in the hazy lights, was equal to my joy and amazement at my birthday evening in London. Just a different type.

I wonder where all this life, this seemingly out of a magazine of the over-the-top and young and fabulous, is going?

11/30/99 1:24 p.m., Bonaventure Hotel, Los Angeles
Had a work flight here yesterday. Went immediately to bed and slept until a few hours ago. Anthony Keadis from Red Hot Chili Peppers was in first class. He irritated me, sucking face with a trashy-looking blonde girl for the whole five-and-a-half hour flight. I told the #5 not to give him a sock. She didn't get the reference I was making to an old *Rolling Stone* cover where he was completely naked except for a sock on his dick.

12/1/99 12:16 p.m., Starbucks, 2ⁿᵈ Ave, Manhattan
Winter is here. It is crystal clear, sunny and cold. Easy flight back to JFK yesterday except for bitchy passengers. I hate working business class. It's all

the people who upgraded from coach and those whose companies paid for their ticket; they are all obnoxious with entitlement. People who fly in first class generally live that type of life, so they are used to all of it and generally polite. In any case, one person in particular was outright rude. Otherwise, I read my book about Van Gogh, sitting up front on the jump seat. One of the flight attendants started telling me his fears and dreams and hopes and secrets. Then he said, "I don't know why I trust you. I never tell people these things." Why does this happen to me all the time?

Heather Locklear was on the plane and as nice as can be. Gorgeous. Smiles and manners. I told her to slip into the galley to hide while people deplaned and her blue eyes twinkled at me when she said thanks. Very genuine. Should I have told her I'm an attorney and knew all of the terms of her *Melrose Place* deal? I laughed at myself as I told her it was a pleasure to meet her.

12/4/99 10:12 a.m., Starbucks, Union Square, Manhattan
Nora arrived from London yesterday. I met her at the Soho Grand and we had wine and salad niçoise at Balthazar. She wore a gorgeous sable coat with flared hem and cuffs. She will speak with anyone, utterly friendly, a flirt. No holding back, but with grace. I want that kind of confidence! To feel that comfortable in my own skin. After our salads and wine, we walked around Soho and found ourselves in a great design gallery on West Broadway. There was a Fabergé egg clock. Silver and gold with an amethyst crystal crown. Gorgeous and unique. I bought it on the spot for my clock collection. Its utter opulence is ridiculous. Whose life do I think I'm leading?

12/11/99 2:31 p.m., Xando, Manhattan
Joanna is planning on being in Warsaw Thursday and Friday. I booked a suite at The Bristol and she said we can either go see "La Traviata" or hear Christmas carols at the Chopin Museum. I also have reservations at The Palace in Prague, but maybe that trip should wait. It's freezing in Czech.

Lisa got me a silver flask for my birthday. It was hysterical and I love it. We immediately bought a bottle of Cristal and filled it up. Mom got me a mini "Doorslam" for Hanukkah. When I was a little kid, Mom got me a hand-puppet in the shape of a lamb. I loved it and still have it in my box of "treasures." I'm sure Mom loathed the day she bought It because I used to open a door with the puppet on my hand, then slam the door shut yelling, "Doorslam!" Charming child. In any case, it was so sweet and warmed my heart. I am so "hard," so "blunt" in such a careless way lately, so into being fabulous and international and absorbing all the attention I can get. And all it took to break down the wall was this teensy present from my childhood.

12/13/99 6:55 p.m., Babba's House, Laguna Beach
I flew here spur of the moment yesterday. Felt like I needed some peace. Some balance. A quiet time. And it has been great. Babba and I talked on the sofa for four hours this afternoon. What a blessing. What pleasure. She tells such stories. We open our hearts. I know more about her than anyone. So many things I'm never supposed to tell, even her sons. She told me she is more content with herself than she has ever been. Happier. She watched her kids grow up and then her grandkids, lives in a beautiful home, and has no serious regrets. To hear her say, "I'm so happy now" made me feel wonderful. I am so hard lately and our time together made me feel softer. Gentle, almost. Although I'm sure it's a passing moment given my lifestyle lately.

Babba: "Jackie, do you know what I'd like to see before I die?"

Me: "World peace?"

Babba: "You wearing clothes that aren't black."

Me: "World peace is more likely."

Babba: "Do you know what I want so that I can die happy?"

Me: "Yes. You want me to wear clothes that aren't black."

Babba: "I can deal with the black clothes. Now I want you married before I die."

Me: "How about if I wear a blue shirt next time and we call it even?"

Babba: "Jackie, I'm serious."

Me: "So am I. I really will wear a blue shirt next time I come to see you."

Babba: "You're not funny."

Mc: "Ya, I kinda am."

Babba laughs and rolls her eyes.

1/2/00 2:41 p.m., Xando, Manhattan

I want to remove my head and put it in the freezer for a while. I am so incredibly hung over from last night/early this morning. Brent was in Boston for New Year's Eve and comes back tomorrow, which is just as well because staying together last night would have felt false. Against everyone's expectations, I decided to spend the night by myself. I was in my jammies, candles lit, two bottles of Cristal and Nancy or Linda crooning on the stereo. I sat there in my huge leather chair watching the lights of the city. Completely content not to be flying around the world or even out tonight with everyone else.

Then, maximus interruptus: Lisa called and demanded my presence at a little Italian restaurant in the Village. I relented after five minutes, messed my hair into a frenzy, wore my grey, crushed velvet jeans from Paris and my Gucci pea-green plush shirt over a simple white t-shirt. I have to admit that I looked great considering it only took me 20 minutes from phone call to out the door. It was one of those times that I looked in the mirror and am exactly the image, at least on the outside, I never knew I'd be. All luster and sheen on the outside and all the experience, fascination, education, emotion, confusion, and insecurities on the inside.

After a tremendous dinner with our usual laughing and banter, we went to a party on 10th Street in the Village. A penthouse with the elevator opening into an apartment filled with pounding music, low lights, tons of people and every "look" you could imagine. The apartment was huge and gorgeous. Breathtaking. Candles. Every type of alcohol. And only Hershey Kisses to eat. In every bowl all over the apartment. Lisa and I met Steph and Rich there and the four of us were lit like the ball over Times Square in no time. We ran around hugging everyone and making tons of new "friends." But what was with having only Hershey's Kisses? Where was the Godiva? The Beluga?

Lisa vaguely recalls being on the balcony waving her arms around and screaming "Happy New Year!" to everyone on the streets below. She sounded all raspy on the phone from all the hollering. I vaguely recall salsa dancing with some girl. And I do not salsa dance. Lisa kept saying, "I am so glad you came. I had to be able to tell my grandchildren we spent this night together!"

I said, "You need to have children first. That's the way it works."

CHAPTER 11

Coming Out

1/14/00 2:30 p.m. (Japan time), on plane from Dallas to Osaka

DAD AND I ARE FLYING to Japan. New York to Dallas to Osaka and then a train to Kyoto. Kyoto is Japan's oldest unharmed-during-the-war city. I'm very, very excited in a way I haven't been for a trip in ages. Excited like a little kid instead of a thrilled to be an international jetsetter. Of course, we'll fly premium class in the sleeper seats on the 777. This flight is almost 15 hours long due to a very strong headwind. I have slept, read my guidebooks, watched parts of movies. Due to the comfort, the service, the pampering, and true lack of any ability to do anything of consequence, I am forced to relax and think. Slowly, at last.

My unexpected interview at DreamWorks the other day went well, I think. I was just totally myself without pretense. I was sarcastic and professional when appropriate. I was completely honest, almost forceful, about my complete lack of television experience. At one point, I said, "I'm really not sure if you want me. I know absolutely nothing about the TV industry." The head of business and legal affairs for DreamWorks TV laughed. She thought my "nerve" to be a flight attendant was "inspiring." Inspiring? Me? I may be a ton of fun, but I'm not sure I'm inspiring.

I got the interview because I was visiting Linda in her office and she introduced me to Amy, her boss. After talking to Amy for about 30 minutes, she suddenly picked up the phone, called this woman at DreamWorks and said, "I have someone you need to speak with." Late that afternoon, I had the interview. Would I want to move? Would I want to leave the airline? Leaving Brent seems almost inevitable now, sadly.

1/16/00 7:56 a.m., Three Sisters Ryokan, Kyoto
I am so utterly lost in thought that I can hardly write. I sit here in a tiny sitting room off the main room of our suite, which is not a suite in the American sense of the term. This area can be closed off from the main room with rice paper screens sliding silently along the floor. There are enormous windows on one side where I stare at a courtyard below. The courtyard is tiny, but cleverly and intricately designed with rocks, plants, a stream, and a large tree reaching up near the window next to me. Huge magenta blossoms. It is cold here, but not snowing and not to the point of discomfort. On our flight two days ago, we flew by Mount Fuji and the view from the plane took my breath away. The sun was low and the clouds hovered below the peak. It was perfectly shaped. Almost flat on top. I was surprisingly enthralled. Dad was literally out of his seat peering, with exclamations of amazement.

1/17/00 8:23 p.m., Three Sisters Ryokan, Kyoto
I am so entranced with this city. The culture seems rooted in gracious rules of formality which come off as kind and gentle instead of stiff and conservative. And the smiles! When a Japanese person smiles at you, his whole face lights up. Those eyes penetrate with kindness even if for the briefest of moments. The first morning, Dad and I walked to the oldest (around 1530 or something) Zen temple in the city. We woke at dawn and got there as the sun was rising. Rock gardens. Molded sand gardens with incredibly intricate designs. Trees with blossoms falling on short dark green grass. Paths of stone perfectly shaped. Shadows on the dew-covered garden as the sun rose. It was quite simply breathtaking.

1/28/00 11:45 a.m., Starbucks, Marina Del Rey, California
Found out yesterday that the DreamWorks position is between me and one other person. Amazing considering I have absolutely no TV experience. Pam, who interviewed me, called Linda and told her she is concerned about me settling down. She also asked Linda, "Is he kind of full of himself?" Linda told her I am not full of myself. I hate to think my presentation of confidence, my blunt way of being myself, came off as pompous. Too much overcompensating because I'm a little scared the job would be too challenging?

DP left an email and he wants to see me when I'm in San Francisco on a layover next week. I'm not going to respond. Meth Matt left a voicemail and wants to see me when I'm back home in NYC tomorrow. I'll call him back, but won't see him. Marta and Joanna called from Warsaw saying, "We're drunk on four bottles of champagne. We miss you! Come over!" I hung up laughing. Oh sure, I'll just hop on a plane for Poland. Oh, wait . . .

Despite being completely addicted to Xanax, I had never done drugs. Not once. Well, in college, my Dad and his girlfriend invited me to smoke a little pot. I don't think I inhaled. It made me cough and didn't do anything. When I was 17, the cardiologist who was overseeing my tachycardia had terrified me when he told me, "If you do drugs, you might die. If you do cocaine, you will die. If you do speed, you will die. If you smoke pot and it is laced with cocaine or speed and you don't know about it, you will die." He scared the hell out of me.

Actually, I did take a drug just once. On Fire Island. July 4th weekend, 1994. How I ended up on Fire Island that weekend is a long story. Even for me. It was probably the first culmination of events and meetings that should have told me, "Things are going to happen to you that don't happen to every-one else." "A kind of a life most people do not have. At that time, I hadn't yet learned to be my own observer.

It took me a long time to know that I got noticed. Singled out. Or, maybe it just took me a long time to believe it. I had been singled out before in not such a great way. In sixth grade, after school, I literally had to run away from three bullies who were shouting, "Fag! Come here, faggot!" How did they know? How did anyone know? I didn't stare at the guys. I didn't lisp. I talked about girls when other guys talked about girls. I talked about girls the same way the boys did because I copied them. The bullies caught up with me. One

Young Jack

punched me. Closed fist right to my cheek. No black eye, which was amazing. They grabbed me and slapped me around and I didn't scream for help. I didn't fight back. I didn't know how. I never even ASKED for help. From anyone. I had learned to be "I'm Jack. I can handle it all" way before this. They picked me up and put me in a garbage can, butt first. Walked away laughing. The one who punched me kept shouting, "Ya! Faggot in the trash where he belongs!"

I was gay. I knew it. I walked home. I didn't tell my parents. I never told them. It was too embarrassing. And if the bullies got in trouble for it, that would spark another thrashing. I was helpless against being gay. I was a fag and in my 12-year-old mind, I had behaved like one. I was disgusted with myself. Same feeling when guys in my gym class wrote "Homo" all over my gym locker in junior high school. Right in front of me, they asked a girl I was "dating" why she was dating a "homo." Or, the guy in Hebrew school who used to box my head between his fists and call me "cocksucker." Or the teacher in high school who commented outright to the class about some actor, "He's a fag."

By high school, I really and truly knew what to call it and what it was. Starting at about 14 years old, I convinced myself that if anyone ever found out, the people who loved me would stop and the people who didn't know me wouldn't want to. Maybe that's why so many gay men are into fashion, styles, set design, loud Broadway musicals. We spent too many years not being able to express ourselves out loud without thinking that it would only lead to pain.

Between college and law school, I met Roy and I came out of the closet.

It is very difficult to describe accurately the terror, trepidation, and insecurity that accompanies a "coming out" moment. Especially if that moment is to a parent. Imagine all the things your parents love about you, all the things they admire and all the things they are proud of when they talk about you to their friends. And imagine feeling that there are two words you might say that could destroy all of that. Two words that could ruin a history of trying to be a good guy and a childhood filled with trying to gain mom's and dad's approval. Imagine thinking that all it takes to eradicate love is to say, "I'm gay." That's how I felt. When it comes to telling parents—even parents like mine who had never uttered a bigoted word about gay people while I was growing up—there is always the voice in the back of your head that says, "What if it's only okay only when it's someone else's kid?"

Jack and Dad

I was basically a decent guy. I had finished college. I was about to start law school. I was, for the most part, someone my parents could be proud of. Yet, when I handed "the letter" to my father, folded up and sealed in an envelope, I was shaking and tears were creeping down my cheeks. All I could think was, "Will everything else about me that my dad is grateful for suddenly be irrelevant once he knows I'm gay?" I told my father to read the letter and said that I would come back in an hour. And without a word, I left him standing in the entryway of the house I grew up in and left. I have absolutely no memory of what I did for the next hour.

September 1, 1992
Dear Dad,
I've tried to write this letter so many times over the last six months (in fact this is the third draft of this one). It seems, however, that every time I do,

the words just don't come out or it's not the right time for me or it's not the right time for you. I realize that I no longer have a clue as to when the "right" time would be.

What I need to tell you is that I'm gay. I think you may have already guessed. You may have guessed a long time ago. I don't know. There are tears running down my face as I write. Why? Relief? Excitement? Fear? Probably a bit of each. I'm so worried that this will change the way you see me. I'm worried that you are jaded and influenced by society's attitudes towards gay people. I'm so scared that assumptions and stereotypes and fears will take over and nothing will be the same between us anymore.

What could possibly be going through your mind while you read this? I'm so afraid that you will feel betrayed, hurt, embarrassed, and angry. You have a right to those feelings, but you need to wipe out all the stereotypes you carry, erase all the rumors you've heard, and realize that I'm the same person I've always been.

Mom has known since she surprised me by showing up at graduation in L.A. I had planned on telling you both at the same time. Unfortunately, it didn't work out that way. When she was there, she could tell I was happier and I guess I was talking about new friends and that I was more comfortable with myself. She asked me directly and I had come too far to lie. She had many questions, but made it clear it did not change how she felt about me. In the wee hours of the morning, though, I woke up and heard her crying. I started to tell her, "Mom, it's okay. I'm happy to be honest finally. You don't have to cry."

She said, "No, honey, you don't understand. I'm crying because of all those years you had to hide this while thinking I might not love you if I knew the truth."

Ironic that I pride myself on being so open and honest about how I think and feel and, yet, I've hidden this part of myself from you. I hope you realize that the reason I'm telling you is so you can be a complete part of my life. I don't want to have to censor myself around you or not tell you about the people I care about or, more important, about the people who care about me.

So, where do I start? In third grade, I sure as hell didn't know what to call it, but I remember knowing I was different. In junior high, I tried to deny it. In high school, I made a conscious decision never to tell anybody as long as I lived. Can you imagine the feelings a 15-year-old has deciding not to tell anyone something so intimate about oneself because the world thinks it's disgusting? I knew the world thought that this part of me that I could not change was revolting. I grew up knowing I was something the world, at best, mocked, and at worst, loathed. All I wanted was to be accepted.

Can you imagine the pain this caused me growing up? The loneliness? The constant worry that someone would "find me out?" I don't mean to sound self-pitying or melodramatic, but you need to know. I always knew I was different and that this difference was, by society's judgments, bad. Imagine having to put on a mask every day and pretend to be someone you're not. Then, one day you realize that the effort it takes to pretend has stopped you—me—from being who I really am. It hurt so much to have to hide half of who I am from everyone I love. I'm so glad that I've finally come to accept it, to accept myself. I'm who I am and whoever can't handle it can fuck off.

If someone told me I could take a pill tonight and wake up straight tomorrow morning, I wouldn't do it. I like who I've turned out to be and some of that is because of the things I've had to deal with in terms of being gay. One's sexuality is not a choice. You didn't sit in sex education class in junior high thinking, "Gee, should I like guys or girls? Time to decide." Ridiculous. I was born this way. It is no more simple or complex than that. You were born straight. I was born gay. I did not choose to be gay. I'm not sorry I am (anymore), but it wasn't by choice. Why would someone choose to be something that society can't accept, something that makes life so much more difficult than it already is?

Dad, for me to be attracted to men is as natural to me as for you to be attracted to women. Look at it this way: You can choose to sleep with a man or a woman. You are physically and mentally able to make this choice. You won't, however, be physically attracted to the man. Your sexual urges are for women. I can and have chosen to sleep with both men and women, but it is men to whom I am attracted sexually. You can choose who you sleep with, but you can't choose who you desire.

I hope you realize that gay men aren't attracted to every man they see any more than straight men are attracted to every woman they see. Gay men who are friends do not automatically sleep together. Gay men are no more promiscuous, gross, or deviant in their sexual behavior than straight men and women (we just get more press time). Ignore all the stereotypes and rumors. Most of it is bullshit. And, contrary to popular belief, you can't always tell when a man is gay.

I hope you understand what a huge effort it takes to tell you this. I'm scared. At the same time, I respect that it may be difficult for you to accept. You may not care (ideally). You may feel really uncomfortable with it. Or, you may have guessed and dealt with it a long time ago. I really have no clue. Also, it's not even that you "have" to know. I want you to know. See the difference?

I've heard a zillion different stories about parental reactions. One father cried, but said it didn't matter. One set of parents completely abandoned their son. One mother wanted her son to be in therapy to heal this "disgusting disease." I don't want you to accept it like some curse, however, because I am your son and you want to be a good dad. I still need your support, Dad. I have friends who say they'll come out to everybody except their families. That's not what I want. I don't want to have to alter my stories so they're "straight." I want you to be a complete part of my life.

So, I've spilled my guts and now it's your turn. You have to be absolutely and totally honest with me about how you feel. It wouldn't be fair to make me guess. You're entitled to every single feeling you have, unless you ask me to be straight (but I think that you're more enlightened than that). Actually, I really hope you'll ask a lot of questions. Anything! I don't want to hide any part of my life from you. Ask about sexual history, relationships, friendships, the truth behind any rumors you've heard, anything. You need to be totally open with me so that I feel comfortable. That's one way you can support my coming out to you. If you're angry, I want to hear it. If you're totally disgusted, I want to hear that, too. If you are brave enough to ask the question, I will be brave enough to give you an honest answer.

Being gay doesn't mean that I'm any different from who you've always known me to be.
Love,
Jack

He must have heard the car in the driveway. When I walked in the house he was standing in exactly the same place he had been when I left him an hour earlier. I stood there by the door and looked at him across the entryway. He stood there, motionless, his hands at his side. He held the letter, unfolded, dangling from the fingertips of one hand. I stood there looking at him. I couldn't move and somehow felt that a large part of how I was going to feel about myself for the rest of my life was about to be determined by whatever words were going to come out of his mouth.

His eyes were wet. No tears, but just barely. In a tone of voice tinged with "what did I do wrong that you don't already know this," he said, "Jack. You're my son. I love you no matter what."

That was a few years before Fire Island.

By the age of 24, I was okay with being gay, mainly because of Roy. I knew I got noticed. I'd sit at a café and watch the guys watch me. I'd be at a gay bar and know I was being inspected. Somehow, though, I didn't get the power of it. I knew I got a lot of attention, but I had no idea what to do with it except get my ego boosted and pretend not to. I did know enough not to flaunt it. I went from being this awkward, closeted guy to someone who was "out" and fine with it and getting attention for his looks. It happened so fast that I had no clue what to do with it.

The Santa Fe guys all knew me and liked me and I liked them back. There was a group of us who would show up at Edge on Saturday nights and play. I was new and cute and immediately part of that crowd, so I met a lot of people pretty fast. Santa Fe is like that. The second you are invited into any segment of its community, you meet a ton of people very fast. I ended up at a Christmas party in Santa Fe in 1993. I wore black Doc Martens, Calvin Klein slim-fit blue jeans, kind of a faded, white, oxford-style Ralph Lauren shirt and a taupe, textured, two-button blazer. My hair, as always, gelled and spiked and messy.

The first person I met was Andrea Dewey—one of the most fabulous creatures I had ever met on earth. She had a deep Texas drawl. From real Texas. Midland, Texas. Oil country. Blonde hair pulled back with blue, blue eyes. Her personality consumed her and it was hard to tell how big she was or how old she was. I don't remember why she latched onto me, but I'm sure it was the usual reason back then: I was new and young and cute.

After a glass or two of wine, I was witty and funny and friendly. A guy was there who knew me from going to Edge. When he saw me talking to this upper-crust gay Santa Fe crowd at an upper-crust holiday party at a gorgeous house high on Canyon Road, he said, "Wow. You're like a chameleon." I ended up fulfilling the prophecy. I became able to adapt myself to pretty much any situation. Didn't matter if it was at a dinner on Park Avenue or at a leather bar on Ninth Avenue. I could pretty much always make myself fit in.

Miss Dewey decided that I had to meet a group of men who were there from New York. Especially Barney. Barney was Indian, as in the country, not Native American. It was like talking to a little boy in an older man's rounded body. I couldn't tell how old anyone was. That is how it is when you're 22. Anyone over thirty is simply "over thirty." I drank more wine and flirted with Andrea, who was squiring me around introducing me to everybody. She said her "knack" was putting the right people together.

Barney came with his friend, Roland, a biting and sarcastic interior decorator. Lots of laughter with fangs hiding right behind the smile. Roland came with Ricky, a 19-year-old Puerto Rican guy with pools of dark eyes and a flawless muscular body. We ended up in my car because he wanted to smoke some pot. I had a glass of chardonnay. Roland was rich. Ricky wasn't. Roland picked him up on the pier at the end of Christopher Street in the West Village (where Ricky was turning tricks) and made him his boy. Got him an apartment and helped him get a job. I had never met a sugar daddy and his boy before.

Barney and Roland spent most of the summer on Fire Island at Roland's house on the beach. To me, Fire Island was folklore. It was gay liberation. It was anonymous sex. It was total and complete acceptance. It was unapologetic hedonistic pleasure. It was at a time when gay rights meant "We have a right to fuck when we want and who we want and we refuse to bow down to het-erosexual concepts of relationships and definitions of life." Not, "We have the right to get married."

I had pictures in my mind of gorgeous men going to parties and having sex and being beautiful and tan and young forever. But, they weren't. Not forever, I mean. So many men from that era died that many gay men stopped counting the number of funerals and memorials they had gone to. Gay men found themselves with a rare form of skin cancer. Gay men found themselves with a rare form of pneumonia. Gay men found themselves with all man-ners of diseases that should have been treatable, but weren't. These men died horrible, awful deaths, often alone in yellowed hospitable rooms shitting on themselves because nurses and doctors were too scared to touch them.

I had never known a gay world without AIDS. When I was graduating high school and all through college, these men were dying. This was before doctors learned how you got it. This was before AZT. Before protease inhibi-tors. This was when AIDS meant a horrible death, relatively soon. Obituaries said these men died from pneumonia, skin cancer, etc. They never, ever said AIDS. Many of them still don't.

I had safe sex partially because I was scared shitless and partially because Roy told me almost every single day, "Do not ever have unsafe sex. Not once. Not ever. It only takes once."

I'm sitting in a law firm's office in Santa Fe doing a summer clerkship writing briefs, researching issues like the death penalty and criminal sanc-tions and piercing the corporate veil, bored out of my skull. The lawyers were so obnoxious and some of them outright scared me. Intentionally, I thought. I ended up not caring about what I did and worked very, very slowly so that the lawyers wouldn't give me many assignments. I was lazy, but only because I hated it.

Barney and I are talking on the phone on a typically beautiful Santa Fe June day and he invites me to come to Fire Island for the July 4th weekend. I tell him I don't have the money to fly to New York. He tells me he'll send me a ticket.

Oh.

It takes me three days to think about it. Barney isn't slimy or slippery. He's the child who really never grew up. It didn't feel like some older man trying to buy me for a weekend. Not in the least. It still felt like I shouldn't accept, but Andrea said, "The boy has to go! We love the boy! The girl wants stories!"

On July 2nd, Barney picked me up from La Guardia with a car and driver and an hour later we were on the ferry from Sayville to Fire Island. But it wasn't exactly the Fire Island that sat in my mind like folklore. It was the generation of men who watched their friends die and the new generation of men who bought their houses.

Ricky met us at the ferry with a wagon and said, to me, "Are you ready for this?"

I said, "I'm not that naive."

He rolled his 19-year-old eyes, "Oh yeah, you are."

We walked on boardwalks through a forest on the sand. I never knew you could have a forest on an island. And no cars. I didn't know that either.

Roland's house was a three-story beach house with lots of glass, lots of sun, a pool fifty feet in front of a beach, and a rooftop deck. We all sat on the deck watching the sunset, drinking vodka cranberries and getting tipsy and hysterical. Barney's hobby was photography and he took pictures of me. He asked me to move this way, turn my head that way. I was objectified utterly. It was terribly fun. People dropped by and walked right up the stairs and onto the deck. That's how it was. Nobody locked their doors. Nobody apologized for anything.

That first evening was the night a guy named Henry came over. The only things I learned about Henry were that he had a huge penis (I was told; I didn't actually see it) and that he had HIV. He knew Larry and Bing, two friends of John's who lived in Manhattan and had been together for a little over 20 years. John met Larry through an email chain for gay Mormons. A year later when I moved to NYC, the connections continued. Both Barney and Larry knew Raul and Peter, a couple who had been together for about six years. Henry knew all of them. That night, I ended up falling in love with Raul and having a nonsexual affair with him. I ended up watching Peter die over the next two months from AIDS. Watched him turn blind and waste away. And I met Brent, who was dating a young guy. Oh wait, the young guy was my age, named, strangely enough, Jack. I barely noticed Brent when I was first introduced to him. I had no idea all these connections would end up meaning so much for me.

The next evening, after swimming in the pool and lying in the sun and sipping vodka lemonade all day long, Ricky told me that we were invited to an underwear party.

"A what?"

"An underwear party," he answered, as if I should know exactly what he meant. "A party. Everybody only wears their underwear."

Oh. *Hmmmm.* I thought about it for a minute and then said, "Okay." How could I not visit Fire Island and do pretty much whatever there was to do? I figured my Calvin Klein black button-up boxer briefs covered more than a lot of bathing suits.

I had never, ever before seen so many beautiful gay men wearing so little all in one place. Ricky disappeared. I couldn't find any alcohol to reduce my inhibitions, so I drank the punch. I wandered around to see if I could find Ricky or Henry or one of the many men who had dropped by Roland's house that day. A lot of people were touching

Jack at Fire Island

each other. It was very friendly. Then it started to get friendlier. And friendlier. Oh my god, there were guys having sex in front of me! It was turning into an orgy! I was in utter and complete disbelief. I had absolutely no idea what to do, but I didn't want to leave. I was fixated on what I was seeing, but I was so inhibited. About all I could do was periodically reach out and touch some of the beautiful, tan, muscled skin of any of the guys, and then walk away, and drink the punch since I couldn't find alcohol. About an hour later I went home.

The boardwalk was dark, pitch black in parts. No light lined the way. Suddenly I was running. Not scared. Not anxious. Just running. I could feel the ocean air on my skin and smell the pine trees. I could see the moon. It was the most glorious night. So amazing! So incredible! My skin was tingling all over and I kept running all the way to the house. By now it was 3 a.m. and both Roland and Barney were sleeping. I stripped my underwear off and jumped in the pool and swam back and forth. The moonlight and ocean air and the water were like nothing I had ever felt before. I could feel every molecule of water washing over my body. It tingled in every pore. Absolutely divine. It was as though I couldn't get the water deep enough into my skin and couldn't take a deep enough breath of the ocean air. Every now and then, I'd stop at one end of the pool and sit in the water and stare, breathless, at the moon. Finally I went to bed.

I didn't figure it out for a few years. The punch. That was the first and last time I ever did a street drug.

CHAPTER 12

Dream Along With Me

2/9/00 12:46 p.m., Starbucks, 2AV, NYC

I walked in the door after my flight from Paris last night, plopped down on the couch and was utterly cranky. Very cranky-spice. I hadn't eaten anything but caviar for almost twelve hours. Lisa calls and reminds me that I said I'd go to a private party at Lot 61. I promised her two weeks ago, which is way advanced planning for me. Lot 61 is very Bret Easton Ellis. He mentions it constantly in the first half of *Glam-O-Rama*. I knew it'd be a must-be-on-the-list-better-look-fabulous party. Brent promptly gets very pissed off that I rush in from Paris and then rush out to Lot 61. Although I did invite him to go with me. We had an enormous fight. He chose to stay home and iron shirts. Me vs. Ironing Shirts. You'd think I would have been insulted.

I wore my grey crushed velvet jeans from Paris, my dark green K. Cole shirt, oversized, black, cap-toe Donald Pliner's, and a black belt from who-knows-where. Messed up my hair all over again, although it was probably hard as a rock from my Paris flight anyway. Drinking a fabulous Bargetto Gewurztraminer the whole time. New Pet Shop Boys album on. It was a good drink. It was a good look. Then again, I had dimmed the lights and had taken god-only-knows how many Xanax.

Flew out the door to grab a cab to meet Lisa and Isabel on the corner of 23rd and 7th Ave. Paying the driver when Lisa called me from across the street. Very NYC. Then all of us took another cab to Lot 61. I walked in and promptly got wasted. Not just tipsy. Not pleasantly drunk. Wasted. On an empty stomach. Caviar does not, apparently, absorb very much alcohol. I left

45 minutes after Lisa, Isabel, and I walked past the velvet ropes. Now I have a general feeling of ennui. Enweeeeeeeeeeeee.

Brent decided, this morning, that he loved me again. Still waiting to hear from DreamWorks. Everything is up in the air. Which means, for me, back to normal.

3/1/00 8:57a.m., on plane from NYC to LAX
So much has happened in such a short time. The short of it is that DreamWorks did offer me the job. When I got the call, Brent and I were sitting at home watching TV. There wasn't even a moment that I thought I wouldn't take it, but it was pretty strange for both of us. I got off the phone and we sat together in silence on the couch. We knew we were over, but it was such a gigantic shock. The reality was so unreal. That was the moment that I think we both knew we would no longer fight. That we would not destroy our last few weeks together.

I went out to L.A., found a place high in the Hollywood Hills to rent, bought a new BMW, and set up bank accounts. I move to L.A. on Saturday. I start DreamWorks on Wednesday. I'm nervous and excited and scared and stressed and happy and sad. I can't seem to convince myself that Brent and I are actually, finally, breaking up and that I'm about to leave NYC.

The fact that I am leaving NYC will not sink in. I grew up here. Well, at least it feels like that. Five-and-a-half years in your twenties is a lifetime. I breathed NYC in so fully. I don't know that there was any aspect of the city that I wasn't somehow a participant in. I had center orchestra seats at the opening of Broadway plays, dinner at the top restaurants in the city (at excellent tables), been to every bar from Soho to Chelsea to the Meatpacking District (before the Meatpacking District was clean or commercial or trendy), rollerbladed through Central Park, been to movie premieres, learned I'm a good lawyer, learned that relationships are a lot of work (which I found really upsetting; seriously, I was that naïve).

The final day of my life with Brent, we had already packed the stuff I was taking and FedExed a lot of boxes. I used my airline ID, which entitled me to a gigantic discount at FedEx. The plan was that I would come back later and we'd divide some of the more controversial things, such as our CD collection, some artwork we acquired, and the bread-making machine. I never really cared about homemade bread because we never ate at home. But it was something that was acquired together while we were together, so if it's between the bread-maker and the electric knife, I'm taking the bread-maker, dammit!

I'm wearing a very faded pair of Gap Slim Fit jeans, my good butt jeans. A shirt that has become my airplane shirt: Banana Republic, long-sleeve polo style, charcoal grey (surprise!) and a poly-cotton blend. It was a huge shock to me when I realized (some time after I began to use it as my airplane passenger shirt) that I was wearing something with polyester in it. By choice! It was also when I realized the benefit: I am not wrinkly when I get off a 13-hour flight to who-knows-where while sleeping most of the flight. Seriously, even in premium class, it's relatively sure that no matter what you do to your face after you wake up, your clothes will look like crap (unless you are one of the brilliant people who bring sweatpants and a t-shirt to sleep in; if you're in premium class, that is totally acceptable). Dark socks and my usual square-toe black, clunky Kenneth Cole shoes. I'm wearing a black *New York Times* baseball hat that Barney had given me years ago on Fire Island. I'm giving up dealing with my hair in honor of the sadness of this day.

It is a crisp and gorgeous clear day. The kind of day that I am so happy to live in Manhattan. The kind of day that I step out of our—his—building and feel possibility is everywhere because everything is so clean. When a dirty, crowded, massive city like Manhattan feels clean and pure and easy, it's a tiny miracle. Too bad today isn't some horrid freezing, wet, windy day when you think it's inhuman that anyone should be required to exit home when it's that bad. But, no, it's clear. It's gorgeous. It's so extraordinarily sad.

I raise my arm for a cab and one is there instantly. I'm going to be rushed in saying goodbye to Brent? Hell with that. "Start the meter," I say, leaning my face inside the cab window.

"Brent, I have always loved you."

"I know," he says. "I have always loved you, too."

We hug for what seems like five minutes. We both have tears in our eyes when we stop hugging. We look at each other, trying not to let the tears spill over our cheeks. Neither of us says anything else because, somehow, we know we've said the only thing that matters. There's nothing left. And love isn't enough anymore. Over the years we've morphed into love without friendship.

I get into the cab and, as we head north on 3rd, Brent stands out in the cold on the corner of 32nd and 3rd. I turn around and stare as I get further and further north. Far enough that I can see the top of our, his, building. Brent still stands out there on the corner. Just a speck, but I know it is him.

I get through the tunnel, take 2 mg of Xanax, and turn around. When I see the city from north to south—the valley of buildings between the Empire State Building to the north and the twin towers to the south—my tears fall. My bond to this city had become unmistakable, almost untouchable. I could not grasp the concept that I would land at LAX in a few hours, pick up my new BMW at the airport parking lot where I had left it three weeks ago, go directly up to a Mulholland "home" and start unpacking. So much began in NYC. My most intense experiences, greatest triumphs, and most embarrassing failures.

I take 4 mg of Xanax and am numb in 20. I cannot go through this too aware. I am leaving everything I was so thankful to have. Brent and I had a home. Oh, maybe we were not good for each other at that time of our lives, but we still had a home. It was my home, and I was leaving.

I don't come back to NYC for a long time. Brent divides the CD collection on his own and sends it to me with a bunch of other stuff. I'm furious that I had no say. I'm furious because he kept some of the CDs I had way before we met. I figure that I still have my keys to the condo. I'll fly home—uh, I mean to NYC—later and take what I feel is fair. I never do this. I'm too scared to go back to NYC. It might hurt.

I have no apprehension about the pragmatic aspects of being in L.A. I had rented the lower floor of a house high in the Hollywood Hills on famed Mulholland Drive. I figured if I was going to move, I would move high in the Hills, with city lights twinkling from a huge deck. I wanted the physical feeling of superiority. I had already signed my employment agreement with DreamWorks. I had bought a new, black, 3-series BMW, with no clue that I had fallen into the second most prevalent cliché in L.A.: Prestigious job at a prestigious studio; new black 3-series BMW; house in the Hollywood Hills. The only thing more of a clichéé is the waiter/actor/I'll-suck-you-for-money group. (I mean that sucking part as a euphemism, of course. In L.A., none of us escapes being a hyphenate of some sort or another.)

The next day I wake up on the floor, covered in only my gigantic down comforter. The sun is high and bright and the city is beautiful. Green and lush and breezy. The city is clear and I can see the Hollywood sign to one side and, way off in the distance, the ocean. When I was planning everything a few weeks ago, I had ordered a sofa. It's down-filled with a velvet-like brown, soft-as-a-feather covering. I fell into it and ordered it at once. It was a genuine replica of Coco Chanel's—even more reason to have it, of course. I love to tell my stories and watch the terror, brilliance, hopeful and joyful moments in my listener's eyes. The delivery guys take two hours getting the sofa inside and end up having to use ropes and pulleys, bringing it in over my deck instead of down the steep stairs to my door. I sleep on it until the mattress arrives.

I go out to Marix with Eric in West Hollywood. I begin to meet people and it's almost always because of my outrageousness. My normalcy in NYC is more outrageous in L.A. Which is quite a shock. I didn't know anyone. Nobody knew me. I had a clean slate. So, I must immediately use that advantage to clean/destroy that slate, right? Too comfortable and I'd be bored and, for me, at this point, being bored means being scared. Fun involves total diversion.

I meet Rob and Paul (and their hangers-on) at Marix every Sunday, and we have so much fun. They seem to love my over-the-topness. I didn't know how to do things any less intensely. NYC was intense. NYC was over-the-top. L.A. was insecure. NYC is "fuck you; this is me and if you don't like it, fuck yourself." L.A. is "Who do you want me to be? Oh yes, that's me. Please love me." My "core group" seemed to love that I was both an entertainment lawyer, an ex-flight attendant, and had just left a five-year relationship.

3/19/00 10:25 a.m., Starbucks, West Hollywood

When I was 19, 20, 21, I told myself I wanted to be an executive in a major entertainment company by the time I was 30. I'm 29 now and here I am at DreamWorks. Way back when, I had no inkling of the things that would happen to me between then and now. The last ten years of my life amaze me. I woke today and sat on my deck on this gorgeous morning listening to the birds in the hills, glancing at the Hollywood sign, and felt so calm. A sense that all is where it is supposed to be at the moment.

4/7/00 10:54 a.m., DreamWorks, my office

I was online with the guy who was with Joanna when we all met in London; we were reminiscing about the fortuitous meeting and our little kiss at the Light Bar in St. Martins Lane. I promptly got offline, drank my Absolut, popped a milligram of Xanax, and called Joanna in Warsaw. We're both horribly excited about our weekend in Paris in May. This morning, nursing my hangover with coffee and four Excedrin, Nora called from London; she sounded awfully depressed. By the time we got off the phone, she felt better. Lots of laughter and feeling like someone can relate to you will do that. Makes you feel less alone in your misery. Lisa is to arrive from NYC tonight for the weekend and we'll go out and have a night bar hopping. My non-sexual common-law wife. My twin. What would I do without her?

4/10/00 9:57 a.m., Starbucks, West Hollywood

I am staring at a piece of paper that lays out the major points for a development deal. DreamWorks hires a writer to write a script that is possibly to be made into a pilot for a new television series. If a network likes the script enough, we do a deal with the network to shoot the pilot. If the network likes the pilot enough, we do a deal with the network to shoot episodes for a new television series. The development deal is somewhat complex and I am staring at it doing nothing. My boss has already asked me where we are on it. I'd like to tell her to leave me the fuck alone and let me do it. I'd also like to tell her that I'm a bit more focused on my fear of heart surgery. However, I say nothing. I don't even return her email or the phone call. Nor do I walk the

20 feet to her office. I stare at the piece of paper, doing nothing about finishing the deal or negotiating it with the writer's agent. It's Friday afternoon. It's four o'clock. I decide to go to Paris for the weekend. This doesn't seem at all strange to me. When I run away from something, especially myself, I run far.

I call American Airlines and buy a business class seat on a nonstop flight that leaves for Paris in three and a half hours from LAX. Ten minutes later I call back and upgrade to premium class. It's not that I can afford this. It's that my credit cards have very, very high limits. I don't feel sad. I don't feel yucky. I feel blank, and I want something to fill up this blankness. At the time, a day in Paris seems quite a reasonable way to do this. It doesn't occur to me that my true excuse is that I'm pretty sure I'm going to die, so I might as well enjoy myself along the way.

On Sunday night when I've returned and go to Marix and tell everybody I've just gotten back from one day in Paris, they will think I'm crazy and fabulous and everybody likes to be around that kind of outlandish energy. Everybody wishes they could be that way, but even the people who are more irresponsible with money than I am wouldn't do this.

I turn off my computer. Ignore the blinking red light on the phone telling me I have messages. Ignore the piece of paper my assistant gave me telling me the agent for this deal called again. I put on my black leather bomber jacket, grab my backpack (I refuse to carry a briefcase because that is far too prosaic for the likes of me) and leave the lights on in my office so it isn't quite that obvious that I've left. Although I don't really care at the moment. I tell my assistant I'm leaving early and to call me on my cell phone if anything comes up. She doesn't seem all that shocked. She's accustomed to me not playing by anyone else's rules.

I take a Xanax in the car to calm myself down and race up the hill to my house. I run in, jump in the shower, jump out and throw half a bottle of gel in my hair to get it spiky and messy. Moisturize my face since the air on the plane is dry. I wear my black, Armani, straight-leg, flat-front pants, black Kenneth Cole square-cap shoes, and a black V-neck sweater I bought at Fred Segal. I always have to look as gorgeous as possible on airplanes. It's too small of a space to not stand out from the masses. This is the only time I actually slow down. To primp. I grab my suitcase, which is battered from flying all over the world, and throw whatever black clothes I can fit into it. I grab my bathroom stuff, being careful to put the bottles into Ziploc baggies in case they pop open inside the suitcase. I grab my current issue of *Vanity Fair* and the book I'm reading, Sylvia Plath's *The Bell Jar* (it is just too ironic that I'm reading this right now; although, as with most things that reflect my fear of death at the moment, doesn't occur to me) and run out the door. I'm in the car, all windows down, sunroof open, blasting Poison's version of the Kiss anthem: "I wanna rock and roll all night and party every day." I realize, with horror, that I forgot my Xanax. I leave the car running and the stereo blasting and run back inside, grab the whole bottle, shove 2 mg into my mouth, swallow them dry, shove the bottle into my pocket and run back into the car.

I am driving as fast as I can without killing someone. Through West Hollywood. Through Beverly Hills. Onto the 405 freeway. Which, I see, is a huge mistake. The traffic toward the airport is awful and by now my flight leaves in two hours. I am frantic and take another mg of Xanax. Swallow it dry. I weave in and out of traffic and close the windows and sunroof so I don't die of car exhaust. I drive fast and cut people off and finally make it to a parking lot near LAX that has a shuttle to the terminal. My flight now leaves in one and a half hours. I'm supposed to be there two and a half hours prior to departure since it's an international flight. Instead of taking the shuttle, I beg a taxi driver to take me to the airport. He refuses since it probably means only a $5 fare for him. I tell him I'll give him $30. Ten minutes later I'm in the terminal. The Xanax has calmed me down somewhat, but I'm frantic that I will miss my flight.

I cut in front of everyone in the check-in line and tell the woman at the counter that I'm going to miss my flight. I flash her my biggest smile and give her puppy dog eyes and she looks at me without caring in the least. She has seen big smiles and puppy dog eyes before. She tells me to get in line and they will do their best. I wipe the smile and puppy dog eyes off my face and put on my intense, withering lawyer look. I tell her I paid an obscene amount for a premium class ticket to Paris and, on top of that, I'm an elite-level member of the mileage club. Fifteen minutes later I'm at the gate. The flight leaves in 20 minutes I am instantly calmed. The Xanax has taken over and all is perfect happiness now. On my way to my favorite place in the world. In premium class. I recognize neither the mania nor, any longer, the privilege. This is simply how I live my life.

An hour later, after I've gone through my amenity kit with its little toothbrush, eye mask, slippers, creams and soaps, after I've let the glorious sleeper seat envelop me, I have a glass of champagne. Champagne. Xanax. Premium class. Paris. I feel over-the-top. I feel glamorous. I feel adventurous. I feel superior. Every need, want, and whim is taken care of for me. I eat my caviar, my filet mignon, my spinach salad, my made-to-request ice cream sundae, and more wine. And espresso. I love the combination of alcohol, Xanax, and espresso. Causes utter and complete euphoria. It makes me calm, hopeful, and powerful. I fail to realize that what it really does is cover up the fact that I am not at peace, not calm, not hopeful, and without any power over my life whatsoever.

The glasses and china are all cleared away. The lights in the airplane are dimmed and I watch the glorious sunset from my window—ribbons of fiery red and orange and pink. There is nothing like seeing a sunset from 35,000 feet in the air. I take my journal out to write about how I am so unconventional as to leave the office early and not care. I write about how privileged and lucky I am. I feel like I deserve this. It has been my life for so long that I don't remember what it's like not to live this way. What I don't write about is that this is my over-the-top life on steroids. I write that I miss Manhattan. I write that Los Angeles is an overgrown cow town. I write that I hate my job. I write that I can hardly wait to be in Paris and have my croissant at the little café I love on Île Saint-Louis the moment I get there. I even write that I know that I'm escaping, but I don't write what I'm escaping from.

I take 5 mg of Xanax, have another glass of champagne, order my breakfast, and ask that I be woken up an hour before landing to eat it, put my seat all the way down so it turns into a flat bed, cover myself with a blanket, put on my eye mask and go to sleep for 10 hours.

At Charles de Gaulle airport in Paris, I zip through customs and revel in the familiarity of it all. I have always been happy in Paris. It has always felt familiar from the first time I was here when I was 20 years old. "Comfortable in my own skin," is what I tell people when I'm trying to describe how I feel.

The day is clear with the bluest sky. After the morning rain, puffy white clouds drift low overhead in the breeze. Paris days are rarely like this. It feels like it is here just for me. I sit on the far side of the square in front of Notre Dame. The cathedral looms high, imposing and intense in front of me. People walk around. The clouds drift by just behind and over the cathedral. This moment is so serene and gorgeous. I start crying. Sobbing. Right there in public, sitting on the ground in front of Notre Dame in Paris. The only thing I can think is, "What if I never get to see anything like this again? What if all the beauty and surprise will be gone for me?" I sit there crying until there are no more tears left.

CHAPTER 13

A Day in Paris

5/28/00 11 a.m., Café Le Flore en L'Isle, Paris

FLEW HERE LAST NIGHT TO meet Joanna, who is flying in from Warsaw for a play weekend. Was kindly upgraded from business to premium class. Declined the caviar and lobster in favor of a few Soma and slept for 11 hours across the pond. The flight attendants were very kind and gave me a fabulous bottle of champagne and a wonderful French chardonnay. I wandered unstopped through customs and took the RER to Châtelet–Les Halles. A short walk to my usual hotel and Monsieur Olivier greeted me immediately with, "Bonjour, Monsieur Freedman." Which I, of course, loved. I took a nap in my usual room, #115, until Joanna called.

Joanna's first words were, "Come upstairs quickly. The ice is melting." Well, I am a functional alcoholic, so I ran upstairs to greet the luscious Joanna and toasted our friendship with Polish vodka and French apple juice in the new fabulous crystal wine goblets she purchased for me in Poland. We dressed and dined at Amadeo. Splendid. Went to Open Café and saw Victor, one of the bartenders. He told me Romain wants me to call him even though he's in Aix-en-Provence.

Later we met Joanna's cousin, a very sexy French filmmaker, and his girlfriend. I stood there speaking to his girlfriend in French while Joanna talked to her cousin in Polish. A smoky bar crowded with different languages, cultures, and nationalities. My vodka in a tall frozen glass. The four of us walked to Île Saint-Louis with her cousin explaining histories and stories, then stood in awe of Notre Dame and the lit facades. No matter how many times I see this, it is always overpowering. After they left, Joanna and I walked by the Hôtel de Ville, lit up so beautifully, and saw the lights glisten down the river. Absolutely riveting. Sensory overload in the most wonderful way. This morning we sit on the edge of the river on an absolutely gorgeous, chilly, cloudless day sipping espresso, listening to the low chatter, quietly talking about life and love and hopes and fears.

I adore Joanna. Fabulous and smart and interested in all aspects of life. Even the scary ones. With all the reasons to be pretentious and, yet, isn't a bit. The kind of person I knew I'd like the moment we met months ago in London. So random. You really never know who you will meet at any moment, then the burst of familiarity leading to a close friendship. Life is bizarre. As frightening as the unexpected can be, life would be boring if all parts of it could be expected.

5/29/00 12:18 a.m., Acacias Hotel de Ville, Paris
The sky was stunning. The kind of cloud and blue sky combinations that enhance the facades, the grandeur and the beauty of this city. Marveled again at Notre Dame de Paris. Waltzed through the Musée d'Orsay and a quick visit to the Musée du Louvre to see the Leonardo da Vinci paintings. Purchased a wonderful clock for my collection—a small, round, silver one with sapphires instead of numbers. Simple and gorgeous. My favorite combination lately. Then we sat in Place des Vosges, one of my favorite places in all of Paris. We discussed friendships and opportunities and how large the world is in all its possibilities and opportunities.

Same 6:06 a.m., Acacias Hotel de Ville, Paris
Our dinner last night with Madame Wasiutynska (Joanna's aunt) was grand in the most non-pretentious, casual manner. Oil paintings hanging on the walls. Emblems of royal crests of her aristocratic heritage and a flat so warm and inviting and glorious. Perfect for our last evening on this jaunt to Paris. Madame was so international. We discussed everything from America's involvement in Vietnam to the French people to the Wasiutynska heritage to my two favorite Degas' at the d'Orsay. Joanna and I think she may assume

we are a couple, but I somehow think she may suspect the truth. I have a feeling not much gets by her. It was simply so enchanting to sit in a true French household with a meal and wine and discussion without pretense. Afterwards, Madame drove us through Paris to see all the sights at night. She drove fast and everything was a blur. As though we were in an Impressionist painting.

My flight back from Paris lands at LAX at 3:20 p. I zip through customs and immigration, run to the Starbucks in the terminal and have a five-shot nonfat latte. With 3 mg of Xanax. I take the shuttle to the BMW, jump in and call Rob on my cell. He and Paul and assorted other boys are at Marix for our usual Sunday afternoon drunk-with-the-boys-at-Marix Texmex in West Hollywood.

"Where the hell have you been," Rob shouts over the loud background noise of music and drunk revelers.

"Paris!" I respond triumphantly.

"You are absolutely insane. We love that about you!" screeches Rob. Then Paul is on the phone saying, "Get your international slut self over here at once! We have Chambord margaritas!" Of course they do. None of us are prosaic. About anything. Including

Rob and Jack

our alcohol. Click. Paul hangs up the phone before I can answer that, of course, I'm coming immediately.

I speed up the 405 as fast as possible since there is no traffic. I am feeling very triumphant. I'm fabulous and crazy and everybody loves it! I can see, in my head, what I look like: Hot, popular guy with spiky hair and Dolce & Gabanna sunglasses as dark as they can be without being opaque. I blast "Kids In America" from the *Clueless* soundtrack. Speeding along in a black

BMW. Just off the plane from a day in Paris. A day! Going directly to see friends at the hot-of-the-moment-be-seen place in West Hollywood to have margaritas and be drunk, high, and buzzed. Knowing that the next day, I'll be back in my office at DreamWorks doing my production attorney work. My life is truly fabulous. The thought of my heart surgery doesn't even enter my drug-swaddled brain. At least, not consciously.

Off the freeway, I turn the volume down on my music. I refuse to be one of those obnoxious people who blasts music when cars next to me can hear. I also switch from the *Clueless* soundtrack to Depeche Mode's "People Are People," which, I think to myself, came out around 1984. My freshman year in high school. At stoplights, I rummage through my backpack for some stuff to put on my face. I find a Kiehl's astringent and Chanel moisturizer. My product obsession is getting out of control.

At the next stoplight, I wipe the astringent on my face with a napkin I find on the floor of the car. At the following stoplight, I put Visine in my eyes and the moisturizer on my skin. At the last stoplight I grab the tiny bottle of hairspray in my backpack and spray my hair to death while messing it up with my fingers. No one would ever know I just got off an eleven-hour flight from Paris from the way I look. But, of course, I'll tell everyone. I valet the car. There is a line to get in. I hate lines. I go to the door guy who is drop-dead gorgeous. A little taller than me with dark hair and blue eyes. Very worked out. I flash a huge smile, crinkle my eyes together and tell him, "My friends are waiting for me and I'm really late. Could I avoid the line just this once?" He looks at me like I have three heads and says, blasé, "No." I think for a moment. "Okay. How about I hate lines and I don't wait in them." He laughs and lets me in.

I pause inside the door to see if I can find Paul and Rob. And to get noticed. Paul and Rob are on the little terrace above the floor of the restaurant. There must be about 100 other guys on this terrace. It's a complete madhouse. I walk toward the balcony pretending I don't notice people watching me. Looking as innocent and approachable as possible. I'm not innocent and I'm way too over-the-top to be approachable, however. I grab Paul on the ass and I hear, without him turning around, "Don't grab my ass unless you mean business." I hug him from behind and he says, "Sweetness! Just back from

Paris? You look fab-a-lus. You obviously didn't fly coach." To which Rob, Paul, and I all break down into hysterical fits of laughter.

I tell Paul, "Please! I don't even like to know there are seats back there, dear!"

Rob says to Paul, very deadpan as usual, "Paul, you don't even know what it's like to fly commercial! Let alone coach!" Paul's family has two private jets. One of the things I love about Paul is that he has more money than god, but you'd never know it. He doesn't flaunt it, doesn't hide it, and his pretension is more for fun than anything else. And he is absolutely hysterical.

The three of us spot a very cute guy right in front of us, wearing some kind of stupid medallion around his neck. I look at Rob and say, "The only thing that is good for is ripping it off during sex." I'm so amusing. We run into someone we sort of know. There are a lot of people we sort of know. I can't remember this guy's name, but he's real cute and he knows I'm usually here much earlier and he hollers over the pounding music, "Where the hell have you been?"

I respond, "Darling! Paris! Just got back!" I really am loving this.

Rob asks if I have a chapstick. I give him the lip moisturizer from the premium class amenity kit and say, "Darling! International lip stuff only! We don't do domestic!" We are all hysterical. The place is absolutely packed. Body to body. In ten minutes I have already had a full Chambord margarita. Paul has gotten another pitcher and pours all of us another glass. I insist on paying for this round and whip out my Platinum American Express and give it to Rob to deal with. As usual, my cocktail of Xanax, espresso, and alcohol makes me feel absolutely in control. All is at peace and fabulous in my world now. I am hot and charming and able to surprise people that I actually have a brain. An enigma. My favorite mask.

Three hours and at least a full pitcher each of the Chambord margaritas later, we've had enough. I hug Rob and Paul goodbye as we all wait for the valet to bring our cars. We ask if each other is okay to drive. None of us are, but we all say, scoffing, "Oh yes. I'm fine." I hop in the BMW, blast "Westlife," a CD of a boy band I bought in London a month ago that is not yet released in the U.S. I speed to the top of Laurel Canyon and turn right at Mulholland Drive. I speed around the curves of the road, glancing at the city views, which are, as usual, gorgeous. I pick up my cell phone and try to call

Nora in London. She doesn't answer. I call Joanna in Warsaw. She answers, is at an afternoon garden party, is drunk and squeaky and we laugh and laugh and talk about nothing. She thinks I'm one of the most fabulous creatures on earth to have flown to Paris for a day. I am racking up a gigantic cell phone bill, I think. Not noticing the irony between being concerned about a cell phone bill after purchasing an $8000 airplane ticket. I click off with Joanna and continue to speed around the curves of Mulholland Drive. I realize I have to start focusing because I'm getting drowsy. I often joke to people that one day I will lose complete control of my car and fling myself off a cliff, killing myself very dramatically like James Dean. When I say this, I think I'm very faux dramatic and amusing; apparently, so does everyone else.

At home, I peel off the clothes that I've been wearing for almost 20 hours. I take a scalding shower to wash away the airplane. Brush my teeth. Moisturize my face. Walk into the kitchen, naked, to check the messages on my answering machine. I grab a bottle of Beaujolais that I brought back with me from Paris, pour it in a glass with two ice cubes, which, as usual, is me being so anti-prosaic to drink red wine with ice cubes, and push the button on the answering machine.

Beep. It's Mom. Beep. It's Tim. Beep. It's Eric. Beep. It's Eric again. Beep. It's Eric again. Beep. It's Lisa. Beep. It's some guy I must have given my number to at Marix. Beep. It's another guy I must have given my number to. So many messages. I feel so loved. I finish my wine sitting on a chair on my deck watching the sun set and wash back 6 mg of Xanax and my Atenolol pill for my heart and finish the glass of wine. See, I think triumphantly, I will not let my heart fear affect me. Not realizing that it clearly already has. Intensely. I set my alarm clock and crawl into bed and pass out. Gloriously.

CHAPTER 14

Bailey on Ice

THE THREE ELECTRODES DR. BAILEY attached to my chest earlier today are itchy. Already. I have to wear this Thing for two days. They are little plastic things with a button that the wire snaps onto. All taped towards the top of my heart a little below my neck. Slightly off to the left. They wind their way down my chest and stomach and plug into the Thing—a small, black box that is slung around my hip as though it were a fanny pack. The black box reminds me of a Sony Walkman, circa 1982. Those "sports" Walkmans that were either yellow or black. My grandmother and aunt gave me a yellow one for my Bar Mitzvah. I loved it. Allowed me to plug into my music, tune out the world, and live in my head. Apparently, being a loner started back then.

This box is recording my heartbeats. With any luck, I will have one of my usual tachycardia "attacks" and the box will record it. I've had them for so long, I can almost predict when they will happen. I hope one or two get recorded. I want Dr. Bailey to know as much as possible.

I light a candle, pour myself Absolut Citroen on the rocks, and put an old Yaz CD on the stereo, which I turn up very loud. The lights are dim and everything glows from the candlelight. I want to become my ambiance. I sip the vodka and go out onto the deck for a few moments. I can feel the moist breeze creeping up from the canyons. It melts against my bare skin. I am naked except for the box, the belt around my hips holding it to my body and the wires. The city lights are twinkling in the breeze. The city seems to go on forever. I am so above it all. I stare at the lights. I touch the wires against my chest and trace them with a finger down my chest, over my stomach, and feel the box gently and quietly whirring inside, recording whatever might go wrong with my heart in the next 48 hours. I sip more vodka. Now, I can feel it. That little warm feeling inside, and I press my hands onto the deck railing and push forward as far as I can without falling off, as though I want to float into the city. All of this—the loud music, the candles, the vodka—dulls the fear that I am ignoring anyway.

I can't take a shower with the Thing on, so I wash myself with a wash-cloth and I get water everywhere. For some odd reason this amuses me. It will dry while I am out and about tonight, anyway. I wash my face with my new Kiehl's face wash. I wash my hair with my Paul Mitchell shampoo. I am, as Lisa so eloquently puts it, a product slut. I go into my dressing area and stare at the clothes. Far too many. At least I'm consistent. I wear baggy charcoal Kenneth Cole cargo pants because I think my butt looks good in them. Black Doc Martens. A random black belt. I take another sip of the vodka and turn up Yaz even higher until the bass is pounding. I wonder if it gets recorded by the Thing. I walk back into the bathroom, shirtless, and look at my abs. Which are looking very good lately. All my desperation to prove that I am healthy is apparently working. At least on the outside, which is all that mat-ters now. Which is all I can let matter now. I look at my chest in the mirror and wonder what it will look like with a huge scar running down the center. I realize that once it is there, I may not be able to push it out of my mind. Ever. It will stare at me every morning. I turn away from the mirror and pour more vodka and take a big sip. "Midnight" is playing. My favorite Yaz song. Fantastic sex music.

I put tons of gel into my hair. Spray it to death. Takes me half an hour to get the oh-I-just-gelled-it-and-ran-out-of-the-house look. All spiky and messy. I put on my pearly grey Gucci shirt I bought last week in the Rodeo store when I was feeling quite fabulous. I have, however, absolutely no business spending $325 on a shirt. My credit cards have been feeling very adored lately. American Express is my friend. Then again, I have no business doing most of what I've been doing lately. Not that I give a fuck. The phrase "reality sucks" has never been truer.

I button up the shirt and leave open the top two buttons. The three electrodes are hard to miss. I feel proud to be so bold. I look in the mirror, considering that I am so brave and bold to reveal the wires on my chest while out having dinner with friends. To prove to myself that maybe I'm not quite that scared. I don't realize, right now, that it's actually the opposite. I am wanting desperately for someone to know that I am scared shitless. Since I can't seem to get past my façade of "I am fine," I want someone else to break through it for me. To shake me and say, "Cry, damnit! This is hell! It's okay to be horrified!" Not that I would let anyone. Which is, I suppose, exactly the point.

I finish my vodka, spray my hair once more, tuck in my shirt and look in the mirror. I see the image of the "it" boy. I am cute and educated and have a good job. I am charming and witty. I don't take myself too seriously. The attention I get lately is staggering.

I turn off the stereo, blow out the candles, pop a milligram of Xanax, get into my black BMW and race down the canyon toward West Hollywood. The sunroof and windows are open and the air is loud as it blows through the car. The turns and curves are deadly, but I know them by heart. I blast Faith Hill's new single, "Kiss," and sing at the top of my lungs. Everything feels intensely wonderful and superior. Which isn't so hard when the real stuff is now tucked safely behind vodka and Xanax.

It is a Thursday morning at 9 a.m. Moriah, my younger cousin, picked me up from the house on Mulholland three hours ago to bring me to Glendale Memorial Hospital. The hospital, oddly enough, in which I was born almost 30 years ago. At the moment, I am sitting upright in something resembling a dentist's chair and waiting for Dr. Bailey to do an esophageal echocardio-gram. In addition to all the other tests I've had so far, Dr. Bailey needs to get a look behind my heart. Apparently blood tests, EKGs, the Thing I had to wear to record the heart beats for two days, and relentless echocardiograms are not enough. My body, I imagine, no longer holds any secrets whatsoever. Although, I don't really believe this. It has betrayed me too much already for me to trust it anymore.

Dr. Bailey will, in a moment, be putting a scope down my throat into one lung to watch and take measurements of my heart from behind. The room is dim with yellowed linoleum tile and pale green walls. Dr. Bailey is, it looks like, doing some kind of paperwork on a counter that runs along one wall in front of me. A nurse is preparing an IV next to me and doesn't say a word. I, usually anxious to charm everyone, especially medical staff, be it nurses, doctors or receptionists, am at a loss for words. I manage to ask Dr. Bailey, "What do you expect to find?"

He turns around on the little black swivel stool that seems to be a requirement in American doctors' offices and says, "Nothing new."

I suppose this should relieve me. I notice, however, the nurse preparing a needle to stick into my vein. I am, strangely, not relieved. This is the most lonely I have felt in a very long time, and I am not alone. But being here in this sterile hospital room in the dim light, knowing that I am about to have the first "big" test, is profoundly lonely. "Lonely" is the only word I can think of right now. Everything about all these tests, as I get further and further into "it," makes me feel more and more lonely. More and more alienated from everything and everyone. Unconsciously, I suppose, I aim to make sure I avoid this feeling as much as possible. I will remember later that I am wildly successful at this.

This test is different from everything else so far. This test is way too hospital-like. For this test, I have to have an IV and be put to sleep for the most invasive test I've had so far. Dr. Bailey won't be cutting anything, but he'll be going into a lung with a little camera. How lovely. I'm a photographer's model. From inside. The last time I had an IV was during my leg fiasco. I hated it then. After the tiny bit of pain wore off, the thought of a needle sitting in my arm, stuck into a vein, disgusted me. One would think that, given the fact that I will be having my chest cracked open sometime in the next few months, an IV needle would be of little concern. That isn't so. Every little invasion is a concern now. Not only am I still grossed out by a needle sitting in my vein, but every little invasion is a reminder that I am coming that much closer to the actual heart surgery. It is not as though I am thinking this at the moment, however. I ask, with utter hope, "What drugs are you giving me to put me to sleep?" Surely this can be the only bright moment of this procedure. Drugs. Oblivion. Peace.

Dr. Bailey answers, "Mostly Versed."

I don't need to ask what it is. Aside from the fact that I know too much about most drugs as it is, I know this because of my dad. During one of my dad's colonoscopies, he was given Versed. I picked him up after the procedure, talked to him briefly, bought him McDonalds because that is what he wanted, took him home and he got into bed of his own accord after eating and went to sleep. A few hours later he woke up and had absolutely no memory of any of it. Not me picking him up. Not the McDonalds. Not getting himself to bed. Not of anything we talked about, which was nothing of importance, but he had no memory of it. Versed, I later found out, has an amnesia effect. The patient not only falls asleep, but he has no memory from a tiny bit of time before the procedure to a few hours, usually, following. When I hear this is what I am getting, I am delighted. I am suddenly rather fond of the IV considering what it will be used for.

The nurse ties one of those beige tuber cords around my trying-too-hard-to-look-healthy muscular bicep. She didn't really need to do that. My veins stick out anyway. The nurses at St. Vincent's in Manhattan were all delighted to find it so easy to keep giving me IVs during that week. I, of course, was not so delighted. Although I guess it would be worse if a nurse had to try and find a vein. Ugh, thinking of that disgusts me. I am so easily grossed out by body stuff. I don't comprehend the fact that after all of this is over, almost nothing about bodies, surgeries, or anything else will make me squeamish. Then again, at the moment, I don't think this will ever be over. Unless I am dead. When I consider this, I do so very casually. As though it's such a real possibility that I cannot help but simply acknowledge it with passing interest.

The nurse sticks the IV needle in my arm and I wince from the prick without looking. I can handle it as long as I do not look. Same as having my blood taken. I only turn and look once I can feel the bandage covering the needle. I am still, however, grossed out. Yeach. I look at Dr. Bailey and say, in my sarcastic if-I-must amused voice, "Okay. Give me the happy stuff." Which is the last thing I remember until I wake up a few hours later.

When I wake up, I am sitting upright in the same chair. My throat is terribly sore and when I try to speak, only raspy air comes out. I can see Dr. Bailey in kind of a haze in front of me, his back to me at the counter writing things down. I rasp out, "Dr. Bailey." It's like a scratched whisper. He turns. I ask, "Did you find anything bad?"

"No," he says. "Nothing we didn't expect to find. Relax. You won't remember this conversation anyway."

It ends up that he told a little lie. I remember him telling it.

Moriah has waited for the procedure to be done and we leave the hospital with my head still swimming in drugs. I insist on going out to eat even though she tries to get me to agree to go home. I insist that I am fine despite almost falling asleep in the car. We stop at a small place on Franklin Boulevard in Hollywood and I order soup. I hate soup. I don't like hot liquids. I am so easily over-heated and they make me sweat. Even in the dead of winter in NYC, I drank iced coffee. Five minutes later I hear Moriah yelp, "Jack!" I jerk my head up. It had come perilously close to landing in my soup. Half an hour later I am back at home asleep. Moriah wanted to stay, but I assured her I am fine and she left. It is remarkable how convincing I can be. It is even more remarkable how long it takes everyone to start to ignore me and to realize they probably know better than I do about what I should be doing.

At 5 a.m. the next morning, I do what any normal and sane person would do after having had a procedure with an IV and heavy sedation the prior day: I leave my house and head to LAX. I had planned this trip two weeks ago, even though I had planned the esophageal echo three weeks ago. So, a day after this procedure, when I still cannot speak with more than a raspy whisper, I am heading to Buenos Aires for a 48-hour visit. I don't feel irresponsible. I feel entitled and fabulous and adventurous. Who but I would have a sedated procedure about his heart ailment the day before flying to Buenos Aires. For only two days. Only me. I really am this grand. Or, rather, really getting more and more cunning in finding grandiose ways to avoid reality. I am, it seems, creating a quite unreal reality for myself. One that is so extraordinarily over the top as to help me to ignore, albeit not forget, the heart thing.

Besides, Monique is going with me.

Monique and I met in law school. For the first time in my life, I was part of the cool kids' club. I was from L.A. and had worked in the entertainment industry. I was gay and out just as being gay was becoming trendy. Who knew that being gay might one day make me popular instead of hated? I had a nice Honda Accord with a car phone. I had a great apartment with a pool and a glorious view and high ceilings and an espresso machine. On top of all that, I actually seemed good at the law stuff. In retrospect, maybe most importantly, I made no apologies for absolutely anything about myself. It's hard to resist being around someone like that.

This group of cool kids at first began to study together. Then we began to have movie night at my apartment. We'd watch a law-oriented movie once a week. *Legal Eagles. Paper Chase.* We'd all lie around on my floor since the one thing I didn't have was a sofa. Monique was part of this group. Slowly, things began to change. I began to realize that I didn't like being part of a study group. Then our schedules changed and we couldn't really gather together for movie night. The girls' became catty toward Monique. I ended up, as I was in high school, being on the cusp. Part of the club, but not really part of it either. Yet, this time, it was by choice. And this time, the cool kids couldn't really figure out why I didn't want to be a complete part of their group. They couldn't figure out why Monique and I became close, slowly but surely. We'd sit in Property Law class making faces at each other and giggling. One time I accidentally threw a pen across the room and hit someone in the head. I tried for about three seconds to look innocent, then looked at Monique and that was it. We actually laughed out loud in the middle of a law school course. You'd have thought we were five years old.

There was a guy who sat in between us in class who had the most horrible breath every morning. Monique and I would lean back in our chairs and make absolutely disgusted faces at each other. In other words, we behaved completely in a way you are not supposed to behave in law school. We didn't take ourselves too seriously, but we still studied and seemed to understand everything. We went to a café all the time to study. We'd go to movies to avoid studying. She had this red sports car and drove like an absolute maniac. Scared me to death on a daily basis. I had a car phone before everyone had cell phones in their pockets. Monique and I would hang out in the law school parking lot pretending to talk on the phone. Pulling the cord out of the window so we could stand next to the car looking as cool as possible. In retrospect, how utterly mortifying. It's amazing how mature we thought we were.

One of my favorite Monique stories is when I told her I was gay. We were walking down the street from the café after a wretched three hours of studying and she said something about me, saying "that is so queer."

I said, "Ya, well that goes naturally with being gay."

She said, "Oh, right." I realized at that moment that she didn't know. How did she not know? I wasn't exactly flaming, but I wasn't exactly hiding it either. She said, shocked but laughing, "You are?"

I said, "Yes, I thought you knew."

She said, "No! I just thought you were really funny." I almost fell over from laughing at that one.

I also found out, although I can't remember when, that she had had open heart surgery as a baby to fix a hole in her heart. I told her about my tachycardia. I had no clue, at that time, that I would be needing open heart surgery for myself. I wouldn't, in fact, find out for five more years. My favorite photograph of her is with her head face down on my desk while studying contract law. All you can see is this ball of hair lying on my desk and her middle finger in the air flipping me off.

Monique and Jack

The Heart Thing

Ten years later here we are meeting up in Miami for a trip to Argentina. She was living in NYC and I had already moved to L.A. Obviously, I knew I would need heart surgery this year. So, with my throat still hurting from the esophageal echocardiogram and my brain still swimming a bit in the narcotics, I was off to Argentina. It is Friday morning and I have decided not to go to work; I have to get to Miami in time to catch the overnight flight to Buenos Aires. I wake up and do my usual product-obsession thing and put on some assortment of my usual black clothes. I spray my hair into its usual rock-hard helmet of a mess and swallow my usual 5 milligrams of Xanax (I've upgraded, as it were, from 2 mg at this point). I throw my black clothes into my black suitcase with my black leather jacket and I'm out the door. It is a nasty, rainy day and I probably shouldn't drive at my usual breakneck speed on the slick rainy streets since people in Los Angeles don't know how to drive on slick rainy streets. But, as usual, I do anyway.

An hour later, I'm sitting in first class on a 757 on a non-stop flight to Miami. This is my least favorite airplane because it really is just a 737 on steroids. When I was a flight attendant, I absolutely hated this airplane. It has more seats than a 3-class 767 and one aisle. I hate it as a passenger also because it is only a 2-class, which means first class is really only a slight upgrade from coach. It's one of those planes where first class is more about ego than true comfort. The food isn't that different from coach either. If the coach passengers are getting an egg omelet wrapped in tin foil on a plastic tray, we're getting an egg omelet on a china plate. Although I know this and I judge most of the other passengers for being in first class mostly for ego, I seem somewhat oblivious that I'm also one of these passengers. As long as I know I'm laughing at everyone else for behaving in a certain way, then it seems okay for me to behave exactly the same way. Not as bad as a true hypocrite, but definitely approaching that general area.

The plan is to get to Miami, take the overnight to Buenos Aires and arrive there on Saturday morning. Monique and I will spend all day Saturday and Sunday there and then take the overnight back to Miami. From there, on what will be Monday morning, I will take the 7 a.m. nonstop back to L.A. (which is blessedly on a 3-class 767 where I can pass out in a sleeper in

155

premium class), arrive in L.A. around 10 a.m. and be at work by 11. It's insane and I have no clue where the energy comes from to keep doing these sorts of trips. Paris. London. Buenos Aires. On weekends. Not to mention constant flights to NYC. Those seemed so prosaic that I didn't count them as part of my insanity. Being in NYC for a weekend was practically provincial, while being in Europe for the weekend fed my inner glamour boy. Which, again, wasn't so inner.

I do a horrible, selfish thing to Monique on the ten-hour flight down to Buenos Aires. We are flying on my favorite airplane: An enormous brand-new 777. Three classes. Premium class has sleeper seats that fold down flat into a six-foot bed and you are swaddled in your own little pod of privacy. Coach is two seats against each window and five seats in the middle. Human luggage. I don't even like to know what's back there anymore. I fly premium class since a flight attendant friend of mine has given me a pass. Monique flies coach since she actually has to pay for her ticket, and a premium ticket on a flight like this is ridiculously expensive. Even by my financial standards, lately. She never lets me forget that I did this to her.

Five years later, in the most bizarre coincidence, Monique has to have open heart surgery. What on earth are the chances that two incredibly close friends, the same age, need open heart surgery in their thirties? Maybe people should stay away from me. Maybe it's contagious. The blessing here is not so much that my friend now can completely understand what I went through. The blessing is that now I get to help her because I understand what she's about to go through. Besides, I've finally learned to cry about it. And when you learn to cry about something, you generally also learn that it's okay to laugh about it, too. That's what Monique and I did before she went into the hospital in NYC. And we did it at 2 a.m. after her surgery when she was in the hospital.

When I was heading toward my own surgery, I felt more vulnerable than I ever could have imagined, more scared than I ever could really express. And really more bitchy than anyone thought possible. Seriously. When you think your sternum is about to break into two pieces and your heart is about to pop out of your body, you really turn into a massive prick. I think this is why God invented pain killers. Not so much to help the patient with the pain, but to help friends and family deal with the patient. I don't know if Monique was a bitch since I wasn't there. I still feel guilty about that. I should have been there in NYC with her. I don't know why I wasn't.

One evening, three days after her surgery, I called the hospital and her husband Bill answered and I asked how Monique was doing. He said, in the most exhausted voice, "I have no idea. You talk to her." That made Monique laugh, which made me smile from 3,500 miles away. I might not have been there, but at least I made her giggle like we used to do together in law school. When she went home, I kept telling her to make the doctor give her Vicodin. The doctor told her to take Tylenol. "Tylenol!" I shrieked (yes, I shrieked). "Tylenol is for headaches! Tylenol is for when you stub your toe! Tylenol is not for when they split you in half and sew you back together!" Strangely, however, she seemed fine with it. Did she have less pain than I did? Did she tolerate the pain better than I did? I think I just liked taking the Vicodin,

and my doctors gave me whatever I wanted because they felt bad for me. Of course, I totally worked it.

A year later, Monique and I were at the Ritz Carlton in Laguna Beach. We do this kind of thing several times a year. Fancy-ass vacations at fancy-ass resorts eating fancy-ass food. This time, when I called to make the reservation, I told them we were married and it was our first anniversary. When we checked in, I imagine they all said, "Does she know her husband is gay?" They also probably wondered why we wanted two beds. But my

Handsome Jack

little ploy worked. We got free chocolates and a free bottle of champagne. The next day, we were out by the pool basking in the sun, drinking strawberry daiquiris. Feeling very privileged because, well, we are. We had learned, by this time, that privilege is gloss, not the stuff that lasts, but it's still fun. I'm not stupid enough to let my insight into the meaning of life prevent me from abusing the fact that I can spoil myself.

The two of us are in the sun, next to the pool, probably a tad past tipsy, and a woman walks by and glances at us. We see her stop because she notices our scars. Two young people with identical scars. This woman had the audacity to stop and stare. I said, very droll, "Pec implants."

Monique said, very droll, "Messed up boob job."

The woman said nothing and quickly walked away with no degree of elegance whatsoever. I loved it, but I still wanted her to trip and fall into the pool. By the time she was out of earshot, Monique and I were cackling like mad. I'm not sure what my scar means to me now. I know that I like getting attention for it. Maybe I just really like attention. *Quel* shock.

Monique and I will have to have more heart surgeries because the valves don't last forever in a young body. We've decided that we will have them in the same hospital on the same day and they can put us in the same room. Like those old commercials for Doublemint gum where they have twins saying, "double your pleasure, double your fun . . ." We'd be twins, but we'd be saying, "double your bitchiness with double heart surgeries." I'm sure our friends and families would stay away from us, but at least we'd have each other.

A day after I return from Argentina, I am sitting in Dr. Bailey's office in Beverly Hills waiting to discuss the results with him. He tells me that from the esophageal echocardiogram he could tell that my heart is "severely enlarged" and that my surgery must be moved up. To immediately after Thanksgiving. He doesn't want me to wait until next year. I am stunned. The word "urgent" is one of the most frightening words a doctor can say to a patient.

I get into my car and drive back to my office at DreamWorks. I am sobbing uncontrollably all the way there. In absolute disbelief. Now it's "urgent." I take the elevator up to the 32nd floor of Universal Tower, walk directly to my office and shut the door. I stare down below to Universal Studios and start crying again. I don't know what to think. I make phone calls in the afternoon and joke to everyone that I now have proof that I have a big heart. But inside, as I get further into this, I am losing my sense of humor. My own laughter doesn't fool me anymore.

My mother is flying here to be with me. My father asks what he can do. I think to myself, "Tell mom not to come!" My father ends up being asked for nothing. My mother ends up coming.

CHAPTER 15

Too Too Fabulous

ALL THE FABULOUSNESS HAS EXHAUSTED me. Back and forth to Paris, London, Argentina. Tonight I'm staying home and drinking. If I sit and am quiet too long, I start to think about it too much. I'm used to thinking about the heart thing in dramatic and fearful terms, but when I'm quiet for too long, the reality starts to set in. I start to consider the scary details as opposed to the broad terror of it all. Relaxing at home is not exactly an option unless I'm drinking or taking Xanax. Of course, I decide to do both. Vodka rocks. On an empty stomach because I am not eating much lately. The beta blockers do that, I think. I've lit candles and put on a Morrissey CD, which reminds me of college when I used to listen to that and Souxie and the Banshees and Modern English and Guns N' Roses (well, only "Sweet Child o' Mine"). I thought that was alternative music. Now, it all sounds so casual and relaxed. Music really went downhill after about 1992, so I have to listen to old stuff.

I go into the kitchen to refill my glass of vodka and realize I've already drunk almost a whole bottle of Belvedere. My tolerance is astonishing. Of course, I run into the corner of the counter on my way into the kitchen and spill a little vodka on the floor since I'm rather drunk, but I don't care. The candles seem to glow brighter and the music seems more intense. The drunker I get, the more meaningful the music becomes—the lyrics seem like they were written just for me, for my situation. When I'm sober and listening to music, it's all abstract. Tonight, it's personal.

I have on my grey flannel Calvin Klein jammie bottoms and one of Brent's U of M tank tops (which he got at his sister's school since she went there, not him). It looks hot on me. Will the top of my heart surgery scar be visible when I wear tank tops? I walk onto the deck and it's cool and breezy and the moon is full and everything glows misty white. Will I be embarrassed by the scar or will I like it? Will it be a badge of courage? I don't feel all that courageous right now. More like a badge of "see what I went through" and "see how unique and different I am." Funny how I have such a love/hate relationship with being different and unique.

It's pretty hard to be unique and different when you're growing up. And I don't mean just the gay stuff. Endless teasing and taunting. Massive efforts at trying to appear like everyone else and being able to fool nobody. Kids are remarkably insightful as to who is different and who is cool enough to be in the "cool kids' club." I took all the advanced placement courses in high school and had the cool land cruiser to zoom around in and go off-roading and I skied—all of which were part of the cool kids' world. But I still didn't go to their parties and I didn't hang out with them. I wish I'd had the confidence back then to be okay with being different. To hang with all the other kids who were different rather than trying so hard to fit in, and failing so miserably. Of course, it didn't help that my Ma got cancer when I was 16. It's no wonder that I escaped to go to college in California a month after I graduated high school at 17. It took me a while to embrace being different, and to flaunt it at people. "See how different I am! See how I only follow my own path! My own rules! See how I'm not embarrassed by myself!" I won't realize until months afterwards that this experience will make me different forever.

The breeze is cold and I have finished my vodka and I'm listening to an old Bangles version of a song, "Time time time, see what's become of me; when I look around at the possibilities; I was so hard to please . . ." and then my tachycardia sets in. It's pounding very hard and very fast this time. I put my glass down and lie down on my kitchen floor and I do something very odd: I call my father. It's about 11p in Santa Fe since it's 10p here.

I am drunk and I tell him so. He doesn't reprimand me. I know I'm incoherent and repeating myself and dramatic. Dad is very concerned that my tachycardia is going full blast and that I'm drunk. I tell him I'll stop it. I tell him I don't want to have the surgery. I am on the cold tile floor in my kitchen staring at the ceiling and tell him I'd rather just let myself die. I don't know if I mean it. I only know that I want to say it. In the back of my mind, I know why I'm doing all this. I'm doing it because I don't feel that he understands the intensity of this, or at least how intense it is for me. There is a pretty big difference between saying, "I know you are very scared" and "Jack, tell me what you are scared of."

Forty minutes into the conversation, I'm still lying on the kitchen floor facing the ceiling. I'm still talking to my dad. I'm still very, very drunk. And my tachycardia is going full blast, pounding into my head. When it gets this bad, I can see my chest beating. Sometimes I point this out to people and they freak out. I don't like it, but I'm used to it. I'm holding the phone in my right hand and my left hand is on my chest. Feeling the beating. Hard and intense and erratic.

Dad tells me to call an ambulance. Being such a great judge of what is good for me at the moment, I refuse. It has never gone on this long. Dad doesn't hang up and call 911 for me. Later, I will resent him for this. Later still, I will understand. There is a very fine line between being dramatic and being cautious. How was Dad to decide, in the moment, if he should believe me when I told him it would stop or if he should call 911? It's so easy in hindsight to judge and feel that he wasn't cautious enough. But, when things are happening so fast and I'm drunk and babbling and telling him I'd rather die than have heart surgery, everything gets all jumbled up. I'm just glad he is talking with me, softly and calmly, without judgment. Somehow I want him to be more scared for me.

As it always has for every episode during the past 13 years, the tachycardia stops suddenly with a huge thud in my chest and then total silence in my body for a few seconds. Then my heart starts beating again. Dad and I hang up. Then, like a proper, upper-class drunk, I go into the bathroom, stick my finger down my throat to throw up the vodka, drink two glasses of water, take four aspirin and 2 mg of Xanax. Eric taught me well. I crawl into the loft and go to sleep.

A day later, I call Cedars to schedule my surgery. I pick December 8th. It is exactly two weeks after I turn 30 years old. And it is the day my mom's brother, who I am named after, was killed in Vietnam. I am thinking that it is a good thing—a connection to someone I never knew who everyone has idealized all my life. That it will be, somehow, a little gift to mom. Mom comes out to see me two days later and I tell her the date. She stares at me and doesn't say anything. I say, "Do you know why?" She says, "Yes" and gives me a gentle, small smile. I pause and say "Okay" and walk away. Alone, she walks outside to the deck overlooking the Hollywood Hills and stays there a long time.

I crawl up into my little loft and open a small, plain, grey metal box and start to read. When I graduated high school, my mom's gift to me was all of her letters from Jack. Her note to me, on May 31, 1988, says, "For my son, Jack—wise, funny, arrogant voice from another Jack who was and is still mine, also. For the ideas and promises you share with him. Congratulations. With all my love, Mom."

The stack of letters from Jack to Mom begins on September 11, 1964, when Jack still lived in Detroit and Mom had moved to L.A. to go to Mount Saint Mary's College. They are funny and poignant and contain wit that was far beyond his age. They continue through November 11, 1967, a day after Jack turned 18. By then he was no longer just "Jack." He was Private John F. Higgins of the United States Marine Corp, training at Camp Pendleton. The letters continue on to June 4, 1968 by which time he was already in Vietnam. On December 1, 1968, his last letter to mom is signed, "Hang easy. Love, Jack." The last thing in the stack is a Western Union Telegram, dated December 11, 1958. It reads, "I deeply regret to inform you that Lance Corporal John F. Higgins USMC died 8 December 1968 in Quang Tri Province, Republic of Vietnam. He sustained a gunshot wound to the head from hostile rifle fire while on patrol. Please accept on behalf of the United States Marine Corps our sincere sympathy in your bereavement." He was awarded the Silver Star "for conspicuous gallantry and intrepidity in action" on December 8, 1968. I still cannot read the whole stack of letters all at once. It's not that I see so much of myself in them, although my mother tells me I am so much like him. It's that I see how special she was to him. He adored her. One day he was part of her life. The next, gone forever.

What I don't realize until a while later is that if I die during surgery, then December 8th will become the day that both her brother and her son died. I feel cruel and thoughtless and short-sighted. I am not quite at the stage where I start forgiving myself for making mistakes about any of this.

Rob and Tim and I are on the roof of Rob's apartment building in West Hollywood. It's about 7 p.m. and the three of us are sitting in the hot tub. The Santa Ana winds have started up as they always do in Los Angeles in the fall. They sweep away the smog and leave the skies crystal clear and blue every day. It's what the rest of the country thinks Los Angeles always looks like. Tall, green palm trees swaying in the winds. Lush foliage everywhere. Flowers. Everything feels fresh and new. The beginning. Maybe not for me, though.

It's chilly enough to melt into the hot water. We've brought plastic cups of vodka and orange juice. We're all pretty tipsy already. Or, rather, we probably crossed the line between tipsy and drunk two hours ago when we left our usual Sunday afternoon at Marix. Rob says we should skinny dip. I have never, ever skinny dipped. I have a profound insecurity about my body. No amount of attention or compliments have ever been able to rid me of this fear. I hate undressing in a locker room. At American Fitness in NYC (and then here in L.A. at Crunch), I put a towel around my waist as quickly as humanly possibly. I shower in a stall, pulling the plastic curtain closed as quickly as possible. I don't know where this comes from. I see other guys completely at ease with their nakedness. Even bodies that aren't perfect, although that was a rarity in Chelsea. I'm jealous of their self-comfort. I don't know, at the time, what it will take to make me love my body.

At first, I am horrified. But I feel so comfortable with Rob that it doesn't matter. I suppose the bubbles help since I know nobody can see anything. Generally, even that wouldn't comfort me. I slip off my underwear beneath the bubbles as do Rob and Tim. Take a huge sip of my vodka. As do Rob and Tim. And lean back with my arms outstretched on the edge of the hot tub and stare at the sky as it gets darker. I think maybe Rob's comfort with himself is infectious. Like being with Roy when I was 21. It is virtually impossible to be around someone totally at ease with himself and not have it rub off.

Rob, he has told me, has been after Tim for a year. Tim, however, was in a very difficult relationship during that year and has recently become single. I also know that Rob slept with Tim last night. Tim is gorgeous. He has dealt with his break-up in the *tres* gay way of devoting himself to his work and his gym, and it shows. He's muscular and lean and tan with dark brown hair waving above his eyes. Seemingly, he is unaware. But as I know all too well, you can get attention and it only makes the insecurities become that much more hidden. Nobody would ever guess you have them. At some point, neither do you.

Tim's leg brushes against my leg beneath the bubbles and I'm pretty sure it is an accident. I "accidentally" brush back. Lightly. Then I feel his foot on top of mine. Caressing it. Now, even as clueless as I can be, I know it is on purpose. I am brushing. He is brushing. I caress. He caresses. I put one hand beneath the bubbles and stretch it out to touch his leg. Rob sits across from us. I look into his eyes to see if he knows. Somehow, I think he'd be fine with it, but I'm not sure "how" fine. It's the danger, the act of being "bad," that is thrilling, even more than touching Tim. Although touching Tim is pretty nice, too. Nonetheless, I move away from Tim and sit in between Rob and Tim, making a triangle of space between us. It's not so much that I want to stop touching Tim beneath the bubbles. It's that the last thing I need to do is get an erection the first time I go skinny dipping. And I never, ever, in a million years, would have messed around with someone a friend of mine likes. Before.

6/17/00 9:17 p.m., my house, L.A.
Tim is a bit put off by the appearance of an over-the-top lifestyle and even said I intimidate him. I suppose rushing into his party the other night, demanding my vodka and apple juice while speaking in French on my cell to Lisa was a bit strange to most people. Despite the normalcy to me. Me? Intimidate Tim? Beautiful, kind, sweet, worldly Tim? That surprised me. I know I can frighten people, accidentally. But, to intimidate them? I don't mean to do that.

6/18/00 2:30 p.m., Starbucks, West Hollywood
Had a long discussion with Mom this morning and she gave me some very good advice about masks and being a pretentious snob. She said, "Honey, you always say, 'But I'm not like that even if I appear to be because of the

accoutrements of my life.' Honey, you are like that; it's because it is your mask. Your protection." Wow.

7/3/00 10:10 a.m., Downtown Subscription, Santa Fe
Rob and I flew here a few days ago. The house, as usual, is empty. We immediately filled it with candles and flowers and music. Opened the sets of French doors in the living room wide so the smell of the mountains and piñon trees floated in. Last night, Mom and Rob and I went to dinner. We all got tipsy and then later Rob and I went to Vanessies after dropping Ma off at her house. This morning I woke up at 4 a.m. with the most wretched hangover. Took four Excedrin and a Valium and went back to sleep until 7. Countess Nora called a few minutes ago. She's in Singapore. She wants me to come to London over Labor Day since I'm not coming for July 4th. I told her maybe. She also promised to be at my 30th birthday party in Paris in November.

I am at Dana's. I am wearing Armani matte black, flat-front pants, a polo-style, black knit short-sleeved shirt, a black leather belt I bought at Century 21 in NYC, and my usual square-toe Kenneth Coles. Dark hair messy and gelled to the point of being able to be a hole punch. Really. Dana's is up in the hills above Sunset Plaza. A really gorgeous place. Very white. A very famous songwriter. A very famous set designer. The party is in honor of the young son of a very famous writer about vampires who lives in New Orleans. We are later to

Jack and Simone

go to the APLA [AIDS Project L.A.] backstage party at Universal. We have VIP tickets. Of course.

I am wearing my six-dollar pair of sunglasses I bought one day in Provincetown (which will always be my favorite pair of sunglasses, although I never buy a six-dollar pair of sunglasses again). I know hardly anyone here. I know Dana, and Jay and I at least semi-know Jim and his boyfriend. Jim and I and his boyfriend end up standing on the deck, sipping from our flutes of Cristal, talking about nothing. I go inside and there are more people talking about nothing. I mush my way into a four-person conversation and one of the guys says, "My belt is from Gucci. It was three hundred dollars."

I say, "My sunglasses are from Provincetown. They were six dollars." Everybody laughs.

This is what I mean about it being contagious to be around people who don't apologize for who they are. It makes you feel okay about most of the bullshit about yourself. There are fewer, if any, greater blessings than to find yourself in a place where you totally accept yourself. Like those people you hear about who used to be shy. They often say that they pretended not to be for so long that they ended up not being shy. So, am I this outrageous, self-aware, self-assured hilarious guy, or am I just cultivating an image? Years from now, as with so many other things that come upon me as I grow older, I will realize that it wasn't necessarily an image of me or me. It just was. Period. End of discussion. Analysis only goes so far. There is a reason for the clichéé: Hindsight is always Sunny/Sunny.

At some point, I am alone on the terrace. I am holding my flute of Cristal. I pop a Xanax. I watch the sunset deep into the ocean. I realize that I am so bored. I know this is the fabulous place to be. I know these are the A-gays and their acolytes. I know that I am invited. With my background and what I look like on paper (and in person, I guess), they expect that I be a part of them. But I am so bored. Nothing interesting is going on here. No fascinating conversations. Nothing but glitter. I know I am a hypocrite to see all this and still want it. To still have it drive my ego. But the "here" that I am experiencing doesn't feel solid. Of course, after realizing this and letting a bit of self-analysis into my head, I turn around, go back into the party, fill up my flute of Cristal, and dive back into the mundane and ridiculous conversations with people who are mundane and ridiculous.

Surely I have not become one of these people. Have I? I do not think I have, but I like that I have the choice. Not so much like being on the cusp of the cool kids in high school, but actually having a choice. I can be a part of it or I can walk away. Choice. I'm so full of crap. It chose me and I let it. My insightfulness is such bullshit sometimes. The irony is bizarre. I'm here because I'm part of it and it is human fuel for my running away from the heart crap. Human fuel. Xanax fuel. Disdaining of L.A. fuel. Hating DreamWorks fuel. Flying to Europe for the weekend fuel. Did I mention Xanax fuel? And consistently, almost every day now, looking at the world through Cristal-colored glasses. There are reasons for silver flasks, like the one Lisa gave me for my 28th birthday. If you're going to be tacky enough to even have one, then you sure as hell are only going to put $300 bottles of champagne in it. People are so dumb not to know this, clearly. I later consider this when I keep one in my desk drawer at work the closer I get to the heart surgery. Let me say that, even for me, buying bottles of Cristal on a daily basis is a little much. And swallowing 3 or 4 mg of Xanax in order to feel normal is not quite enough.

We start to leave for the APLA party and I drive alone, following Dana and Jay and the guest of honor in Dana's Land Rover. What is surely bizarre is that all of this is totally new for me and I usually love new. But my outlandish life has elevated my requirement that "new" be truly and totally unrelated to anything I've done. And I've done VIP and fabulous parties with fabulous people. I turn Westlife on very, very loud. I close the windows and the sunroof because I don't want anyone to hear that I'm listening to a boy band if someone from the party pulls up next to me at a stoplight. Told you I never care what other people think. Clearly.

I call Lisa on the way home from the APLA party and I'm completely blitzed out from feeling above everyone because I wasn't impressed, and because I was so impressed that I wasn't impressed.

"Lisa, I know you're asleep, get the hell up. I need a bitch right now."

"You cunt. What do you want," she answers

"I'm on the way home from the APLA event and it was very Hollywood."

"The kind of Hollywood where it's elegant and a little over the top?"

"No, the kind of people who say, 'have my people's people call your people's people'."

"Anybody hit on you?"

"Yes."

"Anyone hot?"

"Yes."

"D.O.C.?"

"Yes."

"The M?"

"Yes"

"CR?"

"YES, already!"

"Going home with any of them?"

"No."

"Idiot."

"Am not," I pout.

"You woke me up. Don't argue with me. You met hot guys and you aren't going home with them for easy, undemanding sex. You are horrible as a gay boy. You should have been a straight girl."

"True," I say, very sullen and pouty.

"What do you have to say for yourself?"

"That I shouldn't look a gift fuck in the mouth."

Lisa laughs hysterically. "Oh my god. I have to use that!" she says.

I say, mockingly, in a high whiny voice, "Oh my god. You have already done that.'"

"Slut."

"Bitch."

"Ho," she says. Although I thought the discussion was about the fact that I am not being a ho.

I continue. "By the way, you had bad hair at the Studio 61 opening."

"By the way, you're still a lawyer," she says. Drawing it out snake-like, low and grovely.

Eric, Lisa, and Jack

I'm horrified. "Now that was a low blow. Even for you."

"I'm going back to bed to go to sleep," she says."

"Okay, I'm going out onto the deck lounge chair to pass out."

"Loves us."

"Loves us, too."

Click.

My life has become measured by three things: (1) How many times a day I say I hate L.A.; (2) How many times I email and/or call Lisa and/or Eric; and (3) how much Xanax I need to get through what I need to get through at the moment.

CHAPTER 16

You Can Run, But . . .

I SWIPE MY PASS CARD at the parking lot to Universal, drive up three levels and park. I have my backpack and my cup of Starbucks and I dread going to work this morning. There is too much to do and I can't seem to focus anymore. I cannot seem to be able to do my job as well as I know I could. Today, however, I am going to completely focus on getting my work done. Finish drafting this development deal I've been working on for a week and respond to comments on some staff writer agreements for "Spin City."

By lunch, I have done nothing. I have answered emails. I have made phone calls. I even close my door for a little bit, lie down on the floor of my office and take a short nap. I decide that I must say something to my boss. She has a large corner office with French doors. I hate going in there because she is the chilliest person in the department. Which is strange because I can sense her capacity for warmth. My intuition for that stuff is usually pretty good. Yet, this infuriates me since I don't see it exhibited.

"Pam, I wanted to let you know something."

"What." She says it more like an exclamation than a question.

"I have a heart, uh, thing and I'm taking a new medication for it and it makes me particularly sluggish. I wanted to let you know why I'm a little slow lately."

"Are you okay?" she asks. It sounds like she knows she has to say something rather than really wanting to know.

Yes, other than the fact that I told you that something is wrong with my heart and I'm taking medication for it. I'm fine, I think. Instead, I say, "Yes," and walk out of her office.

This little exchange does absolutely nothing to improve her attitude toward me. It's as though she doesn't have the strength to be nice to me. Of course, I didn't tell her I have to have heart surgery. Still, I can't believe I told her I have a heart problem and she didn't have the decency to ask what it is or how I'm feeling or tell me to take it easy and let her know what she can do. Not that she would expect less, work-wise. I don't need to be babied. Not yet.

I sit and stare out at Universal Studios 32 floors beneath me. The Jurassic Park ride has a little fireworks explosion every 20 minutes and I watch it go off. I'm miserable. I want to rise above this obsession with my heart. People have gone through much worse and they continue to work. I know, however, I'm getting barely enough done to scrape by, and that makes me feel like crap. I'm capable of so much more. Still, why the hell can't she be nicer to me? Not as a boss, just as a human being. I stare at Jurassic Park. I feel like I have a right, at the moment, to be a much bigger bitch than she is, but I don't have the strength.

All this fabulousness made me, eventually, feel very alone. As much as it drew everyone in—the energy and enthusiasm and blatant disregard for rules—it also held them far enough away so that I was surrounded by my own invisible barrier of protection. It was utter and complete duality. I wanted so badly to tell everyone I was scared and yet I held them at bay, so they thought I was so strong and handling it all well. The drama I was creating was about this individual, unique, and perhaps fabulous experience I was about to go through. I loved telling people, "Let's drink up! Might not be around to drink up in a few months! Might be dead!" We'd all laugh at this.

What was I going to say?

It's not as though I wanted anyone to feel sorry for me. Maybe Rob was right. Maybe I was being overly dramatic for no good reason. I desperately needed someone, maybe everyone, to realize that I was scared shitless. But when you're on every VIP list for every party and jetting back and forth between L.A., NYC, and Europe, and heads are turning when you walk in the room, it's like the French teacher in high school told me when I tried to explain to her that my homework wasn't ready because I had to take my mom to her chemotherapy appointment: "Jack, you're not a very easy person to feel sorry for." I have hated her ever since for pointing out what would, strangely, get more and more intense as I got older.

8/5/00 8:50 a.m., Downtown Subscription, Santa Fe
Flew here last night to flee the madness of my job and the flatness of L.A. Although it does have its amusements. The other night I was getting ready to go out and through my bathroom wall, I could hear Mason in his dungeon. I started laughing as I heard someone slap someone else, like a spanking, and say, "Feel that, boy?" Then a kind of moan. Oh, my. Too funny. As I was leaving, Mason saw me in the driveway and asked that I put my scented candles out of my dressing area because it perfumes his dungeon. I was silently laughing. I'm drinking wine and listening to loud jazz, "Hmmm, which silvery Gucci shirt and black jeans or subdued D&G charcoal shirt with black K. Cole pants?" And Mason says, "Please don't perfume my dungeon." Lisa says that only I would find a gorgeous place high in the Hollywood Hills with a dungeon on the other side of my bathroom. "These things only happen to you, Jack." She says that all the time.

8/16/00 7:04 a.m., Starbucks, West Hollywood
Well, after wallowing in self-pity and basically bursting into private, hot tears in my car after hearing about the angiogram and ablation I have to have, and the 5% chance of stroke, I decided to suck it up and said, "Jack, it is what it is! Go get a hair cut! Get highlights! Go out for an obscenely opulent dinner with Paul and Rob! Order custom invitations for your birthday party!" And I did all of it. Went to the Beverly Center. Bought new sunglasses and considered buying a new Donna Karan suit, but decided against it. I'm flying to Santa Fe next week for a Bar Mitzvah and I do have plenty of clothes. I will, however, buy one for my birthday. Already found it. Hugo Boss. Black. Three button. Elegant.

The day I am to have my ablation comes near. My fear is so intense that I have to get muscle relaxants to be able to unclench my neck and shoulders. They are so tight that to even move my head a small amount is painful. Each step in this real/unreal adventure brings me closer to the open heart surgery.

This step, however, will be the most intense yet. The ablation is supposed to stop my tachycardia attacks for good. And it is necessary to have this done, successfully, prior to the open heart surgery.

As usual, my terror brings me to a natural way to handle it all: Another quick trip to Paris and back. It is Thursday afternoon. I don't have to ditch work because I've already taken a few days off before the ablation. Once in Paris, I do my usual things: breakfast at my café on Île Saint-Louis; a few hours at the Louvre; a few hours at Musee d'Orsay, croissant sitting in the sun in Place des Vosges; a drink out at Open Café; walking up and down the Seine.

I also make all the plans for my upcoming thirtieth party. I go to a small, intimate restaurant on Île Saint-Louis. Café Amadeo. Van and Rogerio took me here last year. I talk to Claudio, the owner, and make reservations and plan a menu. When I had dinner here on a trip a few weeks/months/something ago, Claudio said I have the eyes of an angel. Kinda hard to resist that. Easy to remember the adorations. Easier to forget them when there's rejection, too. Had to make plans for the whole week my friends will be here celebrating my 30th birthday. They are all flying to Paris from four different continents for the dinner. I can barely wrap my head around it. I had better plan it perfectly. Right down to the flowers and the placement. If nothing else, New York taught me how to plan a beyond-perfect dinner party from the kind of candle to use to who you sit next to whom.

A few days later, I am back at the airport. I am in the American Airlines Admirals Club at Charles de Gaulle airport in Paris trying to get back to L.A. in time for my ablation. It involves putting a catheter into my heart. It will require me to be in the hospital for at least two days. And it can be done no later than 30 days prior to my heart surgery. My heart surgery is December 8th. Today is November 6th. If this gets fucked up, I will have to totally reschedule the ablation and then reschedule the heart surgery. And my cardiologist has already made it clear that the heart surgery must be done no later than December. In other words, I will be so busted if anyone finds out I have gone to Paris for 48 hours before the first procedure. The beginning of this "process" of fixing my heart, or of moving toward possible death.

The airport is completely closed due to horrible winds, storm, lightning and thunder. The Admirals Club has huge windows looking out onto the tarmac and the Paris sky is dark and grey even though it is early morning. My original flight was supposed to get me back to L.A. at 2:34 p.m. this afternoon. I planned for an hour going through customs, half an hour to get to my car, and another half hour to be back on Mulholland Drive, so I'd be home by about 4:30 p. I'd unpack, hide anything that gave away the fact that I just went to Europe for 48 hours, and go to bed, waking up in time for my mother's arrival at about 10 a.m. the next day. The Parisian storm, however, is thwarting my plans and I am a complete stress ball. There is an announcement that the airport is closed indefinitely. I immediately take 4 mg of Xanax.

There are so many people in the Admirals Club that some are sitting on the floor. The waitresses providing snacks and drinks look absolutely wrecked and I feel bad for them. I've been in the Admirals Club here many times. Mostly businessmen or wealthy couples and none are all that demanding. Now, however, it's like a crowded restaurant with everyone in a cranky mood and being demanding. I decide not to ask for anything. I've been here enough times that I know where the diet coke is and I know where the chocolate chip cookies are. Between those and the Xanax, I need little other sustenance. When I go to get a cookie, I put my backpack on the big, brown, leather club seat that I now cherish and ask the nice, older, but very-well-put-together-with-bright-red-lipstick-and-silver-hair-just-so woman next to me to watch my seat. She seems delighted by the fact that I speak French and am so respectful. As though such manners and effort are such a shock from an American. Which, I suppose, they are.

I spend all day in the Admirals Club. Waiting and waiting and waiting, and no flights go out. I call my friend Chris who I used to fly with when I was a flight attendant. She is as sarcastic and obnoxious as I am, takes absolutely no shit from anyone, and feels personally insulted by the lack of manners in society. I seem to form friendships with only these types of people. And she is in hysterics at the fact that I flew here when I shouldn't have and got myself stuck. I am getting zero sympathy from her. "Jack, only you would spend 26 hours in airplanes for 24 hours in Paris," she says while cackling into the phone. I love her. She is on the computer at home in NYC with me on the phone here in Paris and I cannot even begin to imagine how much all these phone calls to NYC are costing me. She has logged into the SABRE computer airline reservation system. I am literally telling her computer codes, letter and number by letter and number, to check all the information about times and seats and passenger loads and she says gently, "Jack, you're fucked." Charming. I hang up the phone and take another Xanax, washing it down with diet coke. Downer. Upper. It's a good combo for me, apparently. I know I shouldn't be here at all and, now, if I miss my ablation, or I miss my mom arriving . . . well, it will be irresponsible in the extreme. At this point, considering everything I've been doing the past six months, if I actually think something is irresponsible, it really must be.

Twelve hours after my flight was supposed to depart, five thousand chocolate chip cookies, four thousand diet cokes, and 10 mg of Xanax later, there is an announcement that my flight is going to depart, not from Charles de Gaulle, but from Orly. Orly airport is on exactly the opposite side of Paris from where we are. They are going to take us there by bus. This sucks.

We are on a bus, absolutely stuffed with sweaty, irritated, exhausted people on our way through the storm, through Paris traffic, to Orly. I am in an absolute panic despite chomping on Xanax all day. I think perhaps the caffeine in the diet cokes neutralized the Xanax. *Quel* waste. If the flight from Orly leaves at the time they've told us, then I'm going to get to L.A. at 6 a.m. on November 7th. Only four hours before my mother arrives. My premium class seat is not available for whatever reason. There are no more business class seats available. How could they have simply given my seat to someone else? I come very, very close to throwing a huge, dramatic, uppity fit about this and then think better of it. I, of all people, know the true power of airline agents. I stay quiet. I am given a seat in coach. A middle seat. I haven't flown coach to or from Europe since I was 21. There was a time, oh, maybe a day ago, when I would have refused even to get on the flight. I'd wait for the next one, even if it meant waiting for a day, in order to avoid flying coach. Now, given the circumstances, there is a note of responsibility in my otherwise irresponsible-but-I'm-entitled-to-it brain that I have to get home. Even in a middle seat in coach.

I take my seat and, luckily, I'm in between two thin people. I push my backpack forward, put the pillow behind my back and try to get comfortable in this little tiny space. It doesn't work. An hour into the 12-hour flight and I'm about to go nuts. I get fidgety and panicky and can feel my heart racing. Naturally when I'm concerned about my heart, I decide to drink a copious amount of liquor. I get up, go to the back of the plane, flirt with the flight attendants and end up drinking nine minis of vodka. Then, I take the three Xanax I have left and go back to my seat and go to sleep, or, as it were, black out. Eleven hours later, I wake up with dried drool on my mouth and I wonder if I've been snoring the whole time. It doesn't really matter. I am thankful that I have gotten through the flight and I think to myself that coach isn't all that wretched. Not realizing, of course, that nothing is wretched when you drink enough alcohol and take enough pills. You'd think I would have already noticed this.

We arrive at around 6:20 a.m.; my mother is supposed to arrive at the house on Mulholland at 10 a.m. I zip through customs despite the fact that I am put in the line where they go through every inch of my suitcase, backpack, person. Luckily, (1) I packed very, very light and (2) I already ate my last unprescribed Xanax. I'm back in the BMW by 7:30 a.m. speeding home, until I get stuck in traffic. I completely forgot about morning traffic into L.A. I sit on the 405 inching along and am despising and cursing everything about L.A. I decide to take surface streets and it takes all of my concentration to speed up and slow down and speed up and zip in and out of traffic in front of and behind cars without killing myself or someone else. I'm jet-lagged, still very high on Xanax, and I would imagine there is still quite a lot of vodka in my system. Of course, all this is not to mention the fact that my heart is probably as weak as it has ever been and I'm completely exhausted. I actually do notice that it's beating very, very fast, but I figure it's from the stress, not the exertion. At least, this is what I tell myself.

I get up to Mulholland around 8:30 a.m., leave my suitcase by the door, put my passport/keys/wallet/sunglasses on the kitchen counter, and jump in the shower to wash off 24 hours of being in two different airports, a crowded airplane, and a 12-hour flight in coach. I open the two enormous, glass sliding doors leading onto the deck because it is a stunning gorgeous day. No smog.

Blue, blue sky. I put on the *Less Than Zero* soundtrack. "Time, time, time. See what's become of me. When I look around at the possibilities. I was so hard to please . . ." I have to have some kind of music at all times. Any kind of superficial, outside stimulation. Being quiet is not an option for me. Allows for too much clear thought, and I'm not into clear thought. The kind of thought that is acceptable to me is fast, unbending, selfish, and completely separate from the rest of my world. As though I am at the top of the food chain and what I do or say is the rule. Not in a controlling sense over the lives of my family and friends, but in a controlling sense of how they will see me and what I permit them to say or show to me. A small part of me knows they are too scared to contradict or criticize. Nobody seems to be able to tell me I'm fucking up or not facing anything. Nobody except my mother.

My mother—who makes so many bad choices for herself, who is so needy and so insecure and who everybody sees as made of faults—my mother is, at the moment, the only person who has the nerve and the guts to tell me that I'm fucking up. She doesn't, however, tell me to stop doing things. She has found the fine line between telling me my actions are fucked up and telling me not to do them. She knows I'll do what I want by now. She's known that for six months. But she also knows that she will inject a little sanity into my head by telling me that I might be fucking up, or to show me that there may be ways of handling things better. Really? Surely you jest. Either way, I wonder if anybody knows how strong she is being. I wonder if anyone would know enough to give her credit for doing so much for me right now. The answer is no. Nobody sees this part of her, and I am too wrapped up in my selfish misery and fabulousness to tell anyone.

I make myself a double espresso with the espresso maker from Williams Sonoma. I wash down a Xanax with the espresso and go sit on the deck, watching the city come to life. At 9 a.m., I lie down in bed and set the alarm for 9:45. When the alarm goes off, I am strangely fine due to the Xanax and caffeine: my favorite daytime cocktail. My night cocktail is Xanax+caffeine+any-alcohol-I-can-find. I stand in my kitchen, make myself another espresso, and there is a knock at my door. I open the door in my sweatpants and a t-shirt, and there is my mother. No suitcase. Just a big backpack hanging off the shoulder of my little 5'2" mother. We hug. I make her an espresso. She sits on the sofa and stares out at the city beyond the deck. I go to the bathroom. When I come out, she is standing in the kitchen putting sugar in her espresso, just so. She stirs her espresso and neither of us says anything. Then she stops, looks toward the deck out to the city, turns and looks at me and says, "You look like shit. I know you just came back from somewhere. I'm guessing it was Europe. I'm guessing it was Paris. I'm guessing you got back a few hours ago."

I open my mouth to speak, absolutely stunned, and she cuts me off.

"Your unpacked suitcase is by the door. Your passport is on the counter. You're completely wired and your pupils are pinpricks."

I stand there feeling guilty and kind of stunned that she figured it out so easily. She says, very gently, "Honey, I know this because I know you. I know what kind of life you have been leading for six months. I don't want you to hurt yourself and I know I can't stop anything that you want to do. Not now. Maybe not ever again. And, honey, a part of me knows, agrees, that you're entitled."

That's it. I absolutely lose it and start sobbing. She comes over to hug me and I shrug her off. I tell her, angrily, "Get away from me." It's completely unfair of me, but it's as though I cannot handle anyone caring for me. As though I wanted her so much to say exactly what she said, that I needed to hear it from someone, that nobody else would say it in such a perfect way. But I can't handle anyone caring about me right now. It's too fucking real. Right now, real sucks.

She doesn't force it. My little, tiny mother stands there. She doesn't cry. She doesn't get upset. She has this very gentle, very caring, very understanding look on her face. I walk out onto the deck. It almost pisses me off that she doesn't force it. If she forced it, I could have a big fight about absolutely nothing that I'm really scared and upset about and get all this emotion out on the pretense of being angry. I could scream and yell and curse and turn it into something that has nothing to do with the heart thing. But mom is smarter than me in this situation, so she doesn't press it, and I don't get to pick a fight. I sit on a chair on the deck and mom sits on the sofa. She is content because she knows this is how it has to be. I am absolutely not content, because I know this is how it has to be.

At night, I am completely serene. I have been properly Xanaxed all day long, stopped drinking espresso, and I am numb to the reality of what is about to happen to me tomorrow. We have talked of my ablation as something "simple" and "fast" and "easy." They are going to make a puncture in my groin and thread a catheter through my body up into my heart. First, they will do an angiogram and take pictures and I've been told I will feel a huge zap of heat that feels like it is coming from inside me. We joke that I will truly know what it feels like to have a "hot flash," much to the delight and amusement of my mother and all her fifty-something friends. How lovely. After that, they will do the actual ablation and use electro-radio frequency waves to essentially "burn" the nerves that cause the tachycardia. It is not simple. Technically, from what I've read on the internet (which is far far too much), it seems to me to be an art form. It only seems simple because the next thing to come is hacking my chest open. Thus, I've chosen to Xanax-out for the whole day. Not that this is much different than any other day the past few months.

We have to be at the hospital at 7 a.m. Mom is going to take me. Uncle Norm (my dad's brother), Aunt Bev, Moriah, Linda, and Roy are going to meet us there. Dad is in Vietnam. Before we go to bed, I try to talk to Mom about driving the BMW and explain the various quirks of a $50K car. It says a lot that my concern is making sure mom can drive the Beemer. I'm terrified, so I will cover it up with caring about the fucking car. She "yeses" me along and smiles warmly and I know she is pacifying me, but what am I supposed to say? I wash my face, pop 5 mg of Xanax and say goodnight. I crawl up to my loft bed and she camps out on the sofa. In five minutes, I am oblivious to life. Well, oblivious to death, which is the point.

Sometime in the middle of the night, I am awoken by a horrible groaning noise. It scares the hell out of me and I lie there, without moving, while I try to adjust to (1) being awake at all and (2) the noise. Absolutely nothing wakes me up after 5 mg of Xanax, so this moment is truly shocking. First I think that the noise is coming from Mason's dungeon and I wonder what the hell they are doing in there. I know the dungeon sounds. I'm used to them.

They amuse me. But this sound is extreme, deep, low, rhythmical. Suddenly it dawns on me: my mother is snoring. There is such a huge thunderous noise coming out of her that I am sure she will wake up Mason if he's not in his dungeon playing. I am truly utterly shocked. I simply cannot believe that this thunderous, deep, intense sound is coming out of my tiny 100-pound mother. It sounds exactly like an elephant.

I get up and go over to her. The stereo speaker is next to the sofa and it is, apparently, acting is a nightstand for mom. I see six empty minis of Bombay Sapphire gin and a bottle of Klonopin. With mom making these huge horrible noises, I sit on the floor of the living room six feet away from her, while looking out the floor-to-ceiling windows onto the twinkling lights of the city, and I cry. For all of Mom's strength and understanding and handling this so gently, she needed to get drunk and take lots of medication to get some sleep; she did it all without complaining to me or even telling me.

The horror of what I'm about to put everyone through who cares about me begins, at 1 a.m. the morning of my ablation, to hit me.

I've written letters to the people closest to me and put them in a pile on the top shelf of a kitchen cabinet. I can't say goodbye now. If I die, these will be my goodbye letters. I've also drawn up my health care power of attorney. If I cannot communicate my wishes to the doctors because I'm a vegetable, I've given my mom power of attorney in this regard. She will have complete authority, without restriction, to make decisions for me. In the document, however, I've provided some guidelines. I don't want to be kept on life support if I'm already brain dead. I don't want any heroic measures to save my life if the chances are high that I'll die anyway. If I am going to die, I want to be given medication to ease any discomfort I might have. I've also said that if I'm paralyzed, I want them to let me die. This is the thing I have the most trouble with. It means that if I'm probably going to die, but that with certain measures they might be able to revive me, but that I will be paralyzed, then I want to be let alone to die. I feel extraordinarily selfish about this. I tell myself that it is a matter of quality of life and how I would want to live, but I'm not sure if that's true. Maybe I'm just weak. I don't know if I could be one of those courageous people who continues to live a full life and be positive and optimistic.

I sit down with Mom and go through the document with her. I get teary. She holds it together. Her strength is amazing sometimes. I explain that she should make decisions she thinks that I would make for myself. Not decisions she wants to make or that she thinks she would make for herself. I trust Mom to handle it this way. I know she would. Mom can be pretty off the wall, but with this kind of thing, I know she would follow my instructions no matter how difficult for her.

CHAPTER 17

The Ablation Blues

THE FIRST TIME I MEET Dr. McKenzie, I dislike him immediately. He is technical and cold and precise. There is no warmth. There is no reassurance. He seems to not care. There is, in essence, no effort on his part to be anything else. This annoys me. I want to be coddled. I want to be babied. I want him to like me. To think I'm a good patient and strong and brave. Perhaps if enough people treat me like I'm strong and brave, then I will be.

Dr. McKenzie is going to be puncturing a hole near my groin and threading a catheter through an artery up into my heart. Strangely, this seems most unappealing to me. Not only do I not want things threaded into my heart, but I also don't need someone doing things near my groin. I have a horror of getting turned on and having an erection right there on the operating table. It doesn't occur to me that I'll probably be drugged and either totally incapable of getting an erection or not caring if I do. I let the erection concern occupy my thoughts because anything else about this gets too scary. Much easier to worry about being embarrassed than to deal with being scared. After all, I'm Jack. I can handle anything. This thought is getting more and more full of shit as the extravaganza progresses, but it's the image I've cultivated all my life. And everybody believes it. I used to believe it also.

Dr. McKenzie draws me a rough picture of what makes my heart pitter pat, as it has done the last 13 years. In a non-deformed heart, an electric pulse enters the top of the heart, runs through it helping it beat, and then exits towards the bottom. I'm looking at the drawing and I have a suspicion that it's much, much more complicated than this. A week ago, however, I finally stopped looking things up on the internet, so I don't press him for a better explanation. He is making me feel like I'm the "little patient" and he's the "big doctor." I secretly look at the drawing and consider poking out one of his eyeballs with his pen. I don't do this since I have massive self-control.

In my heart, the electric pulse enters at the top and gets stuck in the heart. It goes around and around and the heart starts to beat erratically. I am told this condition is called WPW—Wolf Parkinson White syndrome. I don't want to talk with Dr. McKenzie any more than I have to since he's pissing me off. The nerve of him to treat me like exactly what I am: a body that needs help. How rude. It is slightly possible that I don't ask questions because I've also taken a non-addictive muscle relaxant that is strangely soothing. Not quite as soothing as Xanax. Note to self: Get another Xanax prescription from Dr. Wolfe. All of my doctors will essentially give me any prescription I ask for because they all feel sorry for me. I choose to exploit this, of course.

The morning of my ablation, Mom and I go to Glendale Memorial Hospital. It is stunningly gorgeous outside: green mountains, crystal clear blue sky, slight wind, warm. A beautiful fall day. I open the sunroof and put on a CD and blast it. Mom doesn't tell me to turn down the music or try to make me talk. What would we say? But as we pull into the hospital parking lot, Mom turns to me and says, "Honey, you know you're going to be okay."

"Bullshit. I don't know that at all, and neither do you."

"Yes, I do, because I won't let you not be okay."

I look out the passenger side window and say, angrily, "I wish it was that easy and so do you, but it's not."

She doesn't respond. She knows it's true. I should be nicer and less snappish because she is trying to find something to say to make me feel . . . something. The most I can hope for is to go from scared to numb. Numb would be nice. As we get out of the car, I pop 2 mg of Xanax. Numb sets in 15 minutes later. I'm delighted.

Mom, Aunt Bev, and Moriah all hug me and tell me they love me and that it will be okay. The nurse takes me, alone, to the operating room.

I take off my clothes. All of them. I lie down on a very, very cold steel operating table with a cloth covering my groin. Dr. Bailey and Dr. McKenzie both come in. They will do an angiogram first. A large machine above me will shoot me with some kind of x-rays while a catheter is in my heart. This will show them if there are any blockages. Seriously, if there are any blockages, I'd rather die. It would be much more comfortable. I don't know what else can go wrong. The electric system is fucked. The valve is fucked. I will throw a hissy fit if an artery is clogged, too. I keep my mouth shut. I am the good patient, after all. Kind of embarrassing that I only learn how to control my mouth after I learn I'm going to have my chest hacked open.

The doctors explain that after Dr. Bailey does the angiogram, Dr. McKenzie will do the ablation. They anticipate it will take an hour or two. Dr. Bailey is gentle and funny and direct and warm. Dr. McKenzie is cold and precise and makes me feel like a piece of meat. And not in a good way. I do, however, decide that he's kind of cute. I'm beginning, in fact, to have crushes on all my doctors. McKenzie, although an asshole, is kind of cute. Dr. Bailey has the most beautiful, gentle eyes. Dr. Wolfe is so sweet and kind. I cannot believe, however, that the only action I'm getting regarding my groin is to have doctors poking it to get into an artery. Not that I really care. Even if I felt like having sex, I'd probably have to brush away the cobwebs first.

A nurse comes in and is very nice. She is wearing green scrubs and has long brown hair tied back into a ponytail. She comes at me with a tray. A doctor or nurse coming at you with a tray can never be a good thing. Trays are bad. I frown upon them. I am sweet and nice and she is charmed, which was my goal. I'm sincere in this, but I also know it benefits me. I want to be liked. Within about a minute, she has an IV in my right arm and does it so well that I barely feel it. Still, I can't look. I don't mind getting IVs anymore or having blood taken or getting shots. It's not the pain that bothers me in the least. It's the idea. That's why I don't look. Ever.

She then takes off the blue cloth covering my groin and I am now completely naked on a cold steel table with fluorescent lights all around me and a bright operating lamp above me. What a delight. She peers at my groin and tells me she needs to shave it. I stare at the ceiling. Can there be no end to my mortification? I hope I don't get an erection because I'm not quite drugged enough even with the Xanax. Not because she's a woman, obviously, but anyone playing around down there might turn me on. I try to focus on the IV in my arm, stuck into a vein. I'm completely grossed out, but it works. I do not get an erection.

After having my pubic hairs shaved off, Dr. Bailey comes in and explains what they will be doing and shows me some of the lovely accoutrements. I don't have the heart (pun intended) to tell him I don't care and would rather not see what they'll be using to stick things into my heart. Nonetheless, they essentially will be punching a hole, like a paper punch, in my groin. Then they put a small round plastic thing into the hole to hold it open. Thus, they are able to thread things into my heart.

I tell them I need Valium immediately. The nurse tells me they won't be starting for a little while. I tell her, "That's nice, but you had better start that IV or I'm jumping off this table." She starts the IV. I go back to being pleasant.

Dr. Bailey and the nurse are here with me and I am drugged enough to not be as scared or numb as I was, but not drugged to the point that I don't know what's going on. The doctor and nurse are both peering at my groin, swabbing it with alcohol and betadine. It has been a very long time since someone took such interest in my groin, let alone got such a close look at it. I hope that my penis hasn't shrunken into nothing. I hope it's at least kind of plumped up since it isn't erect. It's astonishing how penis-fixated males are. Not a gay or straight thing. Just fixated on having a decent size penis. How lame, though. I'm about to have stuff threaded into my heart and I'm concerned that my penis might look too small. While I'm thinking about this and the nurse and doctor are taking things off the evil tray, I actually say, "I hope my penis doesn't get in the way."

Dr. Bailey says, "It won't."

I am utterly and completely mortified. I say this because I have enough drugs in me to open my big mouth. I'm mortified because I don't have enough drugs in me not to be. Frankly, I think my penis is a perfect size, so I'm going to assume he wasn't being insulting.

Ten minutes later, I'm finally starting to fade. The nurse gives me a few shots to my groin to numb the area before they punch the hole. The shots sting a little bit, but I really don't care. Partially because I'm starting to fade and feel lovely and partially because pain and fear is, now, totally relative. Pain ends at some point. Fear. Fear is the hard part.

When Dr. Bailey punches the hole, I only feel pressure. It doesn't hurt at all, but there's a pushing feeling. I wonder if that means he's about to punch the hole or if he already has?

"I need more drugs," I say to the nurse.

She turns up the IV. Then, I'm out.

Minutes later, could be ten, could be 30, I wake up a little bit. The catheter is apparently now in my heart and Dr. Bailey says, "You're going to feel a pulse of heat, but don't be scared." If one more person tells me not to be scared, I know I'll lose it. How completely insane to tell someone not to be scared when they are lying flat on their back on an operating table? Really. I think to myself, "What the fuck does that mean?" Then I know what he means. The machine I saw above me starts to circle around me and I feel a pulse of heat. It's not like anything I've ever felt before. It feels like it's coming from directly inside me, like this build-up of heat deep in the core of my body suddenly burst forth like a volcano. It is so strange. Then, a moment later it's gone. The machine has turned off. I also know exactly what a hot flash feels like. I now have sympathy for my mother and her fifty-something friends. When they are suddenly fanning themselves with anything in reach, I will understand. I can't imagine having this feeling all the time. I'd go nuts.

After the hot flash, I'm out again. I don't know how much later it is, but I wake up to the scariest feeling I have ever had in my life. Not pain or even extreme discomfort. Absolute fear with the acute awareness that I have no control whatsoever over whether my body stays alive or dies. Now. Right now.

I wake up very woozy. As though I have fainted and I'm just coming to. My heart feels like it is going to burst out of my chest. It must be at 200 beats a minute. I lift my head up and see Dr. McKenzie peering into something. He says, with urgency, "Do. Not. Move." I instantly put my head back down onto the table and I do not move. I am terrified. Even the drugs don't keep me from being completely aware of the situation and very, very scared. Dr. McKenzie tells me they must stop my heart for a second by giving me "something in your IV." I say, or probably slur, "Adenosine."

Dr. McKenzie says, "How did you know that."

I say, "I know everything." Apparently being scared to death and feeling like I'm about to die doesn't stop me from being a smartass.

Next thing I know, my heart stops. It goes from beating furiously as though it will fly out my chest to instantly stopping. No movement. Absolute silence inside my body. My breath literally escapes my body and I gasp, trying to breathe, and I start to cry. They speed up my heart again and then stop it and speed it up and then stop it. I am so out of it and so woozy, but I say, "It's too fast. You have to stop." This comes out very slowly, very terrified, and very urgent. I'm actually crying because I know, I know that I am on the edge of death. I'm being given one heart attack after another. Not scared of being on the edge of death, but actually right there. I know I sound as terrified as I am. I truly feel like I'm about to die. I tell them again, "Please. You have to stop." I know something is going terribly wrong. I can feel it. Not the physical feeling, but the knowledge, the instant intuition, that something is wrong. Something is unexpectedly difficult. I know this. They shouldn't have to do this so many times. I feel like I am on the table for hours. It's not that I'm worried that I might die or scared that I might die. I feel my life slipping away. And it is. Start. Stop. Start. Stop.

I find out later that I'm right.

I wake up in a small room on a soft gurney all by myself. Mom and Roy are in the room.

"Am I okay?"

Mom says, holding my hand, "Yes, honey, you're okay. Dr. McKenzie says it worked. You're fine."

This is the first of me asking this same question many, many, many times: "Am I okay?"

I start crying. Not from relief that I'm okay. Not even from relief that it's over. Not that kind of a relief. It's more of a release—the sober awareness of what I just went through. Now, though, it all comes out. Everything that wanted to come out in the operating room. I look up at Mom and Roy and I see that neither of them knows what to do or what to say. I think this shocks them. I think they had never considered that all the usual things such as "you're okay" and "it's over now" and "we love you" will never, ever be enough. Words, now, will fail. Which is hard for me because I love words. I love the right turn of phrase. The perfect thing to say. The knowledge of how to combine intuition with words and make someone feel better. Now, my love of words no longer matters. If I can't cobble them together in my head to make myself feel better, nobody else will be able to do so either.

It's so out of character. These two usually know what to say and they definitely usually know what to say to me. They know my moods and they know when to argue and when to ignore me. They know how to handle me. Suddenly we all see, I suppose, that they don't know what to say. I realize how much I appreciate that they don't try vague "you'll be okay" crap with me. An instant after realizing all of this, I'm crying again. None of us knew it would be like this. We thought it was going to be simple, relatively easy. But this is the most terrifying experience I have ever had. I was actually on the edge of death. I felt it even through the drugs. Now I'm crying and sobbing. I still feel it. Later, out of all the memories I will have of the Heart Thing, this will be one of the most terrifying of all. None of us would have ever predicted this.

All I say is, "I can't do anymore. I'm not doing the heart surgery."

Mom tells me, "No, honey. You're just getting started."

Roy looks at her, horrified. I, strangely, am appreciative, even though I sincerely have decided I will not have the heart surgery. I will never, ever go through something like this again. It was so terrifying that my life is not worth it. I am that scared. I am that much of a wimp. This was enough. I've had a good 30-year run.

Eventually I stop crying and Mom goes into the hallway to make telephone calls. The idea behind these calls, of course, is to let people know I'm "okay." But that's not what "okay" means anymore. It means, "Yes, he's still alive." That's what everybody really wants to know. They're not being dramatic or hysterical; the possibility is always there. What the hell do I care what the odds are that a heart surgery will be successful? I am starting to feel that I am on the bad side of the odds.

Roy stays with me, holding my hand. He brought me a stuffed bear. One of those things you can get in a hospital gift shop with the little plastic stick that the bear is holding saying "Get well." It's a white bear with a pink bow. Something you'd buy for a little girl. Roy thinks it's hysterical that he got it for me and sets it on my groin. We go from being amused at how obnoxious he is to me yelping in fear, "No! There's a hole there!" Roy grabs the stuffed animal off my groin. It didn't hurt in the least. It just scared me since that's where they made the puncture. Roy says, droll, "I can't believe you just yelled 'there's a hole' while looking at your crotch." We both start laughing. Laughing too hard hurts my groin, so I do a kind of breathy laugh that will become very, very familiar to me as the months go by. I am definitely feeling a little more myself and I like that Roy is treating me like me. Naturally, then, since I am no longer scared for my life, at least for the moment, I demand, "Get my Xanax. It's in my glove compartment. I hid it behind the papers." He won't do it and I am literally begging. I don't want to be here. I don't want to be aware of what I just went through. I want to take Xanax and be serene and brave and sweet again. I want to take Xanax and be everything I'm not.

He doesn't get it for me. I am angry because he isn't being a loyal friend. He doesn't get it because he is, in fact, exactly that.

Linda and Jack

Later, when I wake up in my hospital room, I am attached to an IV. There is also a thing on my thumb to register my oxygen level and electrodes on my chest to keep track of my heartbeat.

There is a big window to my right and it looks like it's the end of the day. I got here at 6 a.m. this morning. Now, it must be late afternoon because the sun is beginning to set. Everybody is at the foot of my bed. Nobody is next to me. They are all looking at me.

Mom, Aunt Bev, Moriah, Roy and Linda. Linda worked most of the day and then left early to come be with me. She is wearing a cream-colored leather coat cropped at the waist. I don't really notice anyone else. I tell Linda, "Thank you for coming. I'm glad you're here."

She says, "Of course I'm here." Then I see tears in her eyes. She widens them like we all do when we try to make sure the tears don't roll down our cheeks. It is the first time I see Linda scared. She has cared for me and loved me like the fantastic friend she is, but now I think she is scared. She is looking at me lying here hooked up to all these machines, woozy from what happened today, and it suddenly feels "real" to her. It's one thing for me to become distinctly aware that I'm not immortal. I will find, throughout this experience, that it's quite another when it hits my friends. Like a ton of bricks. I tell her, "I like your coat."

She gives a tiny laugh at the absurdity of my comment and says, "Thanks." I say, "Ross?"

Then we both laugh because Linda is so frugal and I tease her about it all the time. She further laughs because I'm right. She did buy it from Ross.

I wanted to make her laugh. I know she doesn't like her own tears. I want everybody to know I'm still me. Even though I'm not quite sure myself.

Mom is sitting down in a chair in the corner by the window, watching me. I can't read her face. I can't tell if she's scared or tired or relieved. She's not exactly known for holding in her emotions. I say, weakly, in a very small voice, the only one I have right now, "Hi, mom."

Everybody sort of shifts to the other side of the room. Still at the end of the bed, but to the other side. They didn't need to because I could see mom even where they were standing, but people slowly are starting to treat her differently and this is one of the first ways I notice it. She has gone from being "Jack's mom" to being "the mother of the heart patient." I hate this and I have truly no idea how she will begin handling it the closer we get to the open heart. Er, ahem, even though I'm not going to have it.

She says, gently, softly, with a little smile, "Hi, honey."

"Mom, are you okay?"

This brings tears to everyone's eyes. Including mom. This is not me trying to be the good son or be charming or prove to everyone that I'm still myself. It's such an utterly ridiculous question to be asking her. I should know better. Especially now. Since nobody knows what to say, Linda says, joking, "Now he's delirious."

Everybody laughs. I don't care if it's fake-now-we're-relieved laughter. I don't care if it's a diversion from an awkward moment. I don't care if it's sincere or not. It makes me feel better. Makes me smile. Simple as that.

Later, Uncle Norm and Linnie come. Uncle Norm is always there for absolutely everybody in our family. No matter what is happening. No matter how far he has to drive. He is always, always there. I don't feel like the family gives him credit for this. Later, I won't remember what I talk about with anybody, but I will remember that I don't want anybody to leave. I want someone to sit with me all night and watch over me. When I try to say this, it oddly enough comes out as, "All of you should go home. All I'm going to do is sleep tonight anyway." My brain is become increasingly disconnected from my mouth.

At night the hospital is quiet and dim since only the hall lights are on. I can't sleep and decide to take a walk. I am attached to all sorts of things but they are hanging on my IV pole, so I can walk around dragging it with me. I have little slippers that the hospital provided and I sort of shuffle along. My groin really aches, so when I walk, I feel like I'm stretching it. I limp and shuffle. Limp and shuffle. Some of the rooms have lights on and the people in the rooms look very sick. Lifeless. Attached to more machines than I am. The sounds of television and that bluish tinge from TVs at night come out of some rooms. I stand for a moment at the end of a hallway to catch my breath. My breaths are very shallow and I am scared to make them deeper even though I'm not sure why. I don't think anybody told me not to breathe normally. Of course, they didn't tell me to breathe normally, so I'm definitely going to assume the worst and decide not to breathe. My groin is hurting more now that I'm walking, so I head back to my room.

A nurse turns the corner. She's tiny. Absolutely teensy. Smaller than my mom. She comes up to slightly above my belly button, and that's very, very short because I'm not very tall. She walks toward me at a brisk pace, surprisingly fast for someone with three inch long legs, and gets right in my face. Or, really, right in my chest. She says, in a voice that has absolute authority, "What are you doing here?"

What am I doing here, as in the hospital? Here as in having heart stuff? Here as in the hallway? Whatever she means, I am clearly in trouble. She's going to send me to my room. I'm back to being 10 years old.

"Um, I just, take a walk . . .," I stammer.

She continues to look at me without even blinking. It's very unnerving. Cannot be healthy for a heart patient to be made so uncomfortable.

"There are very sick people on this floor," she says.

I am waiting for her to wag her finger in my face and slap my wrist.

"I, uh, had an . . ." I cannot for the life of me remember the word "ablation." And since I'm not in my room, there is no chart for her to look at.

Suddenly, I find that I can take a deep breath out of sheer frustration. "I know there are sick people on this floor," I say irritated. I pause. She doesn't say anything. "I'm one of them." I hear myself saying the words and I absolutely hate her for making me say them.

I manage to tell her I had an ablation. She thought I was wandering around the hospital on the wrong floor. She explains that this floor is only for cardiac patients and she starts to lead me back to my room, holding onto my wrist since she can't really reach my arm. I decide I don't hate her after all. And when she gives me a Restoril to help me sleep, I decide that I love her.

People say I lead a charmed life. That I have a lucky star. Even my mom says she doesn't believe in luck until she thinks of me. It is the morning after my ablation. I have taken a short walk down the hallway, dragging my IV along with me. I notice so many "sick people." I stop, amazed at how stupid I am: I am one of the sick people now. I turn around and pad slowly back to my room, crawl back into my hospital bed, trying not to tangle my IV, and think about this. Are there two versions of sick? About to die and about to recover? I wonder which group I'm in. I seem to be putting a lot more emphasis on being in the About To Die group than the About To Recover group. I don't go further into this thought, but it is probably the clearest and truest one I have made about this heart thing so far.

Mom walks into my room even though it is barely dawn. She is wearing jeans and my tattered, gray, NYU Law School hooded sweatshirt. She looks so tiny swimming in my huge sweatshirt. I also notice that she looks dreadful. Her eyes are bloodshot. There are huge dark circles and bags under her eyes. She has an exhausted, far away look. She comes over and smiles and holds my hand and asks how my night was.

"Mom, you look awful." She takes a moment to decide how to react and ends up with a little, wry smile. "You look like your kid is about to have heart surgery or something!"

She laughs.

This is my version of handling the situation. The way of controlling what is happening to me and everyone else. I'm not ready to sit back and let them be sad. Not yet.

She sits down by the window and tells me that Norm and Linnie are on their way and that Linda will be at up at Mulholland in the afternoon after Mom has brought me home.

"Mom, I was thinking this morning."

"Nothing good can come of that," she says.

We laugh.

"People always say I'm lucky. That things manage to work out for me. Even you have said I have a lucky star." I stop and try to figure out exactly what I am trying to say. "So, I think all this is payback. That now God and I are even."

The look on her face goes from gentle to barely veiled furious. Her eyes suddenly become clearly focused. Her mouth purses in the way that make little wrinkles form on her top lip. The transformation from gentle exhaustion to focused anger is immediate. Her voice is hard, intense, angry, strong and full. She's pissed and helpless at the same time. I haven't heard this voice for months. She is truly angry at me. Not the situation, but at me. She stands up and speaks slowly. "Don't ever. Don't. You. Ever. Say that again. Don't think for even one second that you deserve this."

We never, ever, mention it again.

Not long after I'm home from the ablation, I'm down in Laguna Beach to visit Babba and stay over a Saturday night. Aunt Freda, who is Babba's sister, is visiting her from Winnipeg, Manitoba. Aunt Freda is a firecracker. She is a widow, has lots of money, says it how it is, and doesn't always say it very gently. I have always liked her, but we've never been around each other or communicated enough to become close. About two years ago, she had open heart surgery for a valve replacement. Apparently, the valve they used wasn't quite big enough. I'm thrilled, for obvious reasons, to have this knowledge. I've never, however, asked exactly what problems this causes her. For all I know, there are none. But the possibility of knowing the details scare me, so I don't ask. I fail to see the simple fact that despite this, she seems fine and is walking around and traveling to California from Manitoba. All I see is that a mistake was made.

I'm in my black-and-white plaid Calvin Klein pajama bottoms. They're a light flannel fabric and they are all floppy around the legs and way too long for me. I love them. I'm wearing a white t-shirt. It's late afternoon on Saturday and the three of us are loafing around. The 29-year-old grandson/grand nephew and the grandmother and great aunt. They've engaged in their favorite activity: feeding me. I'm about to burst.

I'm lying down on the sofa reading Albert Camus, *The Plague*. I've read it before and am reading it again to remind myself that we learn humanity through tragedy. I am getting to the point where I need as much reinforcement as I can get. I'm also to the point where the Xanax and alcohol and being fabulous aren't quite cutting it. It's not pleasantly blinding like it used to be. Not that I'm stopping. I'm going to add something to it, like Albert Camus, my grandmother and my great aunt, apparently. None of this is the least bit intentional. It's amazing how strong our will to get through something is. As though my brain knew I had better start getting my shit together and getting it together fast.

Babba is in a chair reading a book and the sun is streaming through mini-blinds across her face. The chair is at the end of the sofa and I can watch her. I know it doesn't compare to what she dealt with when my dad was in Vietnam, but I wish she didn't have to go through this, too.

When I mention the heart surgery, she takes off her glasses and the sun is in her eyes a little and I see them fill with tears. Not one rolls down her cheek, though. There is no way in hell she'll let it. But I still see them. I don't want to make it this "thing" we cannot discuss, but I also don't want to make her cry. I make a joke about being fed endless food by two little old Jewish ladies and let the Heart Thing drop.

The next morning, while Babba is sleeping, Aunt Freda and I decide to go down to the beach to have coffee and read newspapers. It's one of those gorgeous California days. Blue skies with a few puffy clouds. Bright sunshine. The glare off the ocean is almost blinding. Chilly, light wind. Just beautiful. We go to the Starbucks on PCH across the street from the beach. I have a venti nonfat four-shot latte. Aunt Freda has coffee. We get our newspapers and walk across the street to the main beach and sit down at a picnic table on the boardwalk. We are next to each other, facing the water. Watching the sky. The waves. A few other people. We sip our coffee. Read our newspapers. It's an easy, simple moment.

Out of the corner of my eye, I see Aunt Freda lift up her head and face the water. Then I see her facing her newspaper, taking a sip of coffee. And she says, without looking up from her paper, "You know, Jackie, it will be horrible, painful, and terrifying, but you will get through it and you will be fine because we all love you and because you have no choice." We never talk about it after that. About a month after I come home from the hospital, she sends me a note; all it says is, "Dear Jackie. See, I was right. Love, Aunt Freda."

On another quick trip to see Babba, I walk in the door and yell, "Babba, it's me."

I hear her shout, from the kitchen, "Hi, honey, I'm in the kitchen." I walk into the kitchen, give her a hug and kiss on the cheek and ask her what she's stirring on the stove. "Jackie, I'm a Jewish grandmother. It's chicken soup." Of course. She takes the spoon out of the big old metal pot, takes a little sip of the broth, puts it back in the pot and grabs some kind of spice and sprinkles it into the pot. Just so. I've been eating this exact same chicken soup since I was a baby. A few years ago she asked me if I wanted the recipe. I told her no. It wouldn't be Babba's chicken soup if Babba didn't make it.

She looks at me and says, "You look tired, Jackie." And just like that, in the blink of an eye, all the gloss slips off. Suddenly, I'm not fabulous. I'm not flying all over the world. I'm not getting attention at clubs. I'm not wearing my stupidly expensive clothes and driving my stupidly expensive car. I'm not a lawyer. I'm not charming. I'm not trying too hard to impress people. I'm not the "it" boy. Suddenly, I'm quiet. I'm introspective. I'm simple. I'm that insecure, unsure kid all over again. Not Jack. Jackie. I'm me without any of the other bullshit that is usually so much a part of my life that I forget the difference between who I am and the life I have created for myself. When I'm with Babba, everything that doesn't matter, doesn't matter.

I open the fridge, find a diet coke, and go sit at the table next to the kitchen. Babba continues to stir the pot, taking sips of the broth here and there and adding this and that while adjusting the heat.

"You were in Paris last week?"

"Yes, for four days."

She laughs.

"My grandson. The world traveler. You saw your friend from Poland?"

"Yes. Her name is Joanna. She flew to Paris from Warsaw to meet me."

"You live an amazing life, kid," she gives me a little smirk.

"I know. I'm very lucky."

"Yes, you are. And I already know that you know that. I think other people . . ."

I interrupt her, "I know, Babba. People who don't know me look at me and see fluff. They don't see substance. They see a spoiled brat who thinks too highly of himself."

"That's not what I was going to say," she says, giving me a little smirk, raising one eyebrow and taking another sip of the soup all at the same time. "I was going to say, I think other people know how much you appreciate what you have and that's why they love you. You pretend to take it for granted, but people see through the pretense. They know you aren't fluff, Jackie. Nobody who really knows you would ever think you're fluff." She sighs and adds, still smiling, "But you are making it tougher and tougher for people to give you the benefit of the doubt lately."

I smile almost shyly, a little embarrassed, and quote Dr. Seuss, "Those who matter don't mind and those who mind don't matter."

She laughs. "My grandson the lawyer quotes Dr. Seuss. I'm so proud."

We both laugh. I get up, open the freezer and plop some ice into my glass of diet coke. She continues stirring. I go back to the table and sit down.

She says, "Are you scared?"

I say, "Of the surgery? No. I'm not that scared."

She continues stirring the soup. The steam from the pot leaves a shiny film on her face. I drink my diet coke. We are quiet for a moment and then she says, very gently and quietly, "Don't ever lie to me again, okay, honey?"

"Okay, Babba. I'm sorry. Yes, I'm a little scared."

She pauses for a moment and then adds, "And by the way, Jackie, sometimes those who mind are actually the ones who matter most."

C H A P T E R   1 8

The Birthday to End All Birthdays

EVERYONE THOUGHT I WAS CRAZY to plan a birthday dinner to be held two weeks before my open heart surgery. In Paris. I wanted something unique to mark my thirtieth birthday. Open heart surgery being not unique enough, apparently. I believe in sign-posts. Life is full of them, but people either don't notice or let them pass by. Like rolling through a stop sign: you know you should stop and look around, but you go right through anyway. I don't know why people stop marking their movement into the future. At birth, we're circumcised, baptized, or whatever sized you are. At 13 there is a bar mitzvah to mark a passage into adulthood (although for some people, like me for instance, this doesn't really "take"). We have graduation ceremonies in high school and college. After that it seems like the official signposts largely disappear. I wanted the signpost for my 30th birthday to be a lavish party in Paris instead of fearing for my life on a cold steel table.

Once I heard my body was misbehaving, it was as though I took personal offense. How rude of it. Paris, however, always makes me feel comfortable. Of course, this rude thing was making me feel very Parisian. I've always been sure I was a Parisian in a past life. My disdain for anything that was not at least cultural if not fashionable would seem to suggest this. I would have sat at Café Flore wearing a black turtleneck and a beret. I'd drink espresso and Pernod, smoke a Galouise, and wallow in ennui. I would eat Nutella on French bread. In this life, however, I was about to be, as a gentle and dear friend put it, "hacked into like the Christmas-fucking-turkey." I had a feeling Nutella wasn't allowed at Cedars-Sinai. So, off to Paris I went to see my friends.

My friends are sincere, genuine, adventurous, crazy, and over-the-top. They like the spotlight. As Eric once told me, "Jack, you like people who are either devastated or fabulous! I'm devastatingly fabulous!" He's right. I'm a guy of extremes. I'm not so much for the in-betweens. Wouldn't have a clue what to do with them. But the extremes, I can handle. Not necessarily open-heart surgery extreme, but crying hysterically over a heart attack victim on "ER" one night and eating caviar in first class on the way to Paris the next morning extreme. I'm in touch with my inner bipolar.

Nonetheless, it did not register that this birthday thing was really over the top. Which shows you where my point of reference was (or maybe where it wasn't). Frankly, I wasn't feeling well even months before then. I got tired faster. I had to take deeper breaths. I faked it pretty well. I tried to distract myself by getting my Hugo Boss suit tailored just right instead of with the rudely inconvenient pre-surgery crap. After all, I had to look devastatingly fabulous at my birthday dinner. I never considered not having my party. My parents and my doctors were strangely unenthusiastic. Eric, however, said,

30th Birthday Party in Paris

"Hell with 'em. If you're going to die, you should die in Paris." I told him I would want to be cremated and have my ashes sprinkled over the Paris Ritz. *Bien sur.*

A few weeks later, airplanes were in the sky from Los Angeles, New York City, London, and Copenhagen. I felt very important. Everybody told me I was leading a charmed life. About to have my chest hacked in half, but charmed, apparently.

I dedicate the birthday dinner to my mother. A great flourish of a toast, almost in tears. She has strangely been the most supportive person for me in regards to my heart surgery. Or, at least the most patient. Somehow she found her most unselfish strength and shoved it in my direction. Maybe she has done it before, but I didn't know because I only pay attention to my own strength. The restaurant is a chorus of glasses pinging together with sounds of mirth. I think about my mother. And I never tell her about this moment.

And I can never tell anything more about that extraordinary evening, or the whole time in Paris for that matter. It would have to be its own book. Use every ounce of your imagination. So I'll start again at 2 a.m. the night before we were all to fly back to various cities after four days of being devastatingly fabulous. We were finally tired. Rather, we finally cared that we were tired. Lady Paddy, Countess Nora, Joanna, Svend, Eric and I. The rest of the group had either gone to bed or were still running amuck.

I decided to walk the two blocks back to our quaint, little hotel. As with all things called quaint and little, it was more tiny and plain. More like a dorm room. Which, really, was perfect for us that week. We didn't care because either we were hardly ever there or were too self-absorbed to notice.

After a week of being in every you'll-never-get-in swanky place in Paris, we had all gone to Open Bar, which is a very trendy, popular gay bar in *Le Marais*, a section of Paris that used to be the Jewish neighborhood in Paris. I can't say it was "historically" the Jewish neighborhood, however. In Europe, you usually mean somewhere in between the beginning of time and the 1500s when you say "historically." As opposed to the United States when we mean the '60s. You still can get falafel and a menorah, but now, you can also get t-shirts that say "Mom, thanks for the genes." As with any gay neighborhood in the world, there are trendy, expensive, well-turned-out stores and restaurants filled with fabulous people. And just like when it was "historically" the Jewish neighborhood, every ten years or so, a bomb goes off to display someone's hatred.

Open Bar usually is filled to capacity on any night of the week. Impossible to move sometimes, which isn't saying much since it's not that big in the first place. It's very crowded. It gets loud. It gets smoky. It gets hot. It gets uncomfortable until you're drunk and then you don't care. It's amazing the lengths that groups of people who aren't completely accepted into the world will go to so they can forget what it feels like to always feel "other."

The place is sort of octagonal shaped with a bar in the very center. The floor is, I'm pretty sure, polished cement. There is a flat screen TV on one wall showing videos that are not, strangely, the same as whatever music is playing. The music is contemporary pop and 80s. Ask anyone who is in their 30s and they will refuse to acknowledge that 80s music is no longer "contemporary." Can Journey really have hit its height of popularity back when I wore stonewashed jeans and teachers were telling us we'd get detention for dirty dancing?

The bar was packed with guys from all over the world because that's how trendy gay bars in big cities are. Like moths to a flamer, as the saying goes, the guys find them no matter what. The six of us were quite the motley crew. Among us were two sexualities, four (I think) different decades, three continents, and three substances. All of us ignored everyone else in the bar because, as I said, we're all pretty self-absorbed. At some point, Lady Paddy says we should all go back to the hotel, sit in my room and relax. Eric is having none of this and being that he's already on the road from drunk-off-his-ass to falling down on it, I decide to leave him out. I know this sounds awful. I used to stay out with him until 4 a.m. when I lived in Manhattan—partly because I was also drunk and partly because I would get worried about him. But Eric is a human carrier pigeon. He always finds his way home, always in one piece. Besides, when he's that drunk, there is no telling him anything. I stuck a bunch of the hotel's business cards into one of his pockets (I had put them in my pocket earlier for just this moment. Both he and I, for being very unpredictable people, are pretty predictable to each other.) and said goodbye. He said something like, "Goodbyeitwasafunnightandiloveeveryoneofyou."

Back at the dorm-like hotel, the five of us packed ourselves into my little hotel room. I immediately threw open the immense windows so we could breathe. Svend and Joanna sat on the bed next to each other, leaning against the wall. I stuck myself lengthwise onto a mini-sofa. Lady Paddy sat at the small desk. Lady Paddy smoked so I kept the window opened even though it got a little cold once we calmed down. Lady Paddy and Joanna were drunk. Svend was on ecstasy. I was drunk and on Xanax and espresso—my favorite cocktail at the time. Not surprisingly, I don't have a completely clear memory of everything that happened. I do remember that Paddy and I were talking endlessly and finding ourselves highly amusing, Joanna would switch between giggling and dropping an I'm-such-a-sophisticated-American-living-in-Warsaw witty remark and then giggling again. Svend smiled at all of us and everything we said and kept asking Joanna to touch his forearm because apparently the ecstasy made that particular body part highly sensitive.

At some point, Paddy was telling me a story of a fire that had broken out in her flat in London. I asked her what had started the fire and she looked at me like I was completely stupid and said, quite simply, "Fire." Which put us all, even Svend, into hysterical fits of laughter. Then, as we were all cackling like mad, one of Paddy's false eyelashes started to meander down her cheek. When I noticed, I started laughing so hard, I couldn't even talk. The image of her sipping her coffee, laughing, and oblivious to a false eyelash slowly crawling its way down her cheek was too much.

"What? What are you laughing at? What's going on" When she reached up to brush at it, not knowing what it was, Joanna managed, in between cackles, to tell her. Svend said something through his haze/laughter; it might have been, "What's an eyelash?" but I'm not sure. At which point the eyelash jumped from her cheek and into her coffee. Suddenly she stuck her finger in the coffee and tried to get at the eyelash as though she'd never find another one in all of Paris. To this day, I'm shocked I did not pee in my pants. Even sober, I am pretty sure I would have been in hysterics. There is nothing like seeing one of your friends do something which to them seems completely sensical while to the rest of the world, it would seem berserk. We laugh at our friends' antics. We look down on everyone else's.

Suddenly, the door to my hotel room bursts open. Eric is standing there, all 6'2" of him, wearing his full length sable coat, and I see bare calves. Suddenly, I know. Oh. My. God.

He says, strangely not sounding drunk, "Don't ya love wearing a sable and nothing else?"

It was an amazing night. Amazing because nobody could have scripted something more hysterical. Amazing because, with us together, nothing was more important at the moment. That's the thing about a group of friends. What it all comes down to is you care very much for each other and enjoy spending fun times together. In the long run, it doesn't really matter if it's an over-the-top jetsetting trip to Paris or a movie night on the couch. That's just geography.

The next morning at the airport waiting for our plane to fly back to Los Angeles, Eric and I are both horrifyingly hung over. And there is nothing worse than getting on an airplane hung over. Especially for a 13-hour flight. Even if you are in first class. We're both nursing espressos. In silence. Talking might hurt. I'm thinking about what an amazing adventure the week had been. How incredible that it all came together. That it was better and more memorable than anything I had even dared to hope. And the joy I felt that all my friends, seemingly so incongruous, took so much delight in each other. I knew I was about to have my heart surgery in two weeks. It was hard to forget, considering I had to stop for breath so many times while walking through the airport, but I smiled because, what a time!

Eric's eyelids were only half open. A hand was holding up his forehead. I could hear tiny, whimpering sounds in between sips of espresso. I said, quietly, "In my wildest dreams, I couldn't have planned such a birthday party."

Eric kind of grunted, kind of moaned, while looking into his espresso, "That wasn't your birthday party." Ugh. He's still drunk. "You planned a goodbye party. Nobody could admit it. Including you." Tears. In my eyes. Instantly. "But, Jack. You're wrong."

That's the thing about friends. They surprise you with their antics all the time and you love them for it. Sometimes, though, they surprise you because they know you so much better than you know yourself. And for that, you keep them.

The thing is, how do you prepare for something like open heart surgery? Nothing in thirty years has prepared me for this. I don't mind my friends adding things to my life right now—gifts, subtle suggestions of "stay the fuck sober, you ass," teaching me how to meditate—are all welcome. Maybe it's pretty late, only two weeks before the surgery, but I welcome them. They add. They don't subtract. It's the subtracting stuff I can't handle. I don't mind, "Do this." I mind "Don't do this." It's very easy to say that all the Xanax and the alcohol and the extraordinarily fast life I created for myself are detrimental and self-defeating and are my way of running away from the heart surgery, but maybe it's all okay. So what if I want to run away from it? I'm having it. It's happening. I'm not killing myself with alcohol and pills; I'm taking them to avoid thinking about very much more than being fabulous and alive. That's what people aren't understanding. All this is making me feel pretty fucking alive. If I was only doing meditation and therapy and talking out loud to my heart, well, that's just a different direction. It's still running.

None of this is about balance. It is either black or white. I'm either going to live or I'm going to die. I'm going to have the heart surgery or I'm not. I'm going to end up a vegetable or not. I'm going to focus on my inner self or I'm going to focus on the superficial. I. Do. Not. Want. It. Any. Different!

Parv and I have a long telephone conversation and we do some visualization exercises with light and some exercises about picturing my heart as part of my mind. When I get off the phone, I am so fucking high and balanced. I'm not fabulous and wearing $1000 worth of clothes sitting in the hottest club in Europe, but I feel pretty fucking good and the rest begins to fall away. I don't need it anymore. I don't need to be proving I'm alive to myself. In fact, I don't even need to be defining what I've been doing or what my life has been or what I'm been running to or from. None of it fucking matters, suddenly.

I want to prepare for what I'm going to do. I'm still going to take Xanax, but I'll stop drinking (which shouldn't be hard for two weeks) and I'll sit quietly because this sitting quietly with myself stuff suddenly is okay. Maybe that is because it has to be. I really have no choice. Again, it's not about balance. It's still running. It "looks" healthier because it "sounds" healthier and, although I'm still skeptical, it feels good and my cries aren't as scary, so I'm okay with running in this direction for the next two weeks.

Would it be better if I were meditating every day and being quiet and reading and sitting in therapy once or twice a week? That sounds pretty bleak, right? I honestly think that is how some people think I should have dealt with it. But I am dealing with it in the way I know how. Maybe later, if there is a later, I won't regret any of it. Although, for now, I have to admit that the talking out loud to my heart stuff is pretty fuckin' cool. It's definitely working.

CHAPTER 19

D-Day

IT IS 4 A.M. THE morning of December 8, 2000. Heart Surgery Day. Roy and I get ready. As with last night, I take another 15 mg of Xanax while he is in the bathroom. I also insist on driving the BMW down to Aunt Bev's even though I'm too Xanaxed out for driving and, more importantly, a tad distracted.

Mom, Dad, Aunt Bev, Auntie Lanie, Babba, and Moriah are all there. Aunt Bev, in usual Aunt Bev fashion, has brought muffins for everyone and I can smell coffee. I would like nothing more than to shovel a few chocolate chip muffins into my mouth and get a good buzz going with coffee. I am, however, not allowed to eat. I'd probably vomit it all up anyway. I am so drugged out of

Jack and Aunt Bev

my mind that I barely register everything. It is easy, though. It has all already been planned. We drive to Cedars in three cars. It is about 15 minutes away. Five for driving. Ten for parking. You could walk. If people in L.A. walked.

We get to the hospital and it's all a haze. I am now purely going through the motions with hardly any awareness. I sign all the consent forms that essentially say (1) they can do whatever they need to once they are inside; and (2) I am aware and consent to the fact that the surgery may cause death. I know this, but there is a high irony in the fact that I'm about to have a surgery, which may cause death, to save my life. This, however, is exactly what I have known for the past three years. This is the combination that has fueled everything: I have to have the surgery to live even though it might kill me.

I almost fall off my chair while signing the forms. Mom catches me. When she goes to bring the forms to the nurse, I take the last few Xanax I have and pop them quickly into my mouth. My fear of/need for the surgery is the only thing that is keeping me from passing out.

Fifteen minutes later, I'm lying on a gurney being wheeled toward pre-op. I am Xanaxed out of my mind and nobody knows it. At least they don't know quite how much I've taken. I stare straight up at the fluorescent lights. I can see my mom on one side and my dad on the other, their faces peering down at me. They are silent. What could they say? It must have taken every ounce of strength in their souls not to cry in front of me. It's the kind of strength I never knew my parents had. Unselfish strength. Having nothing to do with themselves. Suddenly, I say, in panic, "Where's my Babba?" I hear, behind me, "I'm right here, Jackie." Her voice is elevated. It is not calm. Only I would notice the slight panic in her voice. That's the last thing I remember. "I'm right here, Jackie." Then, the gurney turns the corner and I am completely alone. The nurses and orderlies don't count. I am alone, but this is a familiar feeling. I didn't realize until this very moment that I've been alone for a very long time. I do not feel guilty or small that I am feeling sorry for myself. All that comes into my head, over and over again, is, "It's here." Well, that and all of them sitting outside at a round table as though it is the last supper.

Eric: "We gather here this morning to grieve the death of part of Jack's heart."

Roy: "Ya. Probably the part that makes him nice."

Linda: "True. Wonder who he'll be when the surgery is over?"

Indeed. I wonder. Who? How terribly existential of me to consider this just as the nurse pokes me with the IV.

Here we go . . .

I am lying on a table. My chest has been sliced open. The blood is no longer circulating through my heart, no longer through my body. It is circulating through the heart/lung machine, which is supposed to keep any foreign particles out, but from what I read on the internet (or what I shouldn't have read on the internet), it isn't perfect. It's close, but not perfect. I wish I could make jokes and be my usual self. Trying to take care of everyone else. Or trying to be fabulous. Or trying to charm people. Or being at home reading one of my many books. Or out at the "it" clubs and the "it" restaurants, being crazy/enchanting/fabulous in either NYC or L.A. or Europe. Or sitting at home crying. Essentially, at the moment, I'm basically dead. If they stopped the heart/lung machine right now, I'd be dead.

They're slicing into my heart. My chest is like a window they've opened up. Saw through the breast bone, open me up, and pull my heart out as much as necessary. What if they do something wrong? What if they cut an artery? Or leave a sponge in me? Or the valve they transplant doesn't fit right? What if my body can't accept the invasion and shuts down? What if, like some small percentage of people, I die for what seems like no apparent reason? My chest is open. Part of my heart is being sliced away. Oxygen is getting to my brain because the blood flows through a machine instead of my heart. I have been, for all intents and purposes, put into a coma. I wish I could make jokes, but I'm not really here.

My mother, father, cousin, aunt, brother, grandmother, and closest friends sit in the waiting room. Fifteen people, with another 10 calling them every hour. If I were alive I could comfort them. Maybe tell them I'm finally okay with it. Maybe tell them that, in some strange way, I've made peace with it, but I haven't really. Never have. I have not been brave and courageous. Why have people been saying I am? Maybe I could at least fake it and tell them I have. Instead, they sit under fluorescent lights in a room set aside for them, waiting, waiting, waiting. Is my mother in hysterics? Is she quietly crying? Is my father finally weak and scared for me? Is my grandmother trying to be stoic or is she letting out the fact that she is scared? How could they not be? Is everyone else sitting there trying not to cry so they don't upset my parents and brother and grandmother? Are they trying to be strong for everyone else? Do they leave the room when they can't take their own emotions anymore? Or do they let it out and then feel selfish? How do they comfort each other? Do they talk about being scared or do they tell each other they know it will be fine even if they are scared inside? Do they sit in silence or are they talking to each other? Do they stay together or do they take walks alone around the hospital? Who is comforting whom? And who truly believes this will work?

Does the nurse come out and tell them step by step what's happening? Does that make it worse or better? Do they realize that this is as helpless as they have ever been in their whole lives as far as their love for me? Does their realization break them apart that they cannot do one tiny, little thing about what is going on while I lie here with my chest open, my blood flowing through a machine, my heart being cut apart, and me essentially in a deep, deep coma for as long as this takes? My eyes closed. My mouth covered with a mask. Wires and electrodes and tubes monitoring everything. I'm not really here.

I am taken away at 6 a.m. and I am back five hours later. And they all stayed. I know none of this; I hear the stories afterwards. At least, what people will tell me. All their versions of how they handled it. How the people around them handled it. Sometimes they are the same, sometimes they are different. But, right now, I know nothing. I am gone, and I will never, ever know what it was like to wait to know if I'm okay.

I wish I could make fun of the situation and of myself and my own absurdities. But I can't. I'm not, essentially, here. I'm not cute. I'm not in Paris. I'm not out getting attention. I'm not flying first class to Europe or South America. I'm not successful. I'm not insecure. I'm not educated. I'm not well-read. I'm not unconditionally there for my best friends. I don't have awkward relationships with my parents. I no longer depend on Babba for security. I am not taking any risks in life. I'm not drunk. I'm not taking Xanax. I'm not doing any spiritual work. I'm not talking out loud to my heart. I'm not observant and smart, although pretending to be innocent and naïve. I didn't have a shitty childhood. I didn't push and push and push through my accomplishments. I didn't learn not to take myself too seriously. I didn't learn that life is too short. I didn't learn that I'm not immortal. I'm not devoted to my closest friends. I'm not arrogant. I'm not a know-it-all. I don't take care of my grandmother. I am not proud of myself for the risks I have taken. I have not just left a five-year relationship. I have not spent the last six months traveling to Europe on weekends for a day in Paris or London or Buenos Aires. I have not stood on my deck with a glass of vodka watching the L.A. lights twinkle in the wind while crying because I'm so scared. I have not been so drunk I could barely stand up. I have not been out every night cultivating everybody's adoration for someone so accomplished, so fabulous and outrageous. I have not cried myself to sleep or faked my way into being courageous. I am not self-absorbed. I am none of this. Not anymore. That's all gone now. I am nothing. Everything that has been "me" is gone. What's true, what has happened, what I have done or not done does not matter anymore. My triumphs and mistakes. They are gone. Thirty years have all come down to this one moment. My chest has been sawed in half. My heart is being sliced apart. My family and friends wait to see if I make it.

I have no idea what time it is. I don't know what day it is. I have no idea how long I've been in ICU. Drifting into consciousness is like being inside a thick cloud with thoughts that leave as fast as they come. I barely register that there are tubes down my throat and I cannot talk. I barely register that I am not breathing on my own. I barely register that my arms are tied down. I don't feel any pain. I register that I have absolutely no control over anything, even my own thoughts, then my little tiny world is black again.

I don't know how much later it is since I last woke up. It could be fifteen minutes. It could be two hours. Right now I can feel, barely, someone's hand holding mine. I don't think about who it is. I only know someone is holding my hand and I can't seem to see who it is. I am barely, barely here. Suddenly, though, I realize my mom is to the left of my bed. I think I hear her speaking to me. There is also someone on the right side of my bed rubbing my arm. I can't see who it is and I don't hear a voice. Only later do I find out it's Linda.

I squeeze my mom's hand twice. I open my eyes and I can see her for a second. We had arranged, prior to my surgery, that I would squeeze her hand twice if I was in pain. I can then hear her arguing with the nurse. Later I find out nobody really believed her that this was something we had arranged. I also find out nobody was sure if I meant to squeeze twice or if I was just hold-ing her hand. But, I did mean to squeeze twice. I am starting to hurt. Which means I am starting to wake up a little bit. I'm now terrified, but only for a second before I drift away again.

Time passes. I know this because I can see the clock on the wall facing my bed. I don't know if it's the same day of my surgery or later. I don't know if it's night or day. I am totally disoriented and, as much as I try, I can't figure anything out. As quickly as a thought comes into my head, it leaves. I am struggling to put things into order, to make sense of what is going on, but it's impossible. I have no concept of present time. I'm barely awake to even care what time it is, but it is a losing battle to try to understand anything, so I lapse back into unconsciousness.

I know Roy has come into my room and is rubbing my hand. I know he is with someone, but I can't tell who it is. I also know my grandmother is in the room at some point and I think she is with my dad, but I'm not sure. I am barely awake enough to begin to try to understand things, to figure out what time it is, how long I've been here. What does not occur to me is to ask if I'm okay. I'm so far away from that concept that it doesn't even enter my head.

Then, I know my mom is to the left and my dad is on the right. I know they are saying soothing things to me in soft, delicate voices, but I can't figure out what they are saying. I can hear something for a second or two and then it is as though I'm back asleep. Everything is disconnected. It is as though there is "me" and then there is the world out "there." I instinctively know I am not a part of the world "out there." I don't know that I will ever again feel a true part of the world "out there."

I feel like there is too much saliva in my throat and that I can't breathe. I know I can breathe, but I feel as though I can't. I even remember that I was told that the breathing tube will breathe for me and that I shouldn't fight it. I make a motion with my right hand as though I have a pen in it and move it in the air as though I'm writing. Only with my wrist since my arms are strapped down. I want to write a note and tell them I need suction.

I don't hear what is being said, but I can feel that someone has put a piece of paper in my hand and a pen and I try to write suction. Even as I write it, I know it is not legible. This moment of understanding that I have no way to communicate makes me despair. It is my worst fear. I am lying here, conscious enough to know where I am and what has happened, but I have no way to communicate. For the first time, I wonder if I'm a vegetable. Stuck in this cocoon forever with no way out.

I hear dad saying, "Let him try again." Does he believe that I can really write? Or believe that I know what I'm doing? Or believe that my brain is working and I have a little understanding of what is going on? But he does, and when I am given another chance, I write carefully and slowly, picturing the letters as I go. I know that it's legible this time and a second later there is a tube suctioning my throat. I only later find out that when the nurse saw this, she told my parents, "Wow. He's definitely going to be okay." I wonder if they believe it.

I keep drifting in and out. I am trying to remain calm. It isn't hard since I'm barely awake, but for some reason, I know I have to be calm and let the machines work. I know people are in and out visiting me, but I don't register who they are. Then I open my eyes and someone is talking to me. Everything is still very hazy and I can't make out who is here or what is going on. There are several people in the room. Maybe three, four, or five. I can't tell. Someone is talking to me and although I don't really hear what she is saying, I realize they are about to pull my chest tubes out, remove the respirator tubes. This is my return to life. I don't know if the heart surgery was a success, but I know I'm okay in some way.

There is so much movement in the room, but I can't really see anything. Bits and pieces of life around me. Nothing is all that clear. I look up and see a nurse. She has a small smile on her face and blonde hair tied back in a pony tail. She is saying something to me, but I can't understand what it is. My brain must hear it because I know she is about to take the breathing tube out. It's awful. It feels like someone is taking one of those round hair brushes out of my lungs and throat. I feel like I can't breathe for a moment and start to gasp and this wakes me up more than anything. I try to lift myself up because I can't breathe, but I am completely strapped down and I hear a male voice telling me to remain calm and breathe. I'd happily breathe if I could. A split second later, I can. I am breathing and coughing and I stop gasping. I have graduated from barely conscious to barely awake. I'm still trapped in my own little world. It's very lonely and very safe all at once. Having all these people around me is somehow reassuring. It's as though they are acting in concert with each other.

The same nurse tells me that they are going to take my chest tubes out. I was told this is extraordinarily painful. The tubes are in my chest through two small incisions right below the heart scar down my sternum. I picture a black hose like the kind you would use in a car engine. I'm sure it doesn't really look like that, but that is how I picture it. I never do get to see what they look like. Somehow I know to relax my body completely. They are about to pull the tubes out and I rasp, "Count to three." And they do. Slowly. By the time they get to "three," I have relaxed my chest and abdominal muscles completely. All my focus, energy, and what little brain power I have at the moment are going into relaxing those muscles as though they are going to slip slowly into the center of the earth. The tubes slide right out. It feels like I'm taking one long deep breath through the center of my chest, and when the breath is over, I know, somehow, that it is amazing that there was no pain.

Next is something I have not expected. There is a wire going through my chest and into my heart. It is connected to an external pacemaker. The nurse gently explains what it is and that they are going to take it out. She tells me it will be "uncomfortable." I am at the point where something that is merely "uncomfortable" would be a gigantic blessing. She counts to three and I try to relax my chest and I can actually feel the wire being pulled out of my heart and out of my chest. I can feel it slip out slowly and carefully. It doesn't exactly hurt, but it is very uncomfortable. I am scared. The more conscious I become, the more scared I am. I'm alive, but I don't know if they did the surgery, if it worked, if anything happened. I'm still in between coherency and incoherency despite being conscious.

I'm in a wheelchair. A wheelchair? No gurney? Does that mean I'm okay? Where are my family and friends? This is all a very bad thing. My thoughts are that simple: A bad thing.

The obvious bad things that happen to you when you grow up are easy. You get beat up. You get caught cheating on a test. You fall down and break your arm. You brag and lie because you're insecure. The worst, of course, is needing headgear with your braces. Not that any of these things happened to me . . .

To me, it was absolutely mortifying that I tried out for the part of Radar in "MASH" in my freshman year of high school and didn't get the part. I was scrawny. I was little. Could I be THAT bad that I didn't get the part? How much more of a "Radar" could I be? Radar was little and knew things other people didn't and was easily scared by other people and totally intimidated. I was Radar, damnit! Give me the fucking part! Instead it went to some over-weight guy with big curly hair who was completely un-Radar-like. Oh. You mean I was supposed to be acting? Who knew? Anyway, it was a bad thing.

Then there was this time I was obsessed with a girl. Not obsessed in a sexual way since I was gay, just totally obsessed. She listened to the coolest music, didn't care who thought what about her, had those pairs of Guess! jeans that were grey with a black corduroy fake rip, and had a strobe light that we'd use while setting mousse on fire outside on the sidewalk. I wanted to be her. One Friday night, on Shabbat when I knew everybody was at services, I kept calling her. Except that I didn't say anything. I was barely even cool enough to be around her. I would call and not say anything and then hang up. No heavy breathing. No strange phrases. I mean, I was so un-cool that I couldn't even think of anything interesting to do while crank calling.

Unbeknownst to me, she was so scared that she called the synagogue and had her father come home. Also unbeknownst to me, my parents came home early because they didn't want to stay for the challah (which to me was the point; why go to services if you aren't staying for candy and pastries as the end?). So I'm in the middle of a crank call. Saying nothing. Not having heard my parents come home at the other end of the house. My mom picks up the phone, hears no dial tone, and says, "Jackie? Is that you? Are you on the phone?" The aftermath is unimaginable. Mortification doesn't even begin to describe it in the least. Suffice it to say, as with other things that happen while you are growing up, it was a bad thing.

There was ditching school. I did this a lot. I didn't do a lot of bad things. I never smoked. I never drank. I didn't stay out late (too often). I did help a friend steal a pair of Revo sunglasses that we were going to share while skiing, but that was pretty much the worst thing I did in high school. Except ditching. I hated school, so I ditched. I managed to get decent grades anyway (although not stellar), so it seemed okay to ditch.

One time I took my Toyota Land Cruiser and decided to climb up the dirt road behind our house. People do not realize that Santa Fe is hot and dry in the summer and cold and snowy in the winter. This was winter. I had a Land Cruiser with four-wheel drive. I was ditching. I put the New Order 1984 tape (having just come out two years prior) into my tape player and blasted my way up the dirt road that was covered in ice and snow. At the top of the dirt road is a view that makes you feel you're on top of the world. Nothing can hurt you. Nothing can get you. Nothing can make you feel bad. You see the snow-covered mountains and the dry desert for miles. It is perfect, safe, and gorgeous. Except I got stuck. Completely stuck. Walked back down the mountain to the house. It was really, really cold.

The conversation went like this:

"Dad, it's Jack."

"Hi. What's up?"

"Well, I was driving up the back road to see the view and the Land Cruiser is stuck."

"Okay. No big deal. We'll get someone to help us winch it out."

Then there was this pause and I thought, silently, "What? He's not even pissed?"

"Uh, Jack."

"Ya, Dad?"

"It's 12:45 in the afternoon."

I don't remember the rest of the conversation. I do, however, remember my car being taken away for two weeks. Again, this falling into one of the "bad things" categories.

My mother got cancer when I was 16. It was March of 1987. It was the most gorgeous spring day in Santa Fe. The desert winds and the blue blue blue blue blue sky and me blasting the *Pretty In Pink* tape. I had gotten out of school, gone to Walgreen's to buy green mint'n'chip ice cream, and was on my way home to Dad's. It was his week. This was part of the divorce agreement.

Nick and I were to be one week at Dad's, then one week at Mom's—back and forth and back and forth. I drove. Nick didn't. So, I did the back-and-forthing and Nick had to do it according to my timing. I don't know who it was more difficult for. Me, who had the responsibility for it, or Nick, who had no say in any of it whatsoever.

I get to Dad's and throw my backpack (full of books I don't usually read unless they are Cliff's Notes) onto the sofa and head into the kitchen to eat my ice cream. Phone rings.

"Hi honey, it's Mom."

"Hi, Mom."

"Uh. I need you to come over."

"Well, can it be a little later? I have stuff to do."

Pause.

"It's important. Your brother will be here soon, too."

I don't know what it was in her voice, but something clicked in me that this "it's important" was different than any other "it's important" she had ever said.

I took the back dirt road with the Land Cruiser at full speed, knowing something was wrong. Not really having a clue. Just a feeling. I got to the house and walked in and all the lights were off and all the curtains were closed. Why was it dark in the house at 4 p.m.?

"Ma?"

"I'm in here, honey," she said from her room.

I walked in and she was lying in her bed with her covers pulled up. It was strange. Nothing on her bed was loose. It was as though she had gotten into bed and someone pulled her covers and everything else on her tight and she was just lying there on her back. The only light was a dim antique lamp with a frosted cover that had a little flower painted on it.

I didn't understand what was happening.

I don't remember if I was kneeling by her or standing there, but all I remember from that moment is her saying, while holding my hand, "Honey, I have cancer." She had breast cancer, stage three, as it had already spread to her lymph nodes. Two days before, she had found a lump in her breast while in the shower. A lumpectomy showed that it was malignant and a mammogram showed that the tumor was big. The size of a wad of bubblegum. I can't remember who told me that her chances of survival at this late stage were pretty slim. I do remember that it was the first time I saw horrible pain. It was the first time I saw helpless fear. It was the first time I saw mortality and had absolutely no idea what to call it. And it was the first time I started to hate the smell of hospitals.

After her mastectomy, her cries of pain were unimaginable. Her tears of helplessness brought on my own tears of not being able to help. She would hold my hand and tell me not to cry. I'd leave the room and cry. What could it feel like to have a huge lump of skin and muscle cut away? And as a woman, the psychological impact? At 16 years old, these thoughts were in my head. At 16 years old, the answers weren't. I don't remember ever feeling sorry for myself; the thought that I might have almost breaks my heart. I think I just felt helpless. I know people came to visit, but I don't remember who they were. I know people sent flowers, but I don't remember who they were from. I know my dad never left, even though they were supposed to sign the divorce papers the day she found the lump. I know Nick was there, too, but I don't remember where he was. I hardly remember any of it. Maybe that's the point: When something that awful happens, you only really remember the parts about the person it's happening to. The problem is that you forget that it's happening to you, too.

See how the "bad things" category keeps getting more intense? Getting caught ditching in the Land Cruiser suddenly didn't seem as much of a "bad thing" as Ma having cancer. Everything is relative. What was bad as a kid wasn't so bad the older you got. Is this because the older you get, the more the bad stuff adds up? Or is this because the older we get, the better we are at shutting down our feelings about the bad stuff?

CHAPTER 20

P.S. (Post Surgery)

I'M BEING WHEELED AWAY FROM the ICU toward a regular hospital room and it feels strange. I want to yell, "What? It's over? That's it? Hello! Excuse me, please! Three years of unimaginable drama for this? What the fuck? Do you know how much money I spent because I thought I'd die? How many people I embraced / blew off / fucked / loved / abandoned / learned from / ignored?" All that angst. All that fear. All the pills and alcohol and excess. All the money and people. All the glory and embarrassment. All the knowing I was going to die. And it was all for this? A short ride from ICU to a regular hospital room with a gown that seriously will not keep shut in the back?

I'm absolutely terrified that I will break into two pieces. There is no reassuring me that I won't break apart now that they have cut me in half, so it takes them twenty minutes to get me from the wheelchair into the bed. I'd be fine sitting in the chair waiting to heal. In fact, I'd rather sit in the chair and wait to heal than take the chance that I will fall into two pieces if they try and get me into the bed. They assure me that I will not and cannot fall into two pieces. I assure them that I am right and they, who do this several times a day, are wrong. People could take lessons from them on how to get me to do something I do not want to do, because they actually get me into the bed.

It doesn't seem to register that I survived the surgery that I had assured myself would kill me. It also doesn't seem to register that I'm in quite a lot of pain. What registers the most is fear. There is nothing worse than fear. They give me a shot for the pain. A shot? I get a shot? Aren't I supposed to be drugged to the point of feeling like I'm God? To the point that I feel like I can

219

hold bolts of lightning? To the point that I feel like the bar exam will not scare me? Can't they give me Demerol? My absolute favorite drug in the world. No. I get a shot. I am told it is a special "new" kind of pain medication and I am neurotic about this. I know all medications. I am a walking PDR. They won't tell me the name of the new medication. The big problem is that as soon as they give it to me. I get a little sleepy and keep forgetting to ask. I don't forget, however, to be afraid. I'm horrified at the thought of falling asleep because I know I sleep on my side and my sides are broken in two, so that can't be good. I'm scared of anyone touching any part of me except my legs and arms. There is absolutely no convincing me that the wrong movement won't break me into two pieces.

A nurse comes in and tries to explain to me that it can't happen. She tells me a story that the only time it has ever happened is when someone tried to lift a television right after open heart surgery. This has a strange effect on me. Rather than make me absolutely in disbelief about what kind of idiot would try to lift a television right after open heart surgery; it makes me realize that I can, in fact, break in two pieces. I am immediately terrified at (1) this knowledge and (2) the fact that there is no way in hell I'm going to be able to get to the three hidden Xanax in my backpack without getting out of the bed. I'm not getting out of the bed because I might shatter into two pieces, but I need the Xanax to calm myself down. It's a very viscous cycle. I tell the story to my mother when she walks into my room very early the next morning (minus the Xanax issue). The nurse is never seen again. Neither, oddly, are the three hidden (I thought) Xanax.

I feel like if I move my sternum will simple divide into two halves and my heart will be exposed. This time, however, not on purpose. So I lie here and I do not move. I have never been this scared in my life. I am way too conscious for this. Can't they just keep me asleep until I'm better? Can't I have a Demerol drip and fly in a cloud for a few days? What's the point of having me be so conscious? Who can imagine this terror? Oh. The people who surround me. What a self-pitying asshole I am not to recognize it immediately. Mom, who has survived a mastectomy, a year of chemo and radiation, followed by a silicone implant that burst inside, poisoning her. Linda who has survived cancer as well. Dad, who was shot three times in Vietnam. Roy, who deals with being HIV positive and having hepatitis C and gives himself interferon shots once a week. Babba, who went through her own private hell while my dad was getting shot up in Vietnam and who lost the love of her life just a few years after they were married. I suppose I'm not alone.

They are all survivors. I wonder: Will I be one, too? Or will I be one of the many who don't make it? I don't know. I just know that if I move, I will split open like a fucking pumpkin with all the goo and stringy stuff pouring out and me living a slow death. Isn't that grand? Living. A. Death. How does someone live a death? Isn't that an oxymoron? Yet, I have lived my death for the past three years. Oh. Wait. That isn't true. I have ignored my possible death for the past three years. I have ignored it very loudly and very obviously. Now I'm fucking alive. Did I embrace those three years or did I throw them away while running from my fear? Who knows? I only know I want a pain shot. Although I don't know what they are. The strange thing is that I'm not really in that much pain. It's like the worst ache you can possibly have, but it is not the excruciating kind of pain I had imagined. It is absolutely nothing compared to the pain of my leg when it was a bag of crushed bones. That was agony. This is more fear than pain, although it does hurt. A lot.

At least I have something to compare it to. In my wildest dreams I never would have thought that my leg surgery would help put anything into perspective. I never thought it would help me get through this. But it did. It made me unafraid of hospitals. Unafraid of IVs in my arm. Most important, it made me unafraid, for the first time in my whole life, to ask for help. And so I do. I ask for food. I ask for pills. I ask for my feet to be rubbed. I ask for water. I ask for my pillows to be adjusted. I even ask for the most difficult thing to give me sometimes: silence.

Babba sits in a chair next to my bed and hardly ever leaves, hardly ever says anything, and every now and then rubs my hand a little. She reads and takes little naps sitting up. She does not cry in front of me. Later, she tells me that there was a framed picture outside my room and she would stand in front of it and watch me in the reflection and cry when I wasn't watching. I suppose there was a lot of crying going on, but not in my room.

It is the middle of the second day after being brought back into the world of the living and I am completely out of it. I cannot focus. I do not care what is on television. I do not care that I stay in bed and am terrified of moving. It's not just the drugs. It's all of it. The intensity of everything. Three years of fear of This Moment. Okay, I survived the heart surgery; now what? My fear of heart surgery was my motivator for so many things, my excuse for so much behavior. I click the channels. Click. Click. Click. There is nothing interesting to watch, but it doesn't matter. Around 5 p.m., a nurse comes in and says, "Time to get you up for your first walk."

"What?" I am sure that I misheard. If she said what I think she said, I'm going to pee on her if she gets too close.

"You have to get out of bed and take a short walk," she says, as she is fiddling with all my cords and tubes and electrodes.

"I'm not getting out of this bed," I say.

She ignores me and maneuvers the little gate-like thing on the side of the bed down. The gate-like thing is completely unnecessary because I'm not going to get out of bed. And since I haven't had regular food in ages, it's not as though I have to go to the bathroom. I did learn during my leg surgery that it is possible to pee into a bottle while lying down. I tell her, "I really don't think I'm ready. I can barely breathe."

She gently says, "Just a very short walk. You need to do this. You can do this. I'm going to show you how to get out of bed."

This nurse has complete power over me now. She gives me her total focus and attention and who can resist that? She must be a witch. She has me hypnotized. She teaches me how to roll over onto my side toward the edge of the bed and kind of slip off onto my feet.

"Are you positive my chest isn't going to pop open?" I ask, just to make sure.

"Yes."

She actually gets me onto my feet. A very strange sensation. I haven't been on my feet for days. It felt like weeks. I could barely breathe and I was very hunched over because I was concerned that if I stood up straight, I'd pull my chest in half. If it was a choice between my chest popping open or having a hunchback, having a hunchback seemed like a fine trade-off.

I'm outside my room, which is pretty close to the nurses' station. My electrodes are pretty cool, actually. Everything is monitored by remote control. The electrodes constantly send my heart information to the nurses' station. This is very reassuring to me. I'm absolutely positive they did something wrong. Once you lose confidence in your body, it is pretty difficult to start believing in it again.

I walk by the nurses and they all smile at me and are very pleased to see me on my feet. I'm definitely the star of the heart patient ward at the moment. I am too young to be here and still reasonably cute enough to look sympathetic. I try to be funny about my fear.

I cannot believe I am standing. I am walking very, very, very slowly. Little tiny steps. And I'm holding a small pillow over my chest. This is in case I fall down, then the pillow will cushion my chest. From now on I refuse to walk around without my little pillow.

We walk a little ways and I get scared and tell her I want to go back to my room; she helps turn me around. I really never contemplated needing help turning around. But try turning around while you're holding your arms as close to your chest as possible while clutching a pillow, with eight electrodes attached to a transmitter box around your chest and three IVs: one in one arm, one in the back of my hand, and one in my neck (the one in my neck really, really grossed me out; the others I could deal with. I was not warned about this IV-in-the-neck possibility). It's not easy, but we manage to get me turned around without pulling any tubes out or setting off any alarms. I take little tiny baby steps back to my room. As I walk pass the nurses' station, there are a lot of giggles and a few laughs.

Once we get me back in bed, I feel like I can breathe again. A huge sigh of relief, but it comes out less like a huge sigh and more like a teensy breathy whistle. I can't even sigh right. This bites. I ask the nurse why everyone was giggling as I walked back into my room. She said, "The back of your gown was open the whole time."

"It was?" I am totally horrified! "Why didn't you tell me?" You'd think all modesty would be completely gone by now.

She looks at me like I have three heads and says, "Do you know how long it's been since we've seen the tight ass of a 30-year-old boy in this ward?"

Oh. Even I was amused at that. I am amused at my expense. I'm so easily amused at the moment. And I walked! I shout (well, raise my voice slightly) as she leaves, "Can I have another shot please?"

Yes, nurses can be abrupt and lax. How can you expect them not to be? There aren't enough of them. Patients are crabby, scared, demanding. Human suffering every day, every moment. Of course they sometimes seem uncaring. For us, the hospital, with luck, is a one time thing. I was as charming and funny and self-deprecating and amusing as I could muster through my fear that my chest would spring apart, flinging my heart across the room. It wasn't that I was charming to get my way. I was treating them like human beings who have a really hard job, and I became not just another patient to them because of it. Amazing the response you get when you genuinely treat them, quite simply, as human beings.

I don't know how to explain what it is like to lie in a hospital bed after surgery. People think you are in pain, helpless, scared. All that is true. After surgery, you don't care that you're bored, you don't care that there is nothing to do, you don't care if the only thing on television are soap operas and talk shows. Life is completely suspended. You do not know what is going to happen, how quickly you'll get better, when you will be allowed to go home, if something might go wrong while you're there. You don't know when your family and friends will come to visit you. Oh sure, you know they will, but you have no control over it. I want to tell my parents to be here at the same time each morning, but I'm embarrassed. I don't want to seem needy. Which is ridiculous since I've never been more in need. But how can I ask them for this? If I could ask them to be here at the same time each day, it would be the one thing I could depend on while I'm here. When everything else is up in the air, having one reliable thing can make a big difference, but I don't tell them and nobody guesses.

It gets more difficult to lie here the better I get. Since you feel a tiny bit better, a tiny bit like yourself, you want to get up and leave. It takes only a tiny amount of energy, or feeling less pain, to make you feel like you can handle it all. It's this moment where you go from patient back to being human and you want to make the most of it.

At the same time, it's very, very scary to leave the hospital. I know what to expect in the hospital. I have no idea what's waiting for me outside.

It is the evening of the fourth day since I've come home from the hospital after my open heart surgery. It has been a rough four days. I am astounded at my lack of strength. Simply walking from the couch to my bathroom gets me completely out of breath, as though I've been working out on a treadmill for an hour. It's hard to breathe. I take little tiny breaths in between huge, deep breaths. Tiny breaths, huge breath, tiny breaths, huge breath. I feel like I am gasping for air. When I lie down, it's much worse. When I lie down, I can't take a deep breath no matter how much I try. And I have terrible fevers. Absolutely freezing one moment and sweating hideously the next. None of us knows that this is not supposed to be happening. How are we supposed to know what a recovering heart patient is supposed to go through? What's normal?

Linda and her boyfriend have brought car jacks and put them underneath the head of my bed so that I am angled downward instead of lying flat. It's like one of those Craftmatic beds you see on television. Where everyone is smiling, zooming up and down, so pleasant with their beds moving at the touch of a button. This is not, however, how I feel. I feel as though I'm sliding off the bed. And I do. Every now and then, I realize I'm halfway down the bed. I try to shimmy back up to the top of the bed, but shimmying after heart surgery is extraordinarily difficult. It's not as though I can use my arms and chest and lift myself up. I really have never shimmied before. I am pulling myself up the bed with my shoulders and feet. By the time I get back up to the top of the bed, I am gasping for air and completely exhausted. I cry little, tiny, quiet tears of frustration.

I sweat and shiver and shimmy. Sometimes all three at once. Body failure multi-tasking. I'm getting to be an ace at this. Today is especially difficult because I had to leave the house. Once a week for three weeks following my surgery, I have to go get a chest x-ray, which I had earlier this afternoon. Me, my sweatpants, and two button-up shirts (since I cannot lift my arms to pull anything over my head) and, of course, the pillow I carry with me everywhere to hold in front of my chest for protection, go off to get the chest x-ray. I gasp for air up the stairs. I gasp for air in the car. I'm getting good at gasping, at shimmying, and sometime soon, perhaps I will be good at making jokes about it. Right now, I hate it. I'm frustrated and I hurt and I cannot get even remotely comfortable no matter what I do. Even sitting in the car seems to exhaust me.

At 6 p.m. that evening, my phone rings and, since I am in the kitchen, I answer it.

"Jack, it's Doctor Bailey."

"Hi."

"I've looked at your chest x-ray from this afternoon. I want you to be in the emergency room at Cedars in half an hour."

I pause, barely understanding what he is saying.

"What? What do you mean? Why?"

"Is someone there to drive you or should I send an ambulance?" he asks.

I panic immediately. "But, why? What's wrong?"

"I'll explain it to you at the hospital. I've arranged probably the last bed in the hospital for tonight, but you need to be there asap."

"But, why?"

I do not understand why he has called and why he won't tell me why I have to rush to the emergency room. I gasp for air, as usual. This time it's more frantic, though. Tears spring to my eyeballs. I am so sick of all of this. It's too much. I can't handle anything else.

"Jack, just tell me you'll meet me there."

"Okay."

"I want you to call me on my cell phone if you can't get there."

"Okay."

I stand there stunned. I can't move. I can't remember why I'm even in the kitchen. Aunt Bev is sitting on the sofa looking at me, startled, waiting for me to explain the telephone call. "It was Doctor Bailey. He says I have to meet him in the emergency room at Cedars in thirty minutes and he wouldn't tell me why."

"What?" She jumps up from the couch in a panic.

"I guess we have to go," I say in a strangely calm daze. I can almost feel that my eyes are glassy now.

She semi-freaks, but holds it together and tells me we are leaving immediately. Then I completely freak out. I go into my dressing area and tell her I'm not going back to the hospital without some things. She urges me to hurry and tells me she'll bring me my stuff. Whatever I need. After I'm at the hospital. I holler at her, "No! I'm doing this myself! I'm not going back there without my own things." I am, as it were, trying to control the situation. I hear her calling my mother. I am standing in my dressing area holding a duffle bag looking at my clothes and linens and not really sure what I want to bring. Gasping. My mind is blank although I am absolutely adamant that we not leave until I've brought what I want to bring. In the most literal sense, I am standing here completely unable to think or move.

Aunt Bev is exasperated, but she cannot physically move me and I refuse to do anything until I'm ready. She keeps saying in that gentle/urgent tone of voice, "Jack, we need to go. I'll bring your things."

I ignore her.

In my duffle bag, I put the pillow I've slept on for six years, which is probably full of disgusting dust mites one shouldn't have in a hospital. I stuff an old twin-size down comforter in there. I put black-and-white floppy legged Calvin Klein pajama bottoms in there. All of this makes sense. I also put a pair of tennis shoes and my favorite pair of jeans and a sweatshirt. I would never use the tennis shoes in the hospital. Nor the jeans. I cannot lift my arms up to put on a sweatshirt. I do not know what I am thinking, but I am absolutely scared shitless. I cannot breathe. I can barely stand up. Aunt Bev is begging me, absolutely begging me to go. Ten minutes later we are in the car. I realize I haven't put any bathroom products in the duffle bag, such as face lotion or my Kiehl's face wash. Which is, of course, a perfect example of the degree to which I'm freaking out and not thinking rationally.

We are in my BMW and I don't know why Aunt Bev doesn't have her car at my house. Everybody has been driving everyone else around for days now. Dad is down at his brother's in Orange County. Mom is at Aunt Bev's condo in West Hollywood, near Cedars. I realize in five minutes that Mom is going to freak out more than anyone. Well, not more than me. Mom's behavior in general is pretty in your face. I can only imagine what she'll be like now. Besides, she must be terrified. Her son is being taken, after open heart surgery, back to the hospital in an emergency. I don't know what could scare a parent more. My cell phone rings in the BMW. I have no idea why or how my cell phone got into the car since I haven't seen it or used it in days. It's Nora calling from London and she is freaking, as well. I have now freaked people on two continents. My terror is international! I'm just that fabulous, apparently. I calmly tell her we're going to the hospital. She is frantic, asking what's wrong and I tell her I'm not sure. I tell her I can't talk as I gasp for air and I hang up on her. I don't feel bad about this. I'm terrified. I can't breathe. And I forgot my fucking Vicodin at the house.

Aunt Bev drops me off at the ER and drives to go get Ma because Ma is so apoplectic with fear that she can't drive. She's only five minutes away, though. I walk into the ER alone, exhausted, clutching my pillow to my chest. The ER is completely overcrowded, just like on the television show. But it's semi-comfortable. This is Cedars-Sinai in Beverly Hills, after all. Muted carpeting and quiet lighting and comfortable chairs, for a waiting room. It's a huge room. Or, at least, that is how it feels to me. I haven't been around this many people in weeks and I stand there, in the doorway, holding my pillow to my chest, not able to breathe very well; I feel more vulnerable than I've felt since I was in the hospital the first time. As though someone might brush past me and touch me. The thought terrifies me. If someone rubs against me or touches me, I will break. I know it.

I go to the desk and tell the lady my name, that I am a patient of Dr. Bailey's and that he has told me to come here immediately. I tell her that I am 11 days out from having had open heart surgery. She doesn't look at me like I'm insane because of my age—that look that says, "What? You? Open heart surgery? You're too young!" I realize I must look, finally, like an open heart surgery patient. My blue lips, sweatpants, and clutching my pillow over my chest must give me away. She has a "seen it all, done it all, am real damn tired, take a damn seat" attitude. I'm not used to this since I've been treated with kid gloves for so long now. Before all this, I'd know exactly what to do and how to handle it. Not now, though. Not anymore. She cannot find my name in the system because it's under John and my brain is not working and I forget to tell her that for a minute. Then, when she does find it, she cannot find that Dr. Bailey had called in ahead and arranged a room for me on an emergency basis. I almost start to cry. This is the longest I have actually stood since I waited for my gurney the day of the surgery. I have to sit down very, very fast or I will fall down. I barely even have the energy to be frustrated. I realize Dr. Bailey has probably called in the bed under "Jack." At this point my mother rushes in, almost runs through the doors, and takes over while I go sit down. I shudder to think what she is putting that woman behind the desk through.

Five minutes later I am on a table in a curtained-off area of the emergency room. The table is cold, black plastic and there is no paper on it. White fluorescent light. And a doctor I've never met or seen before is asking me to turn onto my right side. I ask why. He tells me it makes it easier for the heart. Puts less stress on it. Nobody ever told me that or I'd have been lying on my right side for the past six months! He's doing what must be the 100th echocardiogram I've had lately and I look up at my mom, almost casually. She looks down at me with glassy eyes and turns away. She has never done this before. She has never looked this scared around me. But this moment is happening too fast for all of us. The fact that she turns away from me makes it more seriously real for me. I'm very, very scared. Everything before this had been orchestrated and planned and scheduled. This, however, is not planned. This is an emergency and nobody has told me what is going on. While this new doctor is doing the echo, I ask Mom and Aunt Bev if they know why I'm here and why I can't breathe. I feel paranoid. Everyone knows but me and they won't tell me because it will scare me. I don't know until later that they didn't know at that point either. I only know that I have added frustration to my lovely list of feelings at the moment. Paranoid, scared, frustrated . . . and ya, I really, really need my Vicodin right now.

Half an hour later I'm in yet another hospital room. I have been told there is fluid in my lungs. This is not the whole story, as Dr. Bailey is soon to tell me. Dad has gotten here already; he must have driven at least 100 miles an hour to get here this fast from Babba's, which is 70 miles away. What terror that must have been. Knowing your kid is being taken to the hospital in an emergency after open heart surgery, and not being able to be there instantly. Again, the horror that I am putting them through. I have, however, never, ever seen my dad "jump" at anything before. Later, when things are over, I'm bitter that it took this to make him drop everything on earth for me.

Mom and dad are on either side of my bed and both are holding my hands because I'm pretty well freaked the fuck out by now. Suddenly, Dr. Bailey rushes in carrying a yellow orchid in a nice Japanese-looking clay pot and says, "I can't believe this is happening to you. To someone as nice as you are." He genuinely looks upset and a little flustered and sincere in his wish-this-wasn't-happening-to-you look. And it hits me hard. In a good way. Because he hadn't said anything like that before and patients become very close to their doctors. I even smile a little and say, "Can't get rid of me." I can feel my mother squeeze my hand a little tighter for a moment when I say this.

Apparently viscous fluid and blood have built up in my chest cavity and have (1) filled up one lung completely; (2) filled up another lung, leaving me only a 10% space with which to breathe; and (3) coated my organs in something sticky that Dr. Bailey describes as orange rind. Apparently, this is all very, very bad and very unexpected. It is, however, the reason I have not been able to breathe and the reason for all my fevers. It is also lucky that I (1) had my x-ray today; and (2) that Dr. Bailey was able to look at it. If he hadn't, I am told later, I probably would have suffocated in my sleep and died that night.

I am told that they will do a thoracentesis in a few hours, right there in my hospital room, to get rid of most of the fluid. This involves sticking a tube into my back and basically sucking out the fluid. I am really scared although they tell me it won't hurt and it isn't that scary. Well, fuck that! You hear that someone will be sticking a tube into your back to drain you and see if you're scared! Just once, I would like to have a doctor say, "Jack, this is really going to suck, but you will get through it because you have no choice and we'll try to make it as easy as we can."

I am also told that I will have to have a thoracotomy to remove the gunk that is coating my organs. This involves another serious surgery where they cut into my side by the right lung and basically dig into my chest, scraping everything off and pulling it out. Scraping the chest cavity, my lungs, my organs. Oh lovely.

When I hear this, I let my head sink into my pillow and start crying again. I tell my parents, probably to their horror, "I can't go through this again. I can't do this anymore." They don't say anything, but they continue to hold my hands and that's all I need right now. At some point, the only thing people can do is be present. To everyone's surprise but the patient's, that's all it takes.

I tell mom I need a Valium immediately. I don't know how she does it in a hospital like this, but I have the Valium in five minutes from a very annoyed-looking nurse. My mom is very good at this. My dad is scared. I see a look on his face I've never seen before—helpless and unsure. He's so quiet and doesn't seem to know what to say. My tough, always-in-control-of-emotions, ex-marine father looks downright terrified and doesn't seem to know how to hide it. He's so scared that he doesn't even know it shows.

Another doctor I haven't met comes into the room carrying some kind of apparatus I can't see, but I can see a bunch of bottles that strangely resemble Evian bottles. I am made to sit up in my bed with my feet over the side. They slide a small table against my torso. One of those small, rectangle tables that seem to go in any direction, any height. I am then told that I have to lean over it and my parents are going to hold my hands. It takes me only a second to realize they will be holding my hands to make sure I keep myself curved over the table and my spine and back stretched forward. I beg, literally beg, to be put to sleep. I do not understand why they can't just Valium, Versed or/ and Xanax me to sleep. I've been through open heart surgery. They put me into a coma, practically! Why can't they Valium me to sleep! Nobody listens; instead, they give me a shot in the back to numb part of it and then I feel pressure. When I realize they are sticking a tube in me, I freak. I tell them to stop. My parents are literally pulling me forward because I want to pull back and away. Their eyes must be no more than four inches away from mine as they hold me forward. Their glassy, exhausted, terrified eyes are right there. And this silences me. They don't say anything, but the look in their eyes is identical. I think the last time they had any kind of same look about anything was at my Bar Mitzvah. That was a proud look; this is a helpless look. It shuts me up because it startles me.

They suck bottle after bottle of this horrible looking purple fluid from my back. Six bottles in all, and as they do, even they seem astonished. I cough and cough and cough. It's like the feeling when you've been in a swimming pool for too long and when you finally get out, you cough if you breathe too deeply. That is the feeling I have. When it's over and my coughing has subsided, I see all the fluid they just sucked out of me. I feel better. I can breathe. They pull the tube out of me, put a bandage on my back and I am allowed to lie back in bed. For the first time since they hacked into me, I can breathe well. For the moment, that is all it takes to make me feel strong again. Okay, maybe I can get through the thoracotomy after all. Being able to breathe gives me a tiny bit of confidence back in my body that I haven't had for a long time. Maybe my body isn't an enemy. This momentary confidence is a good thing because I had absolutely no clue how painful the thoracotomy was going to be.

I drift awake. Or rather I drift to something remotely resembling consciousness. It's very strange to wake up from surgery, aside from the fact that someone cut into me and fiddled with my insides. There is absolute disorientation. I know nothing. Not where I am. Not what has happened. Not why I am here. As the haze begins to clear, I notice that there is a plastic oxygen mask strapped to my face. It makes me feel like I can't breathe. My drugged-out brain hasn't yet told me that is ridiculous. The second thing I realize is that I am not in a private room. A nurses' station is in front of me. I lift my head up a tiny bit. It feels like there are weights attached to my neck. I see other people on gurneys and people standing next to them looking concerned. A roomful of people. One group needing help. The other group grasping for ways to help them. The third thing I notice is that my dad is sitting next to me on my right and I can feel him holding my hand, although my arm is strapped to the gurney. As with the open heart surgery, my first words are, "Am I okay?" And, as with the open heart surgery, I hear, "Yes." I feel hot tears running down my cold cheeks in relief. I go back to being unconscious.

CHAPTER 21

Ho Ho Ho

Christmas Day, 2000

AFTER THE ABLATION AND AFTER the open heart surgery and after the emergency thoracentesis, I have now had a fucking thoracotomy. As though three surgeries haven't been enough. Lovely. As my mother has always said, "Jackie, when you do something, you DO it."

When I wake up from the thoracotomy, I'm in a large corner room. Again, on the cardiac floor, not in the ICU. I'm just down the way from my first hospital room. I have more tubes and stuff in me. I have a Dilaudid IV. A drug stronger than morphine. It barely takes away the pain, but "barely" is enough right now. I can press a little button every eight minutes and this machine releases a dose of the painkiller into my bloodstream. I look at the box trying to figure out how to dismantle it and take the Dilaudid as I want, without having to wait every eight minutes. The fact that it's locked would seem to prevent this. Well, that and the fact that I just had all my thoracic organs scraped clean. The insides of my chest have been Brillo-padded. Charming. I'm in a lot more pain than I was after my open heart surgery. Tremendous more pain. It feels like someone punched every part of my body from inside, like razor blades are inside every time I move. I try to stay still. This is almost as bad as the leg surgery pain. Not quite, though. I know I can handle pain. I'm just not sure my body can handle much more.

I'm very woozy, but I see that my Dad, Nick, Aunt Bev, Moriah, and Linda are in the room. Dad is on the right side of me where all the IVs and other machines are and everyone else is on the left side.

"Am I okay?" I ask my Dad. Not knowing how many times I've already asked this.

"Yes. You're doing fine," he says.

I start to cry and say, "I can't do anymore. This is the last one. I can't handle it. I don't care if I die." I mean it. There is only so much someone can take. I don't know if this makes me extremely aware or just weak, but I can't keep going through surgery after surgery. Then again, I've thought this after every surgery. Enough. I've had a good thirty year run. I've had shitty times and I've had times straight out of a *Vanity Fair* article about the young, wealthy, jetsitting crowd; yet, I can't do anymore. I cannot go through anything else.

Even though I just did.

"How are you feeling," says Aunt Bev.

I look at her like she's grown a second head and I'd like to poke her eyes out with hot pokers and think, "Hello! I've gone through seven purposely-induced heart attacks while awake during the ablation with wires and tubes stuck into my heart, an open heart surgery where I almost didn't come out of a coma, a thoracentesis with tubes stuck into my back to drain me, and now an unexpectedly agonizingly painful thoracotomy, and you are asking me how I feel?"

Instead it comes out as: "It hurts. A lot this time. More than the other surgeries. I'm glad you're here."

I'd still like to light her head on fire since it's a dumb question. And I'm sick to death of being asked it.

"Anybody want any Dilaudid?" I ask. I have no energy, am in severe pain, have basically, pathetically, given up by this point and I still try to be amusing. To take care of them. To make sure they're okay and make sure they're comfortable that I'm still me. Uh, who is? There is no end to my absurdity.

Little uncomfortable chuckles from everyone. As I come out of it a little more, the pain is even worse. "It really, really hurts," I say with more tears springing to my eyes. I'm not even trying not to cry anymore.

I feel my heart do a PVT [Polymorphic Ventricular Tachycardia]. Then another one. I see Aunt Bev looking above me where all the monitors are. I see my Dad follow her look. I see them look at each other. The machines above me are where all the fucking wires and tubes under their charming statistics second by second. I try to turn to see what she's looking at and she quickly looks back down at me. I can't really turn, though. I can barely move without agonizing pain. I know something is wrong and I'm starting to panic. Aunt Bev and Dad look at each other and my Dad calmly walks out the door. Thirty seconds later a nurse comes into the room. He tells me he's my nurse today and his name is David. He's very tall. He's very cute, too. Straight out of Melrose Place. By now, however, I seem to think everyone is cute. If I was like this in "real life," I'd probably go on a lot more dates. Then again, it would also be nice to have my little Dilaudid toy all the time.

He's abrupt and tells everyone to step away from the bed. He fiddles with some of the machinery attached to me. Everyone looks worried and I don't understand what is happening. Apparently, my heart rate is suddenly very fast and everyone can tell this because by now everyone knows how to read the various monitors that get attached to me. My heart starts doing PVTs continuously. Those I can feel. I don't have to look at any machines. I know that is very, very bad.

David immediately picks up the phone near my bed and makes a phone call. Then, he tells everyone to get out of the room. He is very abrasive. He looks at me and says, "Something is wrong, but we know what to do." He says it abruptly and does not use that sugary nurse-voice I'm accustomed to. I feel very protected by him. He's blunt, but he reassures me at the same time. Everyone has left the room but my Dad. I can still see them hovering in the doorway, though. He tells my Dad, "You have to leave."

My dad looks at him from the other side of the bed and says, "No." David seems to know that fighting my dad is useless. Dad is in protective-father mode. My dad is also pretty intimidating when he wants to be. The ex-Marine that I usually hate comes out in him immediately. And you don't fuck with that.

David leaves the room and closes the door in everyone's faces. A minute later he returns with two other people. Another doctor and another nurse. They fiddle with all the controls and take an IV out and put it in another place. And put something, with a syringe, directly into my chest. Literally shove it directly into my heart. Hard and fast. Very fast. I fade away.

I wake up. As usual, I have no sense of time, so it could be half an hour later or six hours later or the next day. I don't see a clock in the room and the shade is drawn on the window. I immediately smell something extraordinarily strong. Several smells. Dad, Nick, Linda, Aunt Bev, and Moriah are here and I can see Aunt Bev taking tin-foil wrapped things out of a cardboard box.

It's Christmas day. After my thoracotomy. After my fourth fucking surgery. But I'm still here. I apparently cannot be killed! "Hi. I'm Jack. I can handle anything." I'm just not quite sure how much longer that phrase is going to last. If I'm supposed to die. Fine. I'm done. I keep thinking: I don't know if that's weak or courageous. I also don't give a shit, by this time.

Bev has brought a home-made Christmas dinner to the hospital. She's delighted and gentle and warm about it. I know she thinks it's the most wonderful gesture and it is. It really is. But all these smells . . . it's a bit much.

She says, "Merry Christmas, honey."

"Merry Christmas, Aunt Bev."

They start to eat turkey and stuffing and other things off cardboard plates. David comes in and adjusts the IV and doesn't say anything to any of us. I feel very, very safe with him looking after me, but I know nobody likes him. I can tell he's pissed off about the food, which pisses the family off even more, which pisses me off because they should see that I feel safe with him. I really expect everyone to be able to read my mind. It's highly annoying that they seem not to have this power.

Aunt Bev asks me what I want and I tell her I only want the pumpkin pie. I tell my Dad to raise my bed, so he pushes a button somewhere and I zoom to a sitting-up position and the razor blades start moving around inside me and I think I am about to pass out. Tears again, but I can hold them back a little now. Although I don't see why I should. I should be hysterical by now. I just don't have the energy.

Aunt Bev passes me a plate. I raise my hands, which are attached to several IVs, which also pulls on the zillion electrodes on my chest and legs and arms. I start to eat. I have IVs on the backs of both hands, one in my upper arm and one in my neck. I'm trying not to tangle up the IV tubes and various wires attached to various monitors. Rather inconvenient. I eat fast.

It's really, really good. I don't think I've had real food for a few weeks now. I shovel it down my gullet, and nobody stops me. Nobody would deny me anything at this point. Everybody feels horrible for me. I can feel it and their agony at being helpless about it. But I don't have the energy to help them. I want to. I really do. I'm a caretaker. I love to take care of people. But I can't right now.

Suddenly, I start to feel sick. The nausea starts to wave across me and I put the plate down.

"I don't feel very well," I say.

"What's wrong," asks Aunt Bev.

I answer her by promptly barfing. Projectile vomit all over what remains of my pie. All over Aunt Bev. All over Nick. All over Moriah as I turn my head to the other side forgetting that's where she's standing. All over myself and my bed and the sheets. I had no idea how much I had eaten and how much liquid they were giving me through IVs. Because there is a ton of vomit and it went from my stomach to the people and my bed in about twenty seconds. My stomach immediately feels better. I start to cry anyway. I'll cry at the smallest thing now. Being hacked into like a turkey a third time has strangely made me rather sensitive. Go figure. And yeah, the pain is absolutely beyond obscene by now. I think I'm about to pass out.

David rushes in and tells everyone, sweetly, since it's Christmas day, "Get out! Now!" They obey. Except, of course, for my Dad. There's no point in him leaving since I didn't puke on him. He was, luckily for him, looking out the window.

David starts to remove the puke-covered sheets and I tell him, "I have to pee, too." He says, "Okay, go. You have a catheter." Despite having vomit on my chin and my arms and everywhere else, I'm absolutely horrified! They put a tube into my penis! Oh my god. Through the leg surgery, the ablation, and even open heart surgery, I managed to avoid this. But now some evil fucking doctor stuck it in there while I was comatose. Lovely. So, while David is cleaning me up I decide, fine, I will pee. I hope it gets everywhere just to prove a point. And I do. At least I think I do. It doesn't feel like I do, but I know I am. I don't have to get up I don't have to stress about peeing in a bottle. I don't have to have a nurse harassing me about it. I'm delighted and immediately decide that I'm in love with the catheter. It's marvelous.

I tell David that I want "the anti-nausea stuff." During my heart surgery, they gave me a few shots whenever I'd feel nauseous. He asks if I'm sure. I give him a look. He smiles and says, "Okay." It's the first time I've seen him smile. He's nice. I love him. If I live, I will date him. Because a recovering heart patient who has just had an emergency surgery and barfs and pees through a catheter must be truly alluring. How could he resist?

About fifteen minutes later, after the sheets have been changed and I've been cleaned up and I feel a little better and everyone has come back to loiter next to me, a nurse walks in. Actually, she waddles in. She's short and fat. Despite being in abject pain and very high on Dilaudid—I'm pushing the button continuously to make sure that I don't miss one of the eight-minute opportunities—I notice everything about nurses. I need to know their names and amuse them. I need to make them see me as different and unique so that they remember me. I need to perform. I want them to treat me special.

She sweetly asks everyone to leave. They do. Including my Dad, which is odd. She goes and shuts the door and starts to move the sheet away from my legs. She puts on rubber gloves and I see her rip open a little foil packet. Oh dear.

"What's that?" I ask in a panic.

"Your medicine," she says.

"A suppository?" I ask, whimpering.

"Yes."

I am horrified! "No! Not a suppository! I want the shot!"

"You want a shot instead of this? They can't give it to you in an IV, you know. It's a real shot. Has to be intramuscular."

I've had metal and screws put in my leg, had intentionally been given seven heart attacks to fix the electrical shit, open heart surgery, a thoracentesis, a thoracotomy, and she is shocked that I'm okay with a shot?

"Yes, I want the shot." She shrugs her shoulders and walks out.

I take a huge, relieved breath. I absolutely refuse to have a suppository. I am absolutely not having some short, fat nurse shove a pill up my ass.

Disgusting. I seem to have a shred of bodily modesty left. I don't know why on earth I care, but I do. What if the last thing I have control over is this? Getting or not getting a suppository? I can't possibly pass up the moment.

David gives me a shot. By-product of the anti-nausea stuff is that it makes me sleepy. I pass out again. When I wake up, I see Eric sitting in a chair near my bed.

"Oh, hi!" I say very pleased that he's here.

"Hi, Jackie-sue," he says, not getting up from the chair.

"I'm in pain and post-surgery and you still have to call me that?"

"Yes," he says, very matter-of-fact.

He's wearing a bright red blazer over a bright green turtleneck. Black pants. And bright red socks with patent leather opera pumps. He looks like a Christmas tree in drag. "What are you supposed to be?" I ask with total sarcasm in my voice.

He says, with a flourish, "Dear! I'm the bitch of Christmas!"

I do my breathy laugh thing and say, "You're my Christmas bitch."

He gives me a little present. I open it and it's a clock. A miniature of a fifties-style clock radio someone would have had in a kitchen. It's bright pink.

"Eric, nobody is supposed to buy me clocks," I say I've collected miniature

Jack's miniature clock collection

clocks for years. From all around the world. I have 95 right now. But every one of them has a memory. Nobody is supposed to buy me clocks.

"I know. Don't care," he says.

"I only get them to mark a memory," I say.

He looks at me like I'm utterly ridiculous and says, "Right. And this whole circus isn't going to be a memory?"

Hmmm. He makes a good point.

I look at it and say, "Well, it's actually really perfect." And it is.

Dad comes into the room with Moriah and Nick. They see Eric and smile.

Ever since Eric stayed with them for 22 hours when they thought I wasn't going to wake up after my open heart surgery, they love Eric. Twenty-two hours. Nobody left. I've heard the story by now: When the surgeon came out and pulled my parents aside and said, "He isn't waking up and we're not sure why. We might need your permission to operate again, but there is a very large chance of non-recovery [meaning death] if we have to operate again. A body [being mine] can only handle so much in such a limited time."

My parents didn't know what to do. I can't even imagine being a parent and having to make this decision. Take a chance that I might wake up or that I'll suddenly die? Or take a chance that I can handle another surgery or that it will kill me?

They tell everybody. All of the people who have stayed all these hours for me. Eric says, apparently joking and matter-of-fact, and without tears, "Jackie is not dying! He hasn't prepared! I don't know where he wants his funeral! I don't know what florist he wants to use. I don't know what caterer he wants to use! I don't know where he wants the memorial! He hasn't let me know about the music! I am unprepared for this. I am completely not ready to let him go right now! He hasn't left enough instructions and it would be very inconvenient of him to die." It took the edge off. A little. People smile. At least that's what I've been told. Besides, I woke up ten minutes later.

"Look! My Christmas bitch is here!"

They laugh. I'm still in a lot of pain and even this little conversation exhausts me, but having Eric here gives me a little lift. He reminds me that I'm me. Eric knows me in "real life." When I see myself through his eyes, I feel a little better.

"I think I'm falling asleep again. Merry Christmas, Eric."

"Merry Christmas, Jack," he says.

Pause.

"You called me Jack," I say.

I fall asleep while he rubs my hand a little and smiles gently.

However many minutes/hours later, my phone rings and I pick it up. Dad has placed it on my bed next to me. It's Mom.

"How are you?"

"It hurts a lot."

"I'm so sorry, honey. Do you want me to come?"

Mom has already gone home to Santa Fe after the open heart surgery. Everything looked like it was fine and she was starting to get the flu. The absolute last thing I need is to get the flu. She went home because, even if she stayed away from me, she might have given it to Dad or Nick or someone else.

"No, Mom. It's okay. I'm just lying here."

"Well, I'll come if you want me to. I'm so sorry I'm not there," she says, sounding very guilty.

"Really, Mom. It's fine."

"I feel terrible that I'm not there."

Oh my god. "Mom. Stop. It's fine."

I cannot believe I'm lying here with IVs in both wrists and a tube stuck up my penis and I am reassuring my mom.

"Okay, honey. You'll tell me if you want me to come, right?"

I'm about to snap at her.

"Yes, I'll tell you," I say. I hang up and immediately push the Dilaudid button.

The next day Roy walks in and says, "Can't you stay out of the damn hospital?"

"No," I answer, "I look too ravishing in the hospital gowns to leave."

I'm starting to feel like myself again. I have a tiny bit of strength and they have replaced the Dilaudid drip with periodic pain shots. Like with Eric, Roy silently reminds me that I'm still me.

He says, "Your nurse is cute. The guy."

"I know. Everybody hates him."

"Why?" he asks.

"He's a little abrasive."

"He's cute enough to get away with that."

"I don't think anyone else cares about that."

"That's because their priorities are fucked up."

Breathy chuckle.

"Your Mom called me and asked me how you look," he says. "I told her you look like crap. That you're thin as a rail. That your skin is yellow. That your eyes are droopy. That you are in pain worse than the open-heart surgery. And that you are really fucking irritable and annoying and rude."

"Lovely," I say, sarcastically.

"It pleased her to know that you are feeling more like yourself."

"Fuck you," I say with a smile.

"Let me see your incisions."

"What?"

"Your incisions! Sexy! I want to see them! You have so many now!" he says, excitedly.

I'm horrified. Even I haven't looked at my incisions. Even my chest scar. I can't. Not yet. Makes me cry to think about it. He lifts the sheet back and looks around making little hemming-hawing sounds.

"Will you stop it already!"

He laughs.

"You have a lot of them. The chest scar and the scars from where they put the tubes in. And the incisions on the side from this surgery. And your leg scar. It'll all be very sexy."

"I'm a damn quilt!"

We both laugh.

CHAPTER 22

Aunt Mil

IT HAS BEEN FIVE WEEKS since I've been home from my thoracotomy. I'm back to living by myself. People have slowly returned to their regular lives, albeit calling constantly and coming to see me whenever they can. I am not allowed to drive and I am still absolutely exhausted. I keep ending up on my side when asleep and having to pop my sternum back into place when I wake up. It's gross.

My day consists of sitting on the sofa and watching television. I know the schedule of every television show on most of the 99 channels my cable service provides. I will watch almost anything except infomercials and soap operas. I keep popping my Vicodin, not because I'm in as much pain as I used to be, but because it mellows me out. It makes me feel less antsy about being stuck inside lying on the sofa all day watching television reruns. The Vicodin does not, however, make me high. Not yet, at least. They merely bring me from severe pain to tolerable pain. I feel justifiably bitter because if I'm going to be provided with unlimited Vicodin, the least that could happen is that they'd make me high and delightful all day. I do not feel high and delightful. My chest still aches. I still have almost zero energy. My eyes still do not focus enough to read.

I am aware that I'm recovering. That is, I'm far enough away from the surgeries to be able to concentrate and notice that I'm recovering, but it's very slow. And now that I'm feeling a teensy bit more like myself, I am reminded that I hate slow. Like the rest of my generation, I want immediate gratification. One would think I would simply be immediately gratified that I am alive. I am, but I don't feel like me anymore. The old me is gone. I'm also beginning to realize that I miss me. I am sick of thinking about this, so I watch an "I Love Lucy" rerun. The one where they are in Italy and Lucy is in a vat of grapes stomping on them in bare feet trying to make wine. I laugh. Tiny, little, subtle laughs. Holding the real ones in. The real ones would hurt my chest. The mere thought of sneezing puts me into a panic.

Every few days, Linda comes to take me to lunch. She leaves her office at Brillstein-Grey, one of the top management/production companies in Beverly Hills, and drives all the way to the top of Mulholland. I hold her arm as we walk up the stairs to her car. Linda and I are always sarcastic with each other. We're both supreme smartasses who are very good at covering our real feelings. Yet, we are also close enough to know what the other is thinking, to a certain extent. Although we make jokes about the two of us going from cancer victim (Linda) to heart victim (me), I can see the agony on her face. She hates seeing me like this and it scares her. We are sarcastic, but less so.

"How are you feeling today?" she asks.

"Same. Exhausted. Listless. So tired that I'm not even frustrated by sitting on the couch all day." Pause. "And I'm completely constipated. I think trying to push something out would really hurt my chest."

We laugh and laugh. We love bowel humor. Well, she laughs. I make a sort of breathy "heh, heh, heh" sound. It's as much as I can do.

We go, as we have since she started doing this for me, to Louisa's. It's a small chain of upper-class Italian restaurants. She has chicken parmesan and iced tea. I have seared tuna salad without scallions and a water. I desperately want diet coke, but I am forbidden from having caffeine. I pop two Vicodin and begin to eat. We don't talk much about my heart thing. Not because it's awkward or a difficult subject. There is nothing I wouldn't tell Linda and she knows it. There's just nothing more to say. They hacked into me twice. I'm still scared. I'm still in pain. I still can't see the other side of recovery quite yet. She knows all this. Instead we talk entertainment industry gossip—who is doing whom, who is being set up with whom, and how there is a political "celebrity" interning at the company for a summer and nobody is supposed to know. I never reveal anything that anyone tells me in confidence, so Linda knows it's okay to tell me stuff like this.

When I'm almost done eating, Linda says, "Let's go."

"But I'm not done."

"I don't care. You're getting more tired. Your eyelids are only halfway open, and your arm slipped off the table."

"It did not," I say, rolling my eyes.

She is very serious. "Yes, it did. You need to be home. We're leaving."

This is usually how our lunches go. We may not talk about it, but she is watching me very closely. When she says I'm tired and we're going, it isn't in panic or a fear. It's very matter-of-fact. She knows that I'm not a good judge of how I'm doing right now and she also is not about to let me control the situation like I'd like to. Twenty minutes later, we're back up on Mulholland and I'm back on the couch and she's driving back to Beverly Hills. Every few days, she's up and down, up and down. Taking me to lunch. Two or two-and-a-half hours. It's not that I'm surprised she is this devoted. It's that to see it so blatant and direct is reassuring. There is no way I could ever tell her how lucky I am to have her friendship during this time. To tell her that I will never forget her total devotion, which started when she was at my ablation. Linda and I don't overtly say these things to each other. Most important of all, she brings me double chocolate chip muffins from Trader Joes once or twice a week.

During the weeks that Linda has been taking me to lunch, Aunt Bev has been bringing me groceries, Roy has been visiting every other evening, Eric, Babba, and Mom call every day. Dad has gone back to Vietnam. Marny spends a lot of time in Vietnam. He had first gone as a Marine, in a reconnaissance unit during the war, and had almost died there of gunshot wounds. He still sports a bullet in close proximity to his spine. Now a successful businessman, he had been returning to Vietnam for years, trying to launch various programs to help the villagers. He bought desks for the school, and the first globe the children had ever seen. The night before my ablation, he was in Vietnam trying to cut through the bureaucratic red tape involved in his upcoming marriage to a young Vietnamese woman.

One evening I get a phone call from Auntie Lanie.

"Jackie, it's Auntie Lanie. How are you, honey?"

"I'm okay. Just tired. How are you? How is Aunt Mil?" My Aunt Mil—Babba's sister and Auntie Lanie's mother—has been very, very sick for almost seven years, dying a horrible slow death. In and out of hospitals constantly. I used to say about my Auntie Lanie, "I don't know how she does it." Now I know. When you have to do it, you do it.

"Well, we're here at the hospital and Aunt Mil is hanging in there. If your Dad calls from Vietnam, please tell him that we're with Aunt Mil and she is fine."

I pause. "Why would he call me to ask that?"

"Well, honey, because Aunt Fan (aka Babba) is here with us and he might call you if he calls her house and she doesn't answer."

I pause. Something's up. I ask about Babba, "Babba is with you in the hospital? Why is she with you in the hospital?"

Auntie Lanie pauses.

"She wanted to be here with us. Aunt Mil is having a rough time, but she's fine. Allan (Aunt Mil's son) is here, too. So, if your Dad calls, tell him we're fine and not to worry that he can't reach his mom."

"Um, okay," I say, not really understanding the point of this phone call since my dad doesn't call me when he's in Vietnam. E-mails periodically, but not phone calls.

Aunt Mil, Aunt Freda, Babba, and Jack

"Honey, are you sure you're okay?" she asks.

"Yes, me and my Vicodin and television addiction are fine."

She doesn't laugh. Just a hint of one, maybe.

"Okay, honey, call my cell if you need anything."

I sit there on the steps to my loft in my uniform of button-up flannel shirt (because I still cannot lift my arms to pull something over my head) and sweatpants. Not really comprehending what's going on. Normally, I would understand immediately. My brain used to work quickly. Now, it's slow. After a minute, I get it and I am shocked.

They called me because Aunt Mil is dying. Now. They do not want Dad to find out because they don't want him to feel like he has to fly back from Vietnam. Personally, I think I should try to call him and get him to fly back so he could be with his mother. But that side of the family, including my dad, is strange about death. I don't think he'd fly back anyway. I may be wrong and it's not my business to change what my Auntie Lanie and, most likely, Babba are concerned about with regard to dad.

I decide immediately I'm going. My Aunt Mil treated me like the golden boy when I was growing up. She always had this cabinet in her kitchen filled with goodies, candy, little writing pads I found so fascinating for some reason. I don't want Babba to be without me as she watches her sister die.

I am, however, forbidden from driving for four more weeks. That is not, however, going to stop me. This is too important. I suppose I think I'm being noble and brave. Really, I'm being very, very stupid and taking a huge risk. I am recovering from open heart surgery. I still walk around holding a pillow if I leave the house. I still get out of breath if I take too long in the shower in the morning because of moving around and standing up for so long. I can still feel the two halves of my sternum rub together. It's not that I feel like I'm going to impress everyone with my bravery. It's not that I think this situation is bigger than me. I am, though, thinking like I used to think before my heart surgery. Drop everything and go do what I have to do. It's as though this gives me an opportunity to be my old self and I'm going to grab it immediately. I can be there and do something that makes me feel normal all at the same time.

I put shoes on. Which tires me since I have to lean forward and be careful about not crunching my chest together too much. I put my leather jacket on, which ends up hurting since I have to reach back too hard to get it on and the bones and muscles in my upper neck and back still hurt. I get my wallet from the kitchen counter and, of course, it has no money in it. Why would it? Then I realize, I have absolutely no idea where my car keys are. My car hasn't been driven in weeks. I pop three Vicodin and look everywhere for the keys. I can't remember why we separated them from my house keys. I imagine someone had a good reason. Maybe they thought I'd do something crazy like drive my car before I'm supposed to. Can't imagine why'd they think that.

I finally find the keys in my kitchen junk drawer. Seriously, someone must have purposely hidden them there. Why else would you put car keys in a junk drawer? It has taken me half an hour to find them. I'm completely frustrated, but the Vicodin has kicked in. And since three were good, six will be better. I pop another three Vicodin. My rational is that I will need to be very drugged in order to drive my car. It's a stick shift and it will hurt too much if I haven't taken my Vicodin. The utter wrongness of thinking it's rational that I drug myself to be able to drive does not occur to me at the time.

As I'm about to leave, my Uncle Allan, Auntie Lanie's brother, calls.

"They weren't completely honest with you about what is going on." I decide not to say that I figured that out. "Aunt Mil is dying. She will probably die tonight. Your grandmother was worried that if your dad found out, he would get on a plane and fly back and she doesn't want him to."

Ya don't say.

"Allan, is she in any pain?"

"We don't know. She's in a coma and she's on a morphine drip and we don't even know why she has hung on all day. We just sit with her."

"How is everyone?"

And the moment I ask it, I'm embarrassed because it is such an asinine question and I, of all people, should know better.

He answers, simply and directly, "Very sad."

"Thank you for telling me."

"Well, I wanted to let you know. They don't know I called you."

I pause, considering telling him I'm coming, but realize that he'll talk me out of it. I am not close to Allan because we've never lived near him, but I know he's one of the good guys. He's brilliant and independent and everything I know about him makes me respect him. This phone call, this unnecessary honesty, makes me feel good. It takes me a moment to realize why. He isn't treating me like a heart patient victim. He's treating me like me.

"Tell everyone I love them and you're all in my thoughts."

Now, more than ever, there is no doubt that I'm going. Besides, the six Vicodin have completely set in and, although I still hurt, I don't care that much. Which is the point.

I walk up the steps toward my car. One step at a time. Steps that used to take me about 30 seconds to run up and down now take a full two minutes. When I get to the top of the steps, I realize I forgot my pillow. I cannot go anywhere without the pillow I clutch in front of my chest when I leave the house. Ever. It is my security blanket. I am, apparently, feeling that it's fine to drive my car, but not without a pillow. Vicodin is lovely this way. Everything always makes perfect sense.

After going down the steps, getting my pillow, going up the steps and getting into my car, I am completely and totally out of breath. I buckle myself in with the pillow against my chest with the buckle in front of it. My thinking, if you can call it that at this point, is that if something happens, I'll hit the pillow instead of the steering wheel. I'm brilliant, clearly.

I drive like a munchkin. Holding the wheel from below with both hands. Then, when I need to shift, I try to keep my elbow at my chest and just move my forearm. Little teensy movements driving the stick shift BMW with a pillow strapped to my chest. At a stop light, I take two more Vicodin. I don't realize how extraordinarily high my tolerance is at this point. I get onto the freeway, put it in fifth, and hold the wheel from below with one hand. This way, there is the least movement of my body. *Quel* safe.

I don't remember until I walk through the hospital doors that this is the same hospital in which I had my ablation. As I go toward the reception desk, I wait for the feeling of dread to creep in. The memories of that horrible, scary procedure. The beginning of all that was going to be even more difficult than

I had imagined. I think about it intellectually, but I don't feel anything. I am numb, and it isn't because of the Vicodin. Too much has happened. The ablation, which was eight weeks ago, seems like a lifetime ago.

I am in a huge hallway walking toward the room I am told that Aunt Mil is in when Auntie Lanie comes around the corner. The picture I have of myself is of me as I've always been. I am walking into the hospital, handsome and responsible and fast, ready to be there for everyone. The reality is that I'm standing there, totally out of breath, dirty sweatpants, crazy hair and clutching a pillow to my chest. Auntie Lanie stops about ten feet away from me, stunned.

"Jackie. What are you doing here?"

"You guys are transparent as glass," I say walking toward her, ignoring her shock.

She laughs a little.

"Honey, I need to tell you, she doesn't look like Aunt Mil anymore."

"I've been around hospitals and sick people for weeks. I'm fine with it."

"No, honey, this is different. This is someone who has been sick for a very long time. Who is in a coma. Who is on morphine. And who is on the edge of death." Her voice is very gentle, trying to reassure me and prepare me. She pauses with tears in her eyes. "Honey, she should have died this morning and we don't know why she's still here."

When I walk into her room, I am totally and utterly unprepared for what I see lying there in this hospital bed. She looks dead already. Little wisps of white hair are all that are left of what was once her beautiful blonde hair. One of her eyes is open, but it is milky and has sunk back into her skull. The other eye is closed, but it looks like the eyeball inside must be gone. Her arms are dry, white skin over bones. She looks like she will break if she is touched. Her mouth is open, but only because she has no muscle control. Since her head is back, her mouth falls open. Her lips are the same color as her skin. I'm so embarrassed at myself for thinking that she looks like something out of a horror movie. There is no other way to describe her. Whatever is there in that bed is not Aunt Mil. Not anymore.

I realize I am standing there, staring at her. Not moving. Then I begin to notice everything else. Babba sits next to her, on a plastic hospital chair, holding her hand and rubbing it. Just like she did for me when I was in the hospital. For days. For two surgeries. Then for her grandson, now for her sister. How much is she supposed to handle at once?

She looks up at me and says, "Jackie! What are you doing here?"

Before I can answer, Auntie Lanie says, very droll, "He said we were transparent as glass." Babba gives me the tiniest conspiratorial smile, but she does not leave Aunt Mil's side to come hug me. I walk over, bend down, still holding my pillow against my chest and give her a small kiss on the cheek. Then I go sit down in another chair. I am so exhausted I can hardly breathe. I have gone from being out of breath and exhausted, but handling it, to suddenly, immediately, needing to sit down, breathe, and not speak. The thought occurs to me that if something happens to me because I came here tonight, that it will have been an awful thing to have done to them.

I don't hug anyone else. My Uncle Norm, Babba, and Mill's younger brother, here with his girlfriend, Linnie. Allan is here. I'm still afraid of hugging people. Lifting my arms up hurts and I get scared that they will hug too tight and hurt me. I can drive a BMW, but I cannot be hugged. I love Vicodin for providing this kind of clarity.

I am sitting in silence, not talking, taking big, gasping breaths. This happens to me now. I am suddenly gasping for air and it scares me. I immediately feel that something must be going wrong inside me. When I mention this to whomever is around, the response is that I'm just scared and my body is healing. How quickly they forget that when I said this after the heart surgery, I was right. Something was going wrong. Had I not gone to the hospital, I would be dead right now. Clearly I don't have a whole lot of faith in my body anymore. The "odds" were against anything happening after the heart surgery, but it did. The "odds" are against anything happening to me now, but I am not reassured. After all, the "odds" are against anyone my age ever needing heart surgery in the first place.

I notice that even though I am gasping for air, albeit quietly, nobody comes over to me. Auntie Lanie says, "Jackie? Are you okay?"

"Yes. Tired."

She gives me a small smile and turns back to look at her mother's living death. I realize, very suddenly, that I am no longer the sickest person in the room. I have been the sickest person in the room for as long as I can remember now. Of course, it has only been the past six months or so, but that was Before. This is After. This is Now. And Now is completely different. I know this, but I will spend the next five years figuring out what all those differences mean and how to handle them. It will end up being like an adult me watching a child me. I will learn so much, miss so much, and be confused by so much, but right now I only know that I can't decide if I feel good that I'm not the sickest person in the room or if I feel bad about it. To admit that I still want the attention seems so wrong. I don't want to grow into a new Jack. I want the old Jack. I want to heal, get better, go back to work and have my life back as if all this never happened. But even now, there is a small voice in the back of my head telling me that I will never see myself, or life in general, the same way ever again.

All this goes through my head sitting here in this chair in the silent room while Aunt Mil drifts towards a death that is not coming soon enough. Auntie Lanie tries not to cry and Babba sits without tears, rubbing Mill's arm and holding her hand. I remember that feeling. I remember it well. Life support. Doesn't take much.

The second bed in the room is empty and I go lie down on it. Aunt Mil in one bed. Me in another. Babba in a chair watching over Mill. Lanie and Allan, waiting for their mother to die. Wondering why it hasn't happened already. Hoping desperately she is unaware of what is going on. Hoping desperately that she is not in pain. It is agony for them and I feel very selfish lying here on this bed. My breathing returns to normal. Or, rather, as normal is it gets right now. I breathe small breaths and then, periodically, one big breath. Not too deep because that will hurt my chest. I had no clue that breathing would become an art form. Perhaps that is because I no longer take my own breath for granted.

It is morning now and we are all still here. We don't understand why Aunt Mil is hanging on so long. Why she doesn't let go? Allan thinks it is the pacemaker that it is keeping her heart beating. I am doubtful of this. Her heart will stop when it wants to stop regardless of the pacemaker. We have great control over our bodies. Not as much as we'd like, but more than we realize. I have a feeling she will die when she wants to die. I don't say anything. This is not the place for me to air my know-it-all opinions. This death belongs to Allan, Elaine, and Babba. Not me. I'm a bystander. I have reverted to my usual role as caretaker as best as I can. Of saying the right things and watching over everyone. I do this with sincerity and love. I have a knack for saying exactly what someone needs to hear. I have always been this way. Able to zero in on what someone is all about. It is the Before Jack, who I am starting to realize I miss.

We convince Babba that she must get out of the hospital room and go eat. She is exhausted. We have been taking turns on the bed all night. Neither of us has slept, though. The tension of waiting for Aunt Mil to die is like a vibration. Everything is humming. Nothing is relaxed. There is no way out of here until Aunt Mil dies. In a way, she's already dead. I sit up slowly in the bed, still having to roll onto my side, push my legs over the edge of the bed and roll off completely. I lean back against the bed slightly to catch my breath a little. I take two Vicodin. I don't have many left in my pocket. I did not expect to be here this long. Nobody did. When I look over to the body, the barely breathing body, I realize it's still Aunt Mil.

Elaine insists that Babba have a wheelchair and I am shocked to see that Babba doesn't resist this. She is that tired. By the time we are downstairs, I am heaving huge breaths and my chest is hurting because I am using it, apparently, while pushing the wheelchair. Babba can hear me breathing. I tell her I need to rest a second. We stop and I sit down in a chair while people drift by with dazed or determined looks on their faces. After thirty seconds, Babba gets out of the wheelchair and says, "Get in."

"No. I just need a minute to rest."

"Jackie. Get in now."

Her voice is suddenly strong. Resonant. Sharp. She sounds almost mad. It is not a request. It is a demand. I get in the chair. Our roles have reversed once again. Babba is the caretaker and it will take her mind off the events of the day a little. I am once again the sickest person in the room. A Jack I can deal with. A Jack I know well. It gives us both a little reprieve from what's going on.

Babba and I order hamburgers and fries and soft drinks and sit in the restaurant on the orange and brown plastic chairs. We don't say much.

"Jackie, how are you feeling?"

"Like a recovering heart patient, I suppose."

"Jackie, how are you really feeling?"

I accidentally look into her eyes when she says this and there is such concern, such focus, such love that it catches me off guard. I don't deserve this kind of attention. Not when her sister is across the street at death's door.

"Scared that I won't get better."

"Jackie, listen to me. You are going to get better. It will be a long road. Nothing bad is going to happen anymore." Her voice is strong and insistent.

"Everyone said that before and then I ended up having my chest scraped from inside. I guess I don't have a lot of faith in my body right now," almost daring her to contradict me.

She doesn't say anything. She doesn't try to get me to see it a different way. She doesn't try to protest. She knows I'm right. Instead, she takes a gigantic bite of her hamburger.

An hour later we are back in Mil's hospital room. Mil is still alive. The doctor has allowed the morphine drip dosage to be increased. We all wish, silently, that they would increase it to the point of hurrying along her death, but this is illegal. It is perfectly fine to allow this emaciated barely-human person in a coma to stay that way until death. That's legal. I don't understand. How can we not allow euthanasia in this country? How is it compassionate to allow two children, Allan and Elaine, watch for 48 hours while their mother slowly inches toward death? We know she is going to die. What if she is in pain and we don't know it? What if she can hear us and we don't know it? I am angry to think that we cannot simply hasten her death. That would be the most compassionate, the most self-less thing to do. And even though I am trying to think of these things in the abstract, or as applying only to Aunt Mil, I know that I am thinking of myself, too. If I had ended up as a vegetable (if

I do end up as a vegetable), I want to be euthanized, because I am absolutely terrified of lying there in a coma but feeling pain and knowing what is going on around me, and I would want it for my family.

Babba and I have both taken a short nap on the other hospital bed. We managed to get on there together. Babba on her side and me on my back because I'm not allowed to lie on my side yet. We don't sleep. I drift away in my head a little. Then I realize my chest is really starting to hurt. A lot. I have forgotten to take my Vicodin. Everybody has told me to stay on top of the pain. Once you let the pain become overwhelming, it takes a long time to get it under control again. I get off the bed and go into the bathroom. A typical hospital bathroom, oversized to allow a wheelchair. Smelly with disinfectant. A glaringly white toilet and sink. I shut the door and I stand there unable to move. This could be a bathroom at Cedars. I try not to remember. I take six Vicodin, knowing that I'm completely ruining my stomach and my liver probably wants to jump out of my body and run away in terror. I also know, at this moment, that I am not only taking the Vicodin for the pain. I have progressed to taking it to deal with this moment. This is the first time I am not taking it just for pain, and I don't care.

When I come out of the bathroom, Babba is back in her chair rubbing Aunt Mil's emaciated, barely there arm. We are all very, very tired. Everybody else has been here for two days. I have been here for fourteen hours. We close the blinds on the window because the sun is bright today. A clear gorgeous day outside that we need to shut out. We also shut the door to the room. We turn out all the lights except for the dim one over the bed. We want to make it quiet and peaceful. For her. For us.

Babba leans to Aunt Mil's ear and starts to talk to her. "It's okay to go, Mil. We're all here. I love you." She talks to her for five minutes. Elaine leans over and talks to Mil in a normal voice. The voice she always used to talk to her mother. "Mom, it's okay to go now. We're going to be fine. Allan is here with your sister and Jackie and your brother. We're all here with you. It's okay to go."

Elaine turns to me and says, funny/sarcastic, "You talk to her. She never would listen to me!" We all giggle. Even Babba.

I bend down close to her ear. I remember this smell. It is how I smelled. An acidic, rotting smell. I almost recoil. The morphine bag inches from my head. I wonder what to say. I can't just say "I love you." I can't just say "It's okay to go." If she can hear us, she must already know these things. She is hanging on for another reason. I stand there, leaning over, my chest beginning to hurt from holding my body in this position. I should know what to say. I understand being sick. I understand being scared. I understand what comforts people in helpless situations. But, I quickly realize, I don't understand what it is like to be 86 years old, a breath away from death, leaving behind her brother, her sister, her son and daughter. In an instant, I know what to say.

"Aunt Mil, we're all here. Everything is calm. We're going to take care of Elaine and Allan. I will. Norm will. Babba will. They will be okay. We'll watch over them just like you would. We're all going to miss you, but it's time to go. Elaine and Allan are ready. We'll take care of them. Always."

Before I can say another word, Elaine says, "Jackie. She's gone." It was so quick and quiet and I was so focused on what to say next that I didn't even notice.

Then, the devastation. First Allan sobbing. Babba's quiet tears, still holding Mil's hand. Norm and Linnie stand back and I see Uncle Norm wipe tears away from his face. So does Linnie. I move quickly out of the way. It isn't my place to be this close right now. Besides, I'm already crying. Last is Auntie Lanie.

I stand back, stunned at what just happened. Was it just a coincidence? Did she hear me? Was that really her fear? A mother's fear that her children might not be okay? And she believed me when I said we'd take care of them? Could it be that simple?

I leave the room and go into the hallway. I sit in one of the chairs. I am still crying and I realize how stupid we all have been. How stupid almost everyone is in this situation. We made it so complicated. "Why is she hanging on?" we kept asking. "She needs to let go." In the end, it was the universal thing: She stayed because she was worried that people she loves might not be okay without her. Babba follows me out of the room. I stand up to hug her and she starts crying. Really crying. Babba does not cry. She gets tears in her eyes when she talks about Dad being in Vietnam. She got tears in her eyes when I tried to talk about my heart surgery.

She asks me if I will tell her what I said to Aunt Mil. Nobody else ever asks me. Or, if they did, I do not end up remembering.

A half hour later, I have taken my last two Vicodin and am in the BMW on the way home. The sun is blinding. I barely realize how much time has passed since I left last night. I am in morning traffic and I find it absurd that life goes on. I've had heart surgery. My aunt died a horrible death. How can life be going on? How can all these people not realize how unimportant they are letting their lives be? How have they let themselves get off track as to what is important in life?

As children we know what matters. Long summer days playing. Yummy food. Happiness that seems to breed more happiness because we are open to it. As adults, we are supposed to get smarter, but we don't. Mature doesn't mean smart. I look around at all the cars, stuck in the morning traffic. My Vicodin is setting in. My pillow strapped to my chest. I wonder how all these people forgot all the brilliance they had as children? I wonder if it takes something like open heart surgery to make you remember that brilliance so clearly? That to be childlike is to be as wise as one can ever get, perhaps.

I get off at Lancaster, turn left on Ventura, and take a quick right up into the hills on a very curvy street to Mulholland and home. I try to remember something, but can't. This keeps happening. Maybe I was without oxygen for a second too long while they put me on the heart/lung machine? I try to brush this worry aside. It is only one of many that come from the eradication of my sense of immortality. As I park on the street in front of the little door that leads to the steps that lead down to my front door, I remember what I was trying to remember. Those old phrases, "If the old had the energy of youth and if children had the wisdom of the old…" And it hits me, if children had the "wisdom" of the old, then they wouldn't be brilliant anymore.

I check the messages on my answering machine from Linda, Eric, Roy, and Nora. There are two from my mother, one left late last night about the time I was strapping myself and my pillow into the BMW and another one a few hours ago. She sounds a little frantic. I call Mom back and tell her

I'm fine. I run through what has happened very fast because I don't have the energy to explain anything in detail right now. There is a pause before she says, quietly, "You shouldn't have gone to the hospital. You cannot be driving. It is too soon." She doesn't repeat herself. She doesn't wait to hear if I have an answer. It is something she must say. She does not ask why on earth I would do it. She already knows the answer. Because I'm me. Even now, apparently.

I hang up the phone, take three Vicodin and a glass of milk and crawl into bed. With my clothes on. I lie on my back, staring at the ceiling. While I try to catch my breath and let myself drift off to sleep, I know that I have learned something. I had a small taste of myself again. Maybe, I think, the Now Jack still has some Before Jack left inside. I also realize that my thoughts about everyone else's priorities being out of whack and that they don't see life clearly anymore, make me feel alienated from people. I assume this is because my chest hurts and I'm exhausted. But this feeling of alienation ends up being one of the many lasting effects.

I feel selfish that my last thought before going to sleep is that Aunt Mil's death has reminded me that I'm alive.

CHAPTER 23

Who Am I Now?

"Eric, what are you doing?"

"Honey, I'm gettin' all liquored up. I've had the week of death," he says with his Virginia-Southern accent turned up a notch.

"Nice turn of phrase," I say, rather self-pityingly. I know Eric is rolling his eyes while taking a sip.

He says, "Oh, please. I refuse to watch what I say around you. First of all, I never watch what I say. Second of all, you need to rejoin the living."

"You mean rejoin the drinking."

"That's what I said!"

"Let's go out tonight and be fabulous."

"Now? Why?" Eric says, surprised.

"Because I can!"

"That's always been your excuse for anything that is remotely irresponsible, Jack."

"Yes, you taught me well."

"Bitch," says Eric.

"Slut," I respond instantly.

"I wish! Come get me in an hour. What are you wearing?" Eric asks, which is strange since he usually wouldn't care.

"Black. What are you wearing?"

"Sable," Eric says like the simpering beauty queen that he is.

Now that I have plans with Eric, I feel that familiar tingle. I'm feeling superior. Unique. So above it all. Apparently heart surgery did not make me feel this way. Making it through my fear and presumption of death did not do the trick either. Of course, it couldn't possibly be because I'm not letting them! It couldn't possibly be because I refuse to consider what I've just been through except in the abstract! It couldn't possibly be because I insist on returning to my Before life even though this is now, After. Alcohol and Xanax do double duty now: They bring me back to the days of avoidance before the surgery and help me avoid the days after the surgery. I'm in this netherworld of not-totally-recovered but recovered-enough. I don't know if I'm running away from the past or speeding as fast as possible toward the future. Something in my head tells me the future is now. I love clichés. Beside, I have a new label: Recovering heart patient. I love labels. They make astonishingly good masks.

I light the candles, put on the Westlife CD, make the dim lamps dimmer, and pour myself a vodka rocks. Belvedere. I have graduated from Absolut. Absolut has become too obvious. I hate obvious. Obvious makes me feel like everyone else and that makes me feel approachable and relatable and that makes me feel vulnerable. I have had a bit too much of feeling vulnerable lately. Who am I kidding? I don't *ever* like to feel vulnerable. Scares the crap out of me. I am far too much of a control freak, but I also know that being a control freak has helped me get through this. Years from now, I will find out there are a few, ahem, residual emotions that I hadn't quite dealt with.

5/4/01 8:07 a.m., on plane from LAX to JFK
Although my house is in shambles, I have two weeks of packing left, and I'm unemployed, I decided late yesterday to take a weekend in NYC. I had to get out of my house. Hell, I had to get out of L.A.! Everywhere I look there are ghosts of a former life. When I was terrified. When I was running. When I was high on booze and pills all the time. When I had been resigned to a death that luckily did not come. I have to say, I miss being fabulous all the time with my lofty views of humanity and grandiose comments on society. There is comfort in hiding behind your fear.

I can't seem to explain, even to myself, why my material possessions seem as though they belong to someone else. Their irrelevance is so very clear now. I'm no longer dramatic enough to say I'm totally different. I wasn't reborn; I simply survived—the surgeries, the fear, the running. Surviving changes you. The luxury of feeling immortal is gone. A part of me wants to sell my objects, my things, my car (well, maybe not the BMW), move out of that gorgeous place high in the Hollywood Hills with the spectacular view and lush landscaping. I suppose I'm running now, too. Away from all that terror, that frantic life. I'm just doing it a little slower. And I'm okay with having no clue as to what the next step should be. I'm just glad there will be one.

5/12/01 9:31 a.m., Starbucks, West Hollywood
NYC was marvelous. It was great to be back among the diversity, the rush, the anonymous feeling of being terribly small in a crowd. The first evening, Magda came over. There we were in Lisa's apartment on Jane Street in the Village. Champagne. Music. Noise from the street below. That funky little apartment, a five floor walk-up. The three of us quipping and laughing while sipping champagne and getting ready for a night out. We walked over to Absolutely Fourth, a small, stylish bar near Lisa's apartment. The brownstones, broken sidewalks, old people with their rent-controlled apartments and tiny storefronts were all so very familiar to me. It was as though I'd never left.

The next evening Lisa and I tried to get into Park and didn't. Have we lost our charm? I can't remember the last time we didn't get in somewhere. Instead we went to the Hudson Bar. We walked in front of the huge line as though we belonged. Nobody stopped us. The Hudson is rather beautiful and reminds me a bit of Bon in Paris. Lots of dark wood and white linen and candles and crystal. And a floor that is lit from beneath and glows. I felt old. Not so much in years, but mentality. I'm not "there" in the same way I was, and I miss that feeling. I can't seem to connect to Before Jack and I can't seem to understand After Jack.

Also saw the play, "Dinner With Friends" by Donald Margulies, which won the 2000 Pulitzer Prize. I was less than impressed. Also saw "Fosse," fourth row, center orchestra. Great seat. As usual, it brought me to tears. The exuberance. The purity of the creativity. The utterly hedonistic aspect of theater. When I cried a bit and found myself amazed at the talent, while sitting in my perfect seat for a hit Broadway play in NYC, I kept thinking to myself, "Maybe I am back."

Went to Lesbian Night at Felt on Tuesday. Those lesbians love me. They certainly are more fun than the boys. I sat with Laura's sister, Beth Broderick, who plays Aunt Zelda on the television show, "Sabrina, The Teenage Witch." We sat together all night, drinking martinis. Everybody wanted to talk to her and she was pleasant, but kept giving me sideways, knowing glances. So I had martinis with the TV star and every time someone came up to her to talk, they'd give me an odd look trying to figure out if I was "someone."

Today I'm running to the gym, running to LAX to fetch Dad, zipping down to Laguna and then back up to L.A. to have dinner with Jim. I've delayed my move to Santa Fe a week. Simply not ready yet. There may be a job at Spelling for me. How funny would that be? I try to leave the industry only to find yet another "cool" job handed to me.

5/16/01 9:20 a.m., Starbucks, West Hollywood
I met Jim on the airplane coming back from NYC. He's a flight attendant and we never ran into each other when I was one, too. Black Irish. Dark hair. Blue eyes. Stunning. We talked until the wheels went down and he went tearing back to his jump seat. Neither of us had the nerve to exchange numbers. Shy. Nerves. There was a point in our conversation when we locked eyes. That little spec of time you "know" there's a connection. As though you're looking so closely at the other person's face to find the inner perfections yet to reveal themselves. With all my computer codes that still work on SABRE, I found his layover hotel and sent a fax. I avoided calling his room so as not to be too stalker-ish. We met at his hotel for dinner Saturday night. He gets my humor. I get his. The only thing that made me nervous, and I will try to put it from my mind so I don't run away, is when he said after only three hours, "Why did I have to wait 12 years to find someone like you?" I should have responded, "What? A 30-year-old who is totally messed up and trying, all over again, to find himself?" Kept my sarcastic mouth shut somehow.

5/19/01 11:09 a.m., Crunch Gym, West Hollywood
Was the ultimate cliché at the gym. I purchased a new cell phone, which is something all unemployed people should do: spend money on trendy toys.

Clipped it to my workout pants, Countess Nora calls from Russia. Then Linda about lunching at Sunset Plaza. Ran into Eric, who was going to town on the treadmill.

Yesterday I was at the Abbey. As I was leaving I heard someone behind me say, "Jack?" I turn around to see Joseph. The guy from that amazing, scary weekend in Paris. I was utterly in shock and had no clue what to say. All my shyness and nerves flew to the surface. We exchanged numbers and he left a message earlier this morning that he'd like to have dinner. Just as I plan to leave L.A., it becomes interesting.

5/21/01 1:06 p.m. Starbucks, West Hollywood
Went on a formal date with Joseph last night. Dinner at a French restaurant and a theater performance at the Ahmanson called, "3hree." Dinner was great and the play was atrocious. Joseph is nice, but there is something about him. Almost as though even he is surprised to have made money and traveled so much. His comments on these subjects seemed less to impress me than to let me know he found a glam life despite it not exactly being in his blood. I also think Eric scared the hell out of him at Felt, where we went afterwards. Eric scares the hell out of lots of people. Of course, I fell right into it as well, as I usually do. It's part of our charm. We talked about parties in NYC with Richard Picasso, a gala in Santa Fe, flights to Paris and London, private Gulfstream jets. Joseph seemed to feel the constant need to let me know he wasn't impressed by the "over-the-top" stuff. I wouldn't respect him if he was. At some point he commented that we had the same Cartier watch. I replied, dryly, "Mine's fake."

He replied, way too quickly, "Mine's real."

Eric, sarong and all, said, "Jack, he is smitten with you! Thinks you're the most unique and divine individual."

I said, "He has no idea just how unique I am. I'm sure I'll scare him off immediately."

Eric was showing a bit of leg through his sarong as we were on our third bottle of Veuve and he was screeching, "I still have the most fabulous legs!"

To which I replied, "But who wants to see them?"

Spoke with Jim again last night. He seemed so happy to hear from me and I admitted I've changed my departure plans in order to see him tomorrow on his layover. He is the first person who has managed to crush my wall. I'm not scared to be vulnerable with him. He makes me feel comfortable. It's not that I'm thinking, "He's the one." But to know I'm not necessarily one of those people who has too much baggage to find love and someone to share myself with. Doesn't even matter if it works out with Jim. Now I have confidence that it could with someone.

Hysterical comment from Eric this morning during our usual 6 a.m. dishing conversation. "Oh, Jack," he said. "I couldn't even get drunk enough to make him cute. Couldn't even drink him into not being ugly!"

Jack in his Beemer

It's 5 a.m. and I am driving from L.A. to Santa Fe. I pass Flagstaff and I'm driving straight east through the desert. I've driven this road a million times. Back and forth all during college. The BMW is packed with everything I think I have to have with me, yet I don't even know what I brought. I have been so busy getting ready for my escape and being fabulous and proving I'm okay that I haven't focused on anything.

The sun is rising over the desert. Clean and crisp and bright orange on the horizon against a sky that is indigo with stars everywhere. It is stunningly gorgeous. I press a button and the sunroof slides open. I press more buttons and the windows roll down. The dry desert air rushes through the car. I put in a CD of some mix I made ages ago. The first song comes on—Bruce Hornsby singing "The End of the Innocence." I am in tears instantly. It is as though all the feelings suddenly come at me from wherever I've been trying to hide them. I'm going about 90 miles an hour. There is nobody on the road. It is me and the wind and the sunrise, and a song that is so appropriate I can hardly stand it. I let the tears come and the wind whips them off my face. I press my head back against the headrest and push the pedal faster. Faster. I'm going 100 miles an hour. Away from something. To what? "Happily-ever-after fails. We've been poisoned by these fairy tales. This is the end of the innocence . . ."

I want so desperately for this drive at 100 miles an hour through the desert to be a new beginning. To feel like a new start. The next step to a new experience. But I can't quite get there in my head. I cry harder. I can't get far enough away from what I went through to be ready to see that there is another beginning. The song ends. I turn off the stereo and push the car to 105, thinking that if I get into a wreck or pulled over that I really couldn't give a shit. Is there anything that I couldn't handle now?

I want it all to feel new, but it doesn't. I remember all this. The sunrises over the desert. The drives through the dry desert wind. New beginnings. New starts. Being alone without being lonely. All that was then. So why the fuck am I speeding on the interstate? I can't get back to whoever I was. I can't figure out who I'm going to be. And I sure as fuck don't know who I am anymore.

I am still crying. I am still looking at the sunrise. Fiery red. The deep blue fading into light blue, turquoise, purple. The stars are still bright. I slow down to 80. I give up on my anger. How is this all a new beginning? I can't quite get at it. I'm not even a player in my own life anymore. That's it, I think to myself, I'm an imposter in my own life. Looking so healed. So brave. So able to move forward. And yet, it's all intellectual. I don't feel it . . . in my heart.

There is nothing linear about any of this, and I tend to think in a line. I think in flow charts. It comforts me. I so desperately want to feel good right now. This IS a new beginning! I made it through heart surgery! Through the ablation! The thoracotomy! I made it! I'm going to spend the summer in Santa Fe getting better and better!

The sky is pale blue. Stars twinkle and the moon is up, faded, like a piece of tissue paper in the sky. I roll up the windows, take the car to 90 and speed off into the sunrise. I want it to feel like some dramatic symbol of a new start. Now that I tucked the confusion back inside, it does. I smile. Barely able to fake it. Even to myself.

5/26/01 8:28 a.m., Downtown Subscription, Santa Fe
I'm at "home." At 30, after going through so much, I'm back where I started. Am I failure because I had to come home and just "be" after ten years of so very much? Or, am I success because I've done so much? The house is empty; Dad is in Vietnam. I've left everything in the house—boxes and bags and clothes and frames and candles. Everything I used to use as the vision of my success and individuality now lays in heaps on the floor.

5/27/01 8 a.m., Downtown Subscription, Santa Fe
It sounds horribly self-indulgent and egotistical, but sometimes it's hard to look like this on the outside and feel so hurt and lost inside. Who would know to look at my $500 clothes thrown on so casually, my tan, my messy hair, green eyes, that I've only recently become human again. To begin to pull myself together. To have made a step at altering my fate. How funny. Fate cannot be altered. Maybe it's the path to one's fate that can be changed. When you put so much effort into your looks, no one asks how your heart is. No one asks what it's like to have the luxury of feeling immortal stolen so fast in the dark of night. And it was night for so long. Guess I'm feeling sorry for myself.

5/28/01 9:16 a.m., Santa Fe Baking Company, Santa Fe
I spoke with Jim on the phone for an hour last night. He acts protective and distant all at once. He's sweet, and I'm a sucker for sweet. He said he was at Target and asked a magic eight ball "Is Jack the one?" The ball said "yes." He swore distance was not an issue. That we'd figure it out eventually. It's crazy. We've spent no time together. Why do I still have hope? How on earth have I managed not to become jaded? I'm clearly bonkers to even allow myself to go there.

Nora is coming from London in a week and Eric is coming for two or three days while she is here. We're all going to stay at the house, so I have to clean the house and put the boxes in Nick's old room, and prepare the master bedroom for Nora. If nothing else, I'm a good host.

Same, that night.

I've clearly gone off the wagon. Chardonnay in a martini glass. There is something about a martini glass that is so much more elegant than a wine glass of chardonnay. Besides, who but me orders chardonnay with ice in a martini glass?

Spoke again with Jim. He said, "A relationship is three things: You, Me, and It." Took my breath away because I have always said the same thing. Each needs its own energy and attention. I can't worry about the "what ifs?" I must keep reminding myself that the fact that I even think somebody could be utterly perfect out there is what counts.

Nora left a message on my voicemail: "The Russian is coming!" I love my friends.

The bartender came over and told me that everyone is amused with my chardonnay-in-a-martini-glass thing. The bar dances with light. Candles. A tiny space. That picture of the woman with a hood around her face and eyes that want to say something. I so love being amusing, but being unique is far more of an adventure.

5/30/01 evening, Santa Fe

I am standing in front of the mirror in my underwear. White Polo boxer briefs. I have worked out every day. I have sat in the sun by the swimming pool. My body looks toned and muscular and lean. Anybody who notices the scar will think it's from a surgery from years and years ago. Nobody would ever know it was just six months ago that someone hacked into me a few times. I splash cold water on my face and run my hands through my hair with a glob of gel. I am sure I am losing my hair. I heard that major shocks to the body might cause something like this. What else do I have to put up with! I am back to my looks as my best shield. My best way of fooling everyone, even myself, into thinking all is fine. I look fantastic, even if my hair is thin. I look into the mirror and laugh at my introspection. Now what do I do with all this fabulous self-awareness? As I throw on my black short-sleeve DKNY t-shirt that shows off the vein down the middle of my bicep, I figure . . . nothing. I put on Kenneth Cole beige cargo pants and tuck just the front of the t-shirt into it, letting it look very casual. I wear the sandals that I bought at Walmart a year ago when Rob and I were here visiting mom.

I pour myself a glass of wine in the kitchen and take it outside. I step into the dirt at the back of the house, just above the arroyo. The arroyo I used to play in when I was 15. Where my friend Annette and I used to sit and talk together about our shitty family lives in high school. In the arroyo where I used to go and look at dirty magazines, where I used to escape when my parents were screaming and fighting. Now, it looks gorgeous. The wine is a nice Merlot Dad found somewhere. I know he doesn't think I should be drinking. I also know that nobody will deny me anything right now. They won't risk saying no. They won't risk being critical. We're all convinced I deserve to do whatever the hell I want, at least on some level. Have what I want. And, most important, be whoever I want. Change my colors as often as I want. I'm more entitled now than I've ever been in my life. The biggest difference is that, in my head, I know that a part of this is truly pathetic. I'm supposed to be this incredibly wise person with incredible perspective now. Not this person going back to drinking and taking Xanax and playing like I'm the "it" boy. Apparently, I'm going back to what I know best. I'm very familiar with the Before Jack. The After Jack is new and I don't know what to do with him. So I ignore him.

I take a deep breath and find my leather Coach backpack. I reach into the back zipper pocket and my fingers dig into a pile of pills. Loose. Now that my secret's out, I can't very well risk anybody finding them. I take two tiny blue pills and swallow them with the last sip of wine. I set the wine glass on the wooden dresser, very Santa Fe style. I look in the mirror. The wine has set in a little. The Xanax will take about 10 more minutes since I have not eaten anything for hours. I do look really awesome tonight. In Santa Fe, I know I am the best looking gay guy in town. I know I get attention wherever I go. I decide to take another Xanax. This time dry. This is so *Valley of the Dolls*. And I laugh to myself at such a fabulous, self-aware reference.

Ten minutes later, I am speeding down the dirt road listening to Yaz. Feeling extra sexy and extra hot and extra original. It is amazing to come back to Santa Fe. I was nerdy growing up. I was a closeted fag with parents who were divorcing and I was relatively miserable and getting very, very good at pretending not to be. Now, here I am back, driving my black BMW, talking about being an entertainment lawyer at DreamWorks and how I am so fabulous and survived heart surgery. Looking incredibly hot at the same time. The Xanax takes hold. There is absolutely nobody like me. I don't even realize that I am, once again, making myself different and separate from everybody else. That once again, I am going to hold everyone at arm's length. I don't know any other way. I only know two things from the past year: fabulous and fast or total terrified emotional wreck, and I don't feel like being the wrecked part. Not tonight. I don't want to be damaged anymore. There is a line from the movie, *Damage*, which was out a million years ago: "Damaged people are dangerous. They know they can survive."

The patio is packed. Metal patio tables and chairs sit on bricks. Candles and yellowed lights hanging from vines over the patio. Some kind of alternate cowboy music comes from inside. I walk up the few bricked steps to the patio and stand there, knowing people are looking at me. I'm different and new and people haven't seen me here before. I feel very superior, although I wonder if I'm wearing my terror and insecurity on my sleeve. I see Stacy sitting at a table with a girl and two guys. I walk over and fling myself into a chair, kissing Stacy hard on the lips, and say with a flourish, "I need alcohol immediately!" Which, of course, gets hysterical laughs. It is this very moment that comes to define my summer. I have made myself completely approachable, totally unattainable, utterly different, and I-don't-give-a-shit-what-anyone-thinks—all in the manner of one minute. I have instantly gone from being Jack to being "Jack!"

The girl is someone Stacy has been dating. She is very butch and very drunk. Bored drunk, so I don't say much to her. There are two guys there. I notice one immediately. Gorgeous eyes. Short-sleeved black t-shirt showing off muscular arms. My favorite body part. Very handsome. I know that I'll have him utterly charmed and fascinated within thirty minutes. It doesn't occur to me that I have put this emotional energy into making sure he falls for me before I even know if I would want him to. Stacy sees me looking at him a tad too long and rolls her eyes.

"He's twenty-three!"

"So! I'm only 30! And my heart is practically a baby now!"

She laughs. We're whispering with each other and ignoring the rest of the table.

"He's really nice and comes from a good family."

"As long as he comes, that's all I care about at the moment." Which really isn't true because Xanax and alcohol do not a horny boy make. Fabulous, but not horny.

I am flying high and tell my story very quickly: I'm an entertainment lawyer. I had open heart surgery four months ago. I'm here to relax for the summer. All said with hilarity! I know that Adam is immediately smitten. I can see it in his eyes. I know this look.

Four margaritas and three bowls of tortilla chips later, I announce, "My god! I am three sheets to the wind! They are Frette sheets, though!" Big laughs from Adam and I'm impressed he knows what Frette sheets are. We all agree to go to Adam's house and go swimming in his pool. Just Stacy, Adam, and I end up going. Stacy and I hop in the BMW and Adam hops into his Acura. I am following him and we are driving insanely fast. I am blasting the soundtrack from *Moulin Rouge*, which has just come out, and have all the windows and sunroof open.

"Don't drive so fast!!" says Stacy, laughing.

"I do everything fast! There is no point in doing things any other way!"

At some point, we have to turn around and I get a little too close to a tree. The passenger side mirror goes flying off. Stacy is shocked. I am delighted. I find it highly amusing!

"Damnit, " I say, laughing maniacally. "That is the fourth mirror I've had to replace in five months!" I genuinely find it hilarious. I love, almost even more, the idea that I don't care.

Adam's pool is stunning, from a spread in *Architectural Digest*. I am seriously impressed, and I am rarely seriously impressed. It is indoors with a cathedral-like ceiling that slides open to the sky at the touch of a button. It is huge—a whole entertainment area complete with barbecue, vaulted roof, patio, and guest rooms.

Adam goes to get us more alcohol and we all strip to our undies and hop in the Jacuzzi. I am horrifyingly proud to show off my scar. Stacy and Adam are, of course, impressed that I am so bold and proud of this scar. Inside, I am impressed with myself, as well. Anything to make me feel different, apparently. Which is the exact opposite of what I should be doing, of course.

An hour later, we are done with the alcohol and Jacuzzi and Stacy wants me to take her back to her car. I end up kissing Adam deeply when we say goodbye and we agree to have dinner together tomorrow night.

In the car, Stacy says, "I'm so proud of you. I can't believe you are so healthy and so happy."

"But dear! Why not be! I am happy to be alive! Almost dying will do that to you!"

And I am happy to be alive, but I'm not exactly happy. This experience has alienated me from everyone else to the extreme.

After dropping Stacy off, I speed as fast as possible up to the house. I feel utterly invincible and without a care in the world. It never occurs to me that if I am pulled over, I will be arrested for driving drunk. Consequences are not something I consider. I've spent the past year teaching myself to never, ever consider them. Unfortunately, I'm fabulously good at it. At the house, I walk around the back. When we built the house, they put an outside door in my bedroom. When I was in high school, this was most useful for not only sneaking out, but also for sneaking people in. Tonight, however, I use it to make sure that if Dad is awake, he doesn't see how bombed I am. It's not that I care; it's that I don't want a lecture.

I wash my face, peel off my clothes, take four Klonopin, and then go outside in my underwear. The moon is full and very bright and skims the top of the mountains in the distance. I look up at it and feel the breeze on my bare skin. I think about the night and how fabulous I am and how I love being such an enigma and how I still can't quite believe all I've gone through and that I'm here.

I go to bed crying until I thankfully pass out.

6/1/01 12:46 a.m. Downtown Subscription, Santa Fe
Am hung over from martinis last night. Have got to stay away from alcohol. My body can't handle it like previously. I also find I like my behavior less when I'm drunk. Obnoxious in a charming manner. Few inhibitions. Charming. Loud. Forward. Over the top, completely. I really used to love it, but lately I wake up and think, "silly, ridiculous 30 year old." Met Andrea at Geronimo and spent far too much money. Lobster. Crab cakes. Andrea saw me on the street and screamed from her car, "God, honey, you look gorgeous!" Every diner on the patio turned to look. I was mortified, but still loved it. As we sat in the candle-lit bar listening to the diners quietly talking and the glasses pinging and the music low and soft, Andrea said, "Honey, I remember you ten years ago, less sure of everything. Now look at you!"

I said, "Right! And now I'm even less sure of everything than I was back then!"

She said, "That means you've grown tremendously."

Hmmmm, good point.

CHAPTER 24

Mystic Santa Fe

IT IS A SANTA FE sky without a cloud. A sky that, even after all these years, I have never taken for granted. Mom and I are driving in her RAV to meet Kay and Helmut, who live in El Dorado, an area about 25 minutes from Santa Fe, with many of the houses using solar energy. The houses are on flat earth, far apart, with views on one side up to the mountains and on the other across the desert until it looks like the world ends in a blue sky. It's slightly windy. The windows in the RAV are down and Mom and I are silent. Not for any reason. We're just comfortable in our silence.

Kay and Helmut are husband and wife. Helmut is a maker of the best coffee and cookies ever. Kay is a shaman. It isn't that I'm leery of shamans or healers. It's probably more that I don't understand. Then again, growing up in Santa Fe with dream catchers, crystals, healers, psychics, and all the "woo-woos," maybe I am a little skeptical. This feeling disappears completely and utterly the moment I meet Kay.

Kay and Helmut smile hugely and hug us both. Helmut immediately makes coffee and gives us raisin cookies and we talk about insignificant things.

Kay Whitaker

Mom, Helmut, and Kay talk. I'm quiet. I'm enthralled with Kay already even though we've barely spoken a word. We are sitting in a front room with the desert sun streaming in, making shadows and playing with the light on the floor and the furniture that is all mismatched and somehow still matches. We sit at a wooden table. I keep eating cookies. They keep talking. Kay is a large woman, but she somehow doesn't seem overweight. She wears a bright red dress. Her face is round, but her jaw and mouth are angular. Her dark hair is in wisps around her face. But it's her eyes that have me enthralled.

When I look at her, I fall away from the now. I can feel that she sees me, but that a part of her is in another place and she is looking at me from that other place. The feeling is unsettling and gentle and kind and natural all at once. She is hypnotizing while barely talking. I believe in her immediately. This woman knows things. She is not a psychic. She is not a healer. I keep eating my cookies and Helmut and Mom are talking about the desert and I try to think of what Kay does. I know she is a shaman, but I come up with one word as she silently looks at me from that other place: protector.

I am here for a bone-throwing, an ancient divination system. The main thing Kay does as a shaman is bone-throwing sessions. Bone-throwing is passed down among the women in the culture of the central eastern Andes. She learned about being a shaman during her thirteen years of training. Part of her training involved collecting small bones from animals. Some came from people who gave them to her. Some she found. She had a small red bag with shimmering fabric full of small bones. This was her Bone Bundle and each bone represented one of the Spirit Nations. I thought I would be horrified to see the bones. I thought it was gross to have collected bones over the years. I mean, really, I collect clocks. Seems much more normal to me. Then again, I can't "throw" my clocks and learn about anyone.

Kay turns to me and, without preamble of any kind, asks if we would like to start. "We" is what she says. She doesn't ask if I'd like to start. She says "we," as though we have to understand that each other is either ready or not. I take a breath for a second, look into her eyes that are now gentle and focused and not looking at me from that other place, and I say, "Yes." Off we go into a den-sized room on the other side of the house.

There are books all over and the room is cozy with a high window facing north. Even though it is mid-afternoon, the light coming from the northern window makes it feel like twilight. Not day. Not night. We sit down in the middle of the room and she asks if I'd like to record the session. I take no time at all in declining. This doesn't seem to be something that I should record. I don't know exactly what it will be, but it feels like something I am going to want to hold inside. Something I will want to let seep into me. Recording it feels like a modern accoutrement that shouldn't be used. Years later, I'll wish I hadn't declined so quickly.

Kay brings out a piece of cloth and throws it on the floor, a tight Berber carpeting, between us. Me on one side of the cloth, she on the other. It is burgundy, with symbols and circles and lines and levels, and looks almost three-dimensional. I later learn that this cloth, in Bone Throwing, is called the Ground. The Ground is created by each bone-thrower and is intricate and delicate and personal and unique to that shaman. I also later learn that it is, indeed, supposed to be viewed in a three-dimensional manner.

While Kay spreads out the Ground and lights a smudge stick to clear and purify the air from any previous sessions, I look up to the window, out to what looks like twilight. How odd it is that I am here. A Xanax-addicted, ex-heart patient with a life that seems so far from sitting out here in the middle of the desert with a shaman. Six months ago I didn't think I'd live. Now I'm confused about what my life is supposed to look like. Maybe that is why I'm so open to this: I'm desperate to find out what else is out there. Who is the After Jack? This is my question to Kay.

In each session, a question or issue can be presented and the answers and information are gleaned from the bones, gleaned from each Spirit Nation as they work together in the room and gather to Kay's energy. It is supposed to be, on one level, a healing process. I ask Kay, "Is it too large a question to ask who I am supposed to be now?" She looks at me and simply says, "No. Any question you want is fine. This is all up to you." Her voice is clear and full, but gentle. "Are you ready?" she says. "I guess," I say with an unsure twitch in my lips.

She laughs heartily and says, "Relax. Breathe." Why does everyone say this to me? Although, when I actually do it, it's irritatingly calming.

She holds the Bone Bundle in her hands and closes her eyes. She doesn't prepare me for anything. She doesn't tell me what she is going to do. I sit and watch. The room almost seems misty. She takes the bones out and they fall onto the Ground. She looks at them and adjusts some and moves others. We sit there for what seems like half an hour, but I think it is really only about five minutes. I feel an immense pressure in my head. Tears spring to my eyes. Anything with purity in it these days will make me cry. Anything that wipes away even a few of my layers will make me cry. Whatever Kay is doing is definitely fucking around with my layers. Every now and then, she looks at me from that other place. Then again, if I can make myself truly understand the meaning of the Spirit Nations and their gathering in this one spot, then it's not that Kay is looking at me from another place. It's that I'm being looked at by more than one person/thing/spirit/reality.

When Kay speaks again, her voice is softer. There is more breath in it. She's looking at me and it's just her. What she tells me is not psychic. It's not predictions. It's not guessing games as to what and/or who is or is not in my life. It's connectors, explanations, thoughts. It's like 100 therapy sessions all wrapped up in one without me having to say a word. The things that Kay tells me are healing. They are explanations. They are the connective tissue to so many things I already know.

At first, as she begins speaking, I find my lawyer head analyzing what she says. I think about one thing, "Hmmm, that's vague. Anybody could know that." And then about another, "Well, that is so specific, but she must have already figured it out since she knows all about me." Slowly something happens, and this is when the tears start. I begin not analyzing what Kay is saying. It all makes too much sense for me to tear it apart and put it together again. What she is saying is whole and complete already. And it is, with things that are vague and specific all at once, completely unique. I know this. Without question. In my heart.

I ask some questions. I can tell that some of her answers come from her, Kay, and what she knows about me, and some of the answers come from what she gleaned from the Bones and the Ground. Some she cannot answer and shrugs her shoulders. There is no pretense or subtext to any of this. It is what it is. When we are done, Kay is smiling happily. Almost Jubilant. I am torn apart and put back together. I'm pooped.

We leave the room and come out into the very sunny front room where Mom and Helmut are still sitting talking and eating cookies. They both smile as we come into the room, me in front of Kay. Mom, says, "So, how was it?"

Kay and I sit down at the table again and I say, "Pretty astounding. I'm exhausted." They all laugh. "Why is that so funny," I ask. I'm not upset. I feel like they know something I don't. (*Quel* shock that such a thing could happen at all!)

Mom says, "That is the way most people feel. It's exhausting. And it energizes Kay."

Helmut says, "She won't need any caffeine now!" We all laugh.

I say, "I'll need caffeine just to make it home without falling asleep in the car!"

We drive off down the desert road with Kay and Helmut standing outside their house waving goodbye. We drive east a bit into the dark sky and then turn around going west, heading toward a sun very low in the sky. Mom and I are, again, quiet, except she asks, "So, what did you find out?"

I look into the sky and say, quietly, "Stuff."

She laughs. "Honey, that a six-year-old's answer." We both laugh.

I say, "I think I'll keep most of it to myself." She takes her eyes off the road, smiles at me gently, and nods in respect.

She drops me off at the empty house and heads home to her own place. I go inside, feed the cat and lie down. I pick up the book I'm currently reading, *Rise and Fall of the Third Reich.* The tome I'm trying to get through since I have the time right now. Later that night, I go to bed early. And I fall asleep. Without any pills.

CHAPTER 25

You Can't Go Home Again, Or Can You?

6/19/01 10:24 a.m., Santa Fe Baking Company, Santa Fe

DAD RETURNED FROM VIETNAM TWO days ago. It isn't quite as relaxing with him home. There is a sense of loneliness or sadness around him. I can't put my finger on it because he appears genuinely happy about his marriage to Phuong. I just sense it when I'm around him and I'm trying to trust my instincts. To be as much of an intuit as possible. It is so easy for me to get into peoples' heads and figure out what they are about, and I'm rarely wrong. Sometimes, the logical, linear side of me gets overbearing and I forget to "feel" the truth. Strange though. It used to be Dad with the social life and friends. Now he seemingly has withdrawn from the world. At least the world outside of Vietnam. Mom now has friends that she spends lots of time with. I love to see her laugh. I worry about her job situation since her unemployment ends in a month, but there is not much I can do about that.

There is a potential job for me at the Hallmark Channel. They've called me for an interview. Twice. Part of me thinks I should do it and part of me wants the summer off. Completely. To figure out what path I should take next. I have no plans and it feels, for once in my life, so good. Am I blowing off an opportunity? Or do I trust my instincts and go with "my heart isn't in it?"

6/22/01 10 a.m., Starbucks, West Hollywood

I hopped on a plane yesterday in time to arrive for a 5 p.m. interview at the Hallmark Channel with a very nice and warm person, but she interrupted a lot. It was hard to explain what I'm about and what my qualifications are. Maybe she already decided I'm qualified from my resume? She immediately asked me, however, to fly back next week to do a satellite interview with the COO who is in Denver. Totally interferes with Lisa's visit, but I'll zip out here on Southwest for the interview and zip back to Santa Fe the same day. Not a clue if the job intrigue is ego-driven, money-driven, or genuine desire to see if I can do it since it's cable and I've never done anything with cable.

Last night I was going to see Eric, but we didn't connect because he wanted to stay in. Doesn't really matter since I'll be back in a few weeks for more heart tests. Richard and I went to Marks and had calamari and ahi tuna and martinis. I managed to have only one martini. I have so much faith in my life and choices now. I keep following my heart to a certain degree. Not following convention. And things come together. At least in my eyes, they do. It's astounding how powerful it is to ignore other peoples' opinions of who you're supposed to be.

6/23/01 6:17 p.m. Paris Hotel, Las Vegas
Since I had my 30th birthday in Paris, Lisa elected to have her 30th birthday in the Paris Hotel, Las Vegas. Oh my, this is the most over-the-top, ridiculous, tacky place I have ever seen! I love it! The plane ride out here was filled with equally ridiculous people. I sat next to a very tall woman with diamonds and platinum and Gucci. She chewed gum, had horrible grammar, and never said please and thank you. I thought, "Could you please use some of that money to buy lessons in poise and manners? Hawk a ring or something!"

It's like Disneyland for grown-ups. We hung out mostly at Mandalay Bay, had a delicious dinner at China Grill, cocktails at the Russian ice bar, and then went to a disco, Rum Jungle. The line went on for days! We hate lines! Isabel goes under the velvet rope, in front of the line, and puts an expression of "whatever" on her face. Lisa follows. Then me. Then Jon and Deb. Not one person said a word. They were probably so shocked at our audacity! Lisa said, "They can sense our New York-ness, so they won't fuck with us."

Tonight we're going to Emeril's for Lisa's birthday dinner. I gave her a bottle of Cristal, so we'll bring it and crack it open. I'll wear my square-toe K.

Cole shoes, black Donald J. Pliner belt with the small silver buckle, my silk/linen grey shirt, and Max Azria charcoal pants.

7/2/01 9:36 a.m., Starbucks, West Hollywood

Vegas was so much fun. I must have turned two or three ethnicities darker from the sun. And I didn't gain weight from all the rich, fabulous food we were constantly eating. China Grill. Emeril's. Olive. We all gambled a bit. Jon won $500 at craps! I won $40 in quarters at a slot machine. None of us really drank too much. We were all much more dressed up than anyone else anywhere we went. Looking like we always look to go out in NYC in the evening. Lisa in her Diane von Furstenberg dress and Tiffany jewelry. Me in my Gucci/Max Azria/Donna Karan/Whatever. Of course, all my clothes generally look the same.

Sunday night it was just Lisa and me and Lisa's parents. Everybody else had left that morning. Lisa's parents took us to the very expensive Italian restaurant at the Mirage. Truly lovely dinner and I swear it felt like I was out with the in-laws. Lisa and I look like a young, upscale couple when we're together. We're sure some people think either 1) oh, what a gorgeous couple or 2) I wonder if she knows her boyfriend is gay?

Monday, Lisa and I flew to Albuquerque. I had left the Beemer at the airport, so we raced to Santa Fe, changed into out sweats, grabbed a bottle of Cristal and some sushi and took the Land Cruiser up to the ridge to toast her 30th birthday as the sun set over Santa Fe and the New Mexico desert. Glorious. We laughed and talked about our families, fears, hopes—the usual things such a moment brings out in two close friends. I wanted to give her a really nice memory for her 30th and she said I did. She is, after all, my non-sexual common-law wife. We spent afternoons by the pool at the club, drinks and appetizers at Santa Café, and Geronimo each evening. One night at Santa Café, a woman, rather tipsy, started chatting with us. Her daughter wants to be a film director. It came out that both Lisa and I are entertainment attorneys. Suddenly the bartender was right there, telling us we don't look or act like lawyers. Lisa and I, at the exact same time, answered him, "Thank God!"

Opera night was magnificent! We bought Dom Pérignon and caviar and other goodies, brought a white linen table cloth (actually a stolen hospital sheet from my days of heart hell), and candles. It's a tradition for everybody to have a tailgate party in the parking lot of the Santa Fe Opera on opening night. Lisa wore her red-and-black Von Furstenberg dress and I wore my Hugo Boss suit and black Donna Karan shirt. I must say, we looked gorgeous. It was all such fun. Everybody having dinner on little tables behind their cars or at big tables set up in the parking lot. Glamorous, but in such a very down-to-earth-let's-have-fun-with-it manner. The Sangre de Cristo mountains on one side, a blue sky blue filled with clouds here and there on the other. An orange and pink sunset over the desert. Breathtaking. Lisa saw some girls looking at me and said, "Stop cruising my nonsexual husband!"

I saw guys looking at her and said, "You definitely could find a sugar daddy here." Fits of laughter.

7/4/01 8:46 a.m., Starbucks, West Hollywood
Fourth of July. In NYC, I'd often sit on my terrace high above the city and watch spectacular fireworks over the East River. Turn on the TV to hear the music played along with the show. Mesmerizing light bursts. Usually Brent and I would do it alone without inviting people. I recall one July 4th in Provincetown on top of Gerry and Dean's roof watching the fireworks over the bay. It is easy to think of those days and miss it. To feel nostalgic for the image of what was. Yet, I know in my heart that beneath the ease and gloss was a layer of dysfunction and unhappiness. Stress and tension between Brent and me. He's not a bad person, but I would never go back with him. I've never found myself missing his company. We stopped having fun together. We stopped playing. I realize I only really began dealing with our break-up after my heart surgery. Prior to that I was so busy with my life, with surviving, with DreamWorks, planning heart surgery, and my move to L.A.. So, my "getting over it" only began in the last few months.

7/7/01 11:56 a.m., Buzz Coffee, West Hollywood
Bailey called last night after looking at my heart test results and said that my heart has shrunk back down to normal size. I almost jumped up and down like a little kid. I was terrified that my heart would get bigger and bigger and that I'd need a full transplant one day. Thirty-year-olds are not supposed to have to worry about such things.

7/12/01 11:28 a.m., Downtown Subscription, Santa Fe
Hallmark phoned and I did not get the job. It came down to me and someone else and the someone else had more experience. Myriad Pictures phoned,
however, and wants to interview me for a Director of Business Affairs position. Christine wants to send me a D3 pass to go to Aruba with her. Steve
Badeau invited me to Provincetown with him and friends at the end of July.
Plans, plans, plans. Money, money, money. The confusion of choices gets
overwhelming, but that's not really a thing to complain about. Besides, I don't
have the money for any of it. Poverty is really irritating.

When Nora and Eric were visiting, I organized a brunch at St. Francis.
Nora, Eric, Adam, Mom, and me. It was great! Mom looked gorgeous. All
these people I adore beyond description and I watched them laugh and play
with each other and it made me so happy. Nora told a story about being in
love when she was 25 and living in Russia. They had planned on getting married, but her fiancé was told by the KGB that he had to drop her or he would
lose his business dealings since Nora is Jewish. How can something so cruel
break a love into two pieces, in the name of God?

Adam and I had dinner at Il Vicino the other night, sitting outside on the
patio. At some point he said I was charmed. Not that things come easily for
me, but that they seem to work out one way or another. That I have a lucky
star. How many people have told me that? The irony of being told I lead a
charmed life six months after open heart surgery is thick. Then again, I lived.
That's pretty damn blessed.

I'm high strung again. The whole reason for spending the summer in
Santa Fe was to relax from my life. Yet, I've allowed myself to be fast again. I
told Lisa and her response was, "Fuck fuck fuckity fuck fuck fuck." I told Eric
and he said, "But dear, you ARE fast!"

7/14/01 9:31 a.m., Starbucks, Santa Fe
My optometrist told me yesterday that I have the very beginnings of glaucoma.
Glaucoma? At 30? It's not so much the actual fact that shocks me, I suppose.
I've had open heart surgery, a thoracentesis, a thoracotomy, an ablation. But

really? Now glaucoma, too! I do think I've been medically challenged enough. So, great. I'll live because my heart now works, but I'll be blind when I'm old. Lovely. My morbid sense of humor is my only protection against the pity party I seem to so often be invited to!

Karen Green may have a consulting job for me at Mattel Toys. We're going to talk about it more in depth next week. I'd rather declare bankruptcy and go back to being a flight attendant. Yet, I couldn't afford my student loans on that job, so it's pie in the sky. All these opportunities and I want to go back to zipping through the air at 30K feet in a metal tube all the time. Who on earth would understand that it was my favorite job of all?

7/16/01 9:30 a.m., Downtown Subscription, Santa Fe

I have been spending entirely too much time with Adam. He's so nice and kind and he kisses like a god. Yet, I'm not in love. I'm not thunderstruck. I haven't been hit over the head. He seems almost innocuous. Isn't that a horrible thing to say about someone? He hasn't had enough life experience for me. He's an old soul, but he's only 25 and some things come with age. I'd rather have poor and over-the-top than rich and innocuous, which clearly means I'm fucked in the head about relationships. Richard tells me, "Jack, you're a non-dater." Am I that afraid of rejection? There is still so much to learn about myself that it's almost annoying.

Matt called the other day and wants me to go to Argentina with him for a few days. He'll give me a pass. Adorable Matt. Why is he so irresistible to me? The fact is that he is semi-closeted, a huge flirt, cute beyond words and knows it. I will never forget him giving me a blowjob on the 777 simulator during training. And in the hallway of the hotel. The hallway! We were inseparable. Then training was over and I was back in NYC and my life with Brent and left Matt to fend for himself in NYC. Not a proud moment for me. But those memories of our little affair (which Brent knew about and was fine with; I should have known that was the beginning of our downfall), the Hyatt, the wine tasting, the bars in Dallas, making out on all the airplane simulators. Fun memories.

7/18/01 10 p.m., Il Vicino, Santa Fe
Decided to have dinner here alone on the patio. It's breezy and clear. A table of two chatty women nearby. A table of two guys in their 20s discussing girlfriend problems. A waitress lights a lamp for me. I have begun to feel a little frantic lately. As though I must begin making decisions again. The point of a summer in Santa Fe was no decisions. As Lisa pointed out, I'm probably not ready to make them yet. I feel drawn back to L.A. and the entertainment industry again. A return to my former life, but not to my former self because I don't know where he is. I want to feel the calm, the centering I feel when I think about what is truly meaningful for me, but a part of me is pulled back to the fast life into which I fit so easily. Expensive car. Designer clothes. VIP invites. Premieres. First class traveling at the drop of a hat. Ya know, all those things are fine, but only tangentially. They are, for better or worse, part of my life.

Mom said, "People parade you around and you let them because it feels good." It's fine, but seeing life through the eyes of a 30-year-old survivor of such extensive terror makes it a mockery. And I never want to be ridiculous. Dana paraded me around, but also told me I live life in the present better than anyone he knew. But, didn't I have to? The choice, then, was victim or grand boy diva, since I didn't know how to be anything but extreme.

Today I raced around Santa Fe in the Beemer, tan skin, CK white t-shirt, dark sunglasses, music loud and fun, sipping my iced Americano, taking calls on my cell phone. A cliché image of the hot, privileged, snotty boy. Then I sat at Starbucks on the plaza and read Anna Quindlen's new book, *A Short Guide To A Happy Life*. I cried right there in Starbucks because I have already learned so many of those lessons too fast, too forced. Now I have to put them into action and I don't know how. Maybe that's the point of the After Jack—not only to acknowledge that I've learned a lot, but also to do something about it.

7/29/01 10:52 a.m., Starbucks, Santa Fe
I told Adam we have to cool it. As nice and sweet as he is, and as much as I wish my feelings were stronger, they are not. Annoying when someone has all these great qualities, yet your heart isn't in it. I really do irritate myself.

The Executive Vice President of Legal Affairs at Paramount Studios called me the other day and left a message to call her back. I hadn't even applied there and I had no clue who she was. Once I did call her, I found out she had gotten my resume from someone at Viacom and wanted me to come interview for a production attorney job in the television division. I'm winging out to L.A. for the interview.

8/2/01 10:55 a.m., Koffee Klatch, Laguna Beach
My interviews at Paramount went, I think, very well yesterday. I drove through the main gate of the studio into the venerable old lot, parked, looked around and remembered so vividly when I used to work here as an intern in a casting office. Seems like an eternity ago. I was only 17. In the closet. Unaware of so much. It was magic to me. The facades and cavernous sound stages. Costumed actors walking around. Filming here and there. The energy. People rushing to a set, to an office, to the world "outside." I almost laugh to remember how important I felt.

I met with nine lawyers, one after another. They all appeared casual and good-humored. Of course, they are lawyers, so I'm not fooled. Nonetheless, it felt comfortable. Like I'd fit in. Milinda, the head of the department, seemed like the perfect boss. Then again, so did Pam at DreamWorks and she turned out to be a total nightmare. We didn't discuss salary or when I'd start, but I already have decided I'd take it. My instincts, which I am endeavoring to trust once again, tell me it'd be right for me. I have no idea why, but I feel it. Even though I still would love to figure out how to afford serving drinks at 30K feet in the air again. Am I insane?

8/12/01 11:19 a.m., Downtown Subscription, Santa Fe
Each time I think I have recovered from the heart thing, on all levels, I realize a few hours/days/months later that I haven't. Emotionally. Sometimes I'm pulled to such vivid memories and images and I cry a little. Nothing like before. But it's still there and I wonder if it will ever go away. I do find I have less need to tell people. Even three months ago I managed to fit it into every

conversation. Now, I keep it to myself more. Maybe I want to be treated like everyone else. To blend in. That'd be a first.

8/18/01 C.G.s Coffeehouse, Magazine Street, New Orleans

Stacy and I flew here two days ago to have fun. Last night we walked along the river and it was so musty, so humid. The atmosphere reeked of being lazy and hedonistic. Jazz bands played in restaurants and bars, the horns and voices seeping into the streets. The foliage overflowing from behind iron lattices and fences. Everything damp. Fortune tellers beneath gas lamps in Jackson Square. Boys tap dancing shirtless and glistening with sweat in the streets. The galleries and antique stores on the classy and relaxed Royal Street. The frat house atmosphere and sex shops and bars on Bourbon only one block away. Even the humidity is bearable. It seems to fit with the rest of the ambiance.

Last night Stacy and I went out to the Quarter. Stacy wore black jeans and a black t-shirt. I wore black jeans and a black tank top. Stacy said I looked like a gymnast. I had to laugh. I'll always, no matter how I look, feel like the skinny guy. Once in the quarter, we began drinking immediately. Alcoholic slurpees. We ended up at Oz and Parade—clubs directly across the street from each other. Exposed brick. Iron latticework. Balconies overlooking the dance floor. Archways and little rooms. An outside balcony where I went to have a breather at one point, watching the action below me on Bourbon Street. The quaint houses and how French it all looked except for the clapboards and lack of stonework. So wonderful to stand on that balcony in the New Orleans night seeing the gas lamps and people in the Quarter, not minding the moisture against my skin. Stacy and I ran around and got very, very drunk. It was marvelous.

I get drunk so easily now. Ever since my heart "enhancement," as I've begun to call it. Being drunk and all, I elected to participate in the Calendar Boy contest at Oz, which was to be at midnight. Unfortunately, I didn't understand what I was supposed to do and I was the first one called up. I assumed I'd get up there, take my shirt off, and get down. But, no. All of a sudden in my drunken haze, I was up there with this enormous black drag queen telling me to take my clothes off. ALL of them! She gave me a cup to hold over my penis. I got as far as taking off my shirt and the drag queen tried to take off my pants and I didn't let her. Thank goodness that even through my drunken haze I knew I would not want to stand naked on the stage at a bar in New Orleans. Tacky! I jumped off the stage, put on my shirt, grabbed Stacy and ran out. Stacy said I looked hot, but very shy. The drag queen said, as I zipped off the stage, "Well, I never in all my years saw somebody get up here and not do a thing!" We left before I found out who won. Another one of those experiences I cringe at, but don't really regret. Knowing me, though, I'll run into someone who will recognize me somewhere. "You kind of stripped in New Orleans. Wasn't that you?" Oh dear. We did go back later and found out that I came in second place. First place was a muscle boy who was a professional stripper.

8/22/01 11:10 a.m., Downtown Subscription, Santa Fe
Our remaining time in New Orleans was slightly less eventful. And no alcohol. We drove around Magazine Street, walked around Tulane, strolled in the parks and walked by the river. Ate what seemed like a thousand beignets at Café Du Monde in the French Quarter. This city combines the utmost elegance and grace with the most uneducated crassness. On Saturday evening, we went back to Oz, where I had my lovely, semi-uninhibited stripping extravaganza. I can never tell anyone about this. I'd be mortified. The guy who won the contest was up on the bar stripping and strutting around; he recognized me, took my hat off, took his underwear off, and covered his penis with my hat. Seriously, that would be a lovely way to get crabs. In my hair! The hat got thrown out. I did meet the most gorgeous guy I have ever met and kissed wildly on the dance floor. He said his name was Rocky and he lives in Mississippi. Twenty-three years old. A model. He asked what I "do" when I go clubbing. I guess not doing any drugs was incomprehensible to him. Truly the most stunning and beautiful guy I have ever touched.

8/25/01 11:25 a.m. Starbucks, West Hollywood
I'm back out here to have dinner with the group of lawyers from Paramount. It's a spectacular, sunny day. Breezy and warm. Upon arrival at LAX yesterday,

I rented a Jeep Cherokee 4x4. Very fun. My first car was a land cruiser and then I had the Bronco II for years. What can I say?

Met Eric at the Abbey. He drank. I did not. He quipped and told stories and I was aloof and uppity, so above it all. I don't like to feel that way and it's even worse that it comes naturally now. Seriously, I cannot quite figure myself out lately. I've never felt more like an adult in my life. Sure of myself, able to be helpful to others, confident about my future in whatever form it may take. Safe in the knowledge that I'm healthy, and even a little proud of myself. I feel no need to defend myself, to tell anyone of my accomplishments (so many of which feel so little and small in the face of the enormity of this past year), or even discuss my surgeries anymore. It's a little unsettling. It all feels genuine and very easy, serene, yet the image of me without the grandiose over-wrought views of life, constant witty comments, being loudly "above it all" instead of quietly "above it all" takes some getting used to.

After a short nap between the Abby and Felt, I ended up having calamari and two glasses of wine at Marks. Then, back to the Abby and everyone rushed to say hello and welcome back. AJ said I looked "luscious." I cackled. That's what I do. It's so ridiculous, I either cackle at compliments or shy away from them. I haven't learned how to take a compliment gracefully. I could have run around doing Jack-Fabulous, but was simply quiet and enjoyed myself, by no means the Jack-of-Old. A part of me missed it.

Roy left me a voicemail saying his t-cells are very high, but that his viral load is undetectable. I think back ten years ago to that summer of 1992 when I was just coming out and Roy was mentor, best-friend, non-sexual lover. It seems almost unreal that we've both gone through so much since then. So much that would have been beyond anything we could have imagined, both good and awful. Maybe that's why, at 30, I am finally beginning to feel like an adult.

Fuck, I know I have a hernia. Must go see Dr. Wolfe on Monday. Just what I fucking need: Another damn surgery.

8/31/01 12:00 p.m., The Big Cup, NYC
Absolutely astounding to be back in this place. I couldn't even begin to count the number of mornings I sat here writing in my journal, ecstatic at the day,

confused with my life, confident, insecure, and every other emotion I could possibly imagine. I love the diversity here and it's such an unlikely place to find it. Boys in suits, women with kids, grungy boys, muscle boys, girls, people reading books, studying, cruising. A little microcosm of life. Above it all, though, it is another representation of my time in NYC.

Last night Lisa and I walked through the Village on cobblestone streets amidst trees blowing in the breeze and clusters of people scurrying in and out of the charming restaurants on every corner. We ate at Nadine's with its wood paneling, crystal chandeliers, dark wood tables, lack of pretense, and delicious food. We had considered going to Menu or Pastis, but decided against it. Food no longer impresses me and few of the "it" restaurants do either. I've done it all, usually without waiting in a line or for a reservation. My own ability to do this no longer impresses me. So, we chose quaint and cozy and yummy over fabulous and chic.

The best thing about this trip is that I don't long to be living here like I used to. I miss it terribly and still think it's the ultimate city, yet I don't wish to be any place in life other than where I am right now. I suppose I'm content. What a concept! And the funniest thing about it is that I don't really have any outside stability. No job, no permanent place to live, etc. Everything is up in the air. And yet, inside, I feel at peace.

9/3/01 11:22 a.m., The Big Cup, NYC
I went to see the revival of "42nd Street" yesterday. Sitting there in my 4th row center orchestra seat, I realized with a slight degree of shock that I'm now old enough to have seen the original of a show that is now a revival! I saw the touring production at the National Theater in DC when I was 13. It was one of the musicals I used to escape from the hollowness of my life without friends, from mom and dad fighting, the misery of being in the closet (which I had yet to define).

Walking back to Lisa's down 8th Ave after the show, I saw the remnants of Wigstock. Drag queens in all their finery. A tall black man wearing only a magenta-sequined G-string, short grey fur coat and spiked heels was the most fabulous. Just walking in the street. Some people watched. Some people didn't blink an eye. This is Manhattan, after all. I loved it! The freedom and diversity. You see someone being themselves and not giving a shit what some-one else thinks, and that confident sense of defiance rubs off a little. Yes, that is a quality I like in people: Quietly, confidently defiant. I will forever, I think, love the diversity of the human condition. It never fails to amaze me.

9/5/01 7:21 a.m., on plane to Buenos Aires, Argentina
Monday evening I took a long walk down the promenade by the Hudson River to Battery Park. I remembered the thrill of rollerblading there when I first moved to NYC. I was only 24. I never found myself anything less than positively filled with life at seeing the twin towers zoom toward me as I raced down the promenade faster and faster. Majestic is the only appropriate word for what Manhattan looks like from that vantage point.

I took Lisa to Sushi Samba for lunch. Took a bit of a nap, packed, and decided to go to Argentina with Matt on his work trip. I didn't sleep at all last night, but it doesn't matter. I'm in premium class on the 777 in my "flagship suite" with tons of room, full length bed, chair that swivels to look directly out the window. I have been pampered, complimented, and loaded down with nine bottles of wine. The sun is coming up and I've swiveled my chair to look directly out the window at a layer of clouds turning orange in the early morn-ing light.

It's early in the morning on September 7, 2001. I have just arrived in JFK after an all-night flight from Argentina with Matthew. I was so exhausted that I slept on the floor in Business Class since Premium was full and I couldn't get comfortable in my business class seat. *Quel* glamour. As a former flight attendant, not to mention someone relatively intelligent, I should know that airplane floors are dirty. Very.

The plan is that I will take the 8 a.m. to Boston this morning and stay with Tom and David. Then I'll go back to L.A. on the morning flight five days later. I haven't seen them since my open heart surgery and I miss David's laugh and his self-awareness and how funny and open he is. There is a huge part of me, however, that wonders if the people who loved me before will love me now. I feel like I used to be so full of energy and passion and craziness. Now it doesn't seem to be here. I keep wondering where I went.

Turns out I am too exhausted to go to Boston, so I take the 8 a.m. transcon to L.A. instead. Then back to Santa Fe a few days later. It's too gorgeous to miss Santa Fe at the beginning of Fall. I'm in Santa Fe when the twin towers are hit and thousands of people are killed. It is only later that afternoon that I do the math. Had I gone to Boston to see Tom and David, the flight I was going to take back to L.A. from Boston would have been the morning transcon to L.A. on American Airlines. At 8 a.m. On September 11, 2001. As Lisa has said for years, "These things only happen to you, Jack." Or, rather, this thing did not happen to me. Since it didn't happen to me, I have a hard time telling the story. Too many people died to make it about myself.

9/10/01 10 a.m., Downtown Subscription, Santa Fe

I keep waiting for this feeling of enlightenment to lessen: this belief in goodness and how amazing life is to such an extreme. The further away I get from the heart debacle, the stronger this feeling becomes. Not that I don't have "down" feelings, but they are always tempered by this consistent feeling that all will be okay. Perspective. That's it. My perspective seems to always remain in place.

My hernia is acting up and I am to see a surgeon this afternoon to possibly have surgery next week. I tell everyone I am completely unconcerned. How can I be upset over a little hernia after all I've been through? How can I complain? There is only so much people can take. To tell them something that would inspire even more showing of love and sympathy and "being there" would be selfish. Yet, I am scared something will go wrong. It's stupid, I know, but things do go wrong in surgeries. I really hate the idea of another surgery, no matter how simple. The feeling of the operating table in another crowded operating room with the bright light overhead before I go under is all too familiar.

I still cry when I think of my heart stuff. It comes on suddenly and always with the feeling of, "I can't believe I almost wasn't here." Not self-pity. Overwhelming gratitude. Tremendous disbelief that I went through it. On one hand, it all seems so unreal. On the other hand, it's too real, even six months later. Hard to forget when I see the gash on my chest in the mirror every morning.

9/21/01 10:46 a.m., Downtown Subscription, Santa Fe
Hernia surgery over. All is well. I had a little bit of a panic when I was in recovery. "Is my heart okay? Did it keep beating correctly?" I even demanded to see my chart to determine if it kept a normal rhythm. That was the point at which the nurse elected to give me a huge shot of Versed. Probably more for her own sanity than mine.

The next day I decided to go to a Rosh Hashanah luncheon given by one of the synagogue members. All these people I haven't seen since I was little were there. And word had, apparently, gotten around about my heart surgery. Everyone seemed genuinely pleased to see me and know I was okay. Of course, I behaved like the victim-with-grace and I know they all thought I looked great. Someone said everybody should have my attitude. I do have a good attitude. At least, I try. It's difficult, though, to convince myself it's not manipulation simply because I know the effect of my actions.

9/29/01 1:10 p.m. Downtown Subscription, Santa Fe
Milinda McNeely from Paramount Studios emailed me that, after two months of interviews, I am on their short list of four candidates. Flattering, but at both Viacom and Hallmark it came down to me or someone else and someone else got it.

10/5/01 12:07 p.m. Downtown Subscription, Santa Fe
Still no word from Paramount. KTG did, however, make a preliminary offer to work as a temporary attorney at Mattel Toys. Approximately three months at a very good salary. I'll be screwed if this doesn't come to fruition. My finances are completely fucked at the moment.

Have decided that if I do work at Mattel, I need to keep my eye on the prize. Get out of debt, save to buy a condo, find stability. My 20s were over the top and crazy ridiculous fun. Wouldn't trade them for anything. But now I want something different. Stability doesn't have to be dull. I've always been a proponent of balance (despite failing miserably at finding it in my life).

CHAPTER 26

What's Paramount in Life?

I'M BACK IN L.A. WORKING at Paramount Studios. It is one of those clear, breezy Spring days. I love driving onto the studio lot and walking underneath the arch—the original Paramount arch that predates the big double arch everyone sees in publicity photographs. I like that I know it is the original and a lot of people don't. I like even more that it is part of the story I tell when I give tours to friends.

I don't ever get bored of walking around the studio, the oldest actual movie studio. Gigantic sound stages. Freighter-like, sound-proof doors and red lights flashing outside letting you know something magical is going on inside. A story is unfolding. Everything is a story, except here the stories get put on film. Here they become permanent, stuck in time.

My favorite part of the studio is New York Street. It isn't really a street; it is part of the back lot. The Huxtable home is here. The school where Rizzo, Sandy, and Danny went to school is here. I saw a Gap commercial with Madonna one day that I noticed was filmed here. Part of New York Street can be made to look like the upper east side, the lower east side, the village, or midtown. There's even a subway entrance that actually goes underground. I like to go to the café underneath the huge waterpower that says "Paramount Studio," get lunch and then sit on the stoop of one of the facades. If you go inside the facades, it's still magic. There are ladders and electrical grids and lights set up from whatever was shot here last. There are curtains hanging in some of the windows. Some of them are new from something just shot; some are in tatters because they were never removed from something shot a while ago. I'll have a friend go into one of the building facades, climb a ladder or staircase, and I'll take a picture of them looking out one of the windows. You'd never know he/she wasn't actually in NYC at the time. When friends come to visit, I walk them around the lot, pointing out where *Star Trek* was filmed or *Sunset Boulevard* or "Frasier" or "Cheers," or any number of famous television shows or movies. I like to say "Stage 18, Ms. Desmond" when we come to the sound stage where most of *Sunset Boulevard* was shot. It's fun. It's a game. It's magic.

Movie and TV stars walk around so much that it becomes ordinary. The "Nip/Tuck" show was shot in the soundstage next to my office building. Their dressing room trailers were outside and I always saw the guys, who were even hotter in person. Robert Evans' office was in my building. I'm more impressed seeing him than a lot of stars. He's a legend. I saw Sydney Poitier in Whole Foods one time and was very impressed, but seeing an actor shop for organic vegetables is just not the same as seeing them about to walk into a soundstage to shoot a scene the whole world will be watching at some point. But still, when Sydney bought the organic blueberries, I decided I should buy them, too.

One day I'm in my office and Ma calls to tell me someone's sister, who she works with on the Indian reservation, has major heart problems and is at St. Vincent's Hospital in Santa Fe and may need a heart transplant. She adds, "I've told them that you will go see her in the hospital." She volunteered me without asking me first. Lovely.

The woman's name is Renee. She has three daughters, a husband, a family. She is 40-ish, I guess. Way too young to need a heart transplant, I think to myself. Funny how that works. All of a sudden, I have a way to brush off my own experience, "Well, even though I was 30, that was just me. But you? At 40? A heart transplant? A family? There's the true tragedy." A subtle way of telling myself that her death would be a worse tragedy than mine.

I fly to Santa Fe, but I'm pissed at Ma for volunteering me. She knows I want to help, but she shouldn't volunteer me for something this sensitive. This emotional. I never know what I can handle from one moment to the next. Ma is sitting in the chilly fall sun on her patio drinking coffee, her hands wrapped around the mug. Sunglasses on. Looking very chic and hip for someone who spent part of last year worrying that her kid might die and the other part worrying about how he would choose to recover. I say hello and I mention Renee and we have this staccato conversation without any pauses.

"Ma, why did you promise I would help this woman?"

"Because you should do it."

"It's very difficult for me."

"It's more difficult for her."

"You don't understand."

"I probably don't."

"I have to make my own choices about things like this."

"You don't always get to make choices."

Now I'm pissed and I throw my hands into the air, back up a step, all exaggerated gestures and drama.

"You're saying this to ME? That I don't get to make choices? That I haven't somehow, strangely figured this out?"

She gets up and gets right into my face. All 5'2" of her. And whips her sunglasses off.

"You just made my point. You of all people know that sometimes there isn't do or do not, there is just do."

Oh. Right. I wonder if she meant to sound like Yoda.

Two hours later I'm in a hallway in St. Vincent's Hospital trying to find Renee's room. I've been here before, I think to myself. At first I think that it's because any hospital will feel familiar now. The slightly sweet disinfectant smell. The fluorescent lights glaring onto a polished beige linoleum floor. The whirring sound of a floor waxer down the hall. The worst part, the absolutely worst thing I hate about hospitals, is looking into rooms and seeing people lying there helplessly. The people who look really, really sick. Not the people who are simply watching TV or reading or sleeping, but the people who truly look like they can't move, like they are all alone. Like nobody comes to see them. I feel so guilty. Should go in and say something for five minutes to each one? Five minutes would never be enough, so I don't do anything. Why is it that we think we'd feel guiltier if we did only a tiny something to help than if we do nothing at all?

I walk like a zombie down the hallway. Little bits of sunlight come from the windows in the hospital rooms. Then it hits me. I know why this is all so familiar. I know why I am getting a creeping sense of terror and feeling almost out of control. Like I'm about to lose it. It's not because I'm scared of hospitals. It's because I just passed the room where, fifteen years ago, my mom had been after her mastectomy, when we were all preparing for her to die from breast cancer that was caught much, much too late.

During the actual operation, I left the hospital. I went to synagogue and sat in the empty sanctuary. Just sat there. I didn't even cry. It was all so beyond my 16-year-old head that I don't think my emotions knew what to do with themselves. I went from driving my jeep home from high school blasting "Depeche Mode" one moment to, an hour later, finding out mom had cancer and had to have a breast removed. So, during the surgery, I ended up at temple.

I'm not a particularly religious person. I like being Jewish. It seems to be a nonjudgmental religion. It doesn't seek to inspire fear. I never had to "recruit" people to be Jewish or tell them it was a "better" religion. It was simply the way I was taught to see God. I have nice memories of growing up with this. In fact, the only nice memories I have of us as a family, all four of us together, involve the synagogue. I'm glad my parents didn't ruin that. Because when I think of being Jewish, it still makes me feel good, safe, accepted and accepting. Like religion is supposed to, right? My dad isn't religious at all. I think if you asked him, he would say he's Jewish, but I don't know for sure. He doesn't even go to Yom Kippur services. But Dad told me that he spent time in the little synagogue at Cedars. Did he pray? Or did he just sit there and think?

When I walked into Renee's room, her sister and husband were there. I awkwardly introduced myself, feeling like such an intruder. I introduced myself to the woman lying in bed in an ugly blue hospital gown. She had big, brown eyes, an oval face, dark brown hair pulled back and a huge, wonderful smile. Very Native American. I told her who I was and why I was there. As I sat down next to her bed, her family left the room so It was just the two of us alone. Despite helping others and talking on the internet to heart patients and their families, this felt different. Renee got into my head immediately. Instant connection. And it scared the hell out of me to care suddenly on a more personal level for someone who was probably going to have a heart transplant. I knew right then and there I would have to stick with it until . . . well, until whatever was going to happen, happened.

I was all hunched over in my chair like I was five years old. The first thing that popped into my head was the only thing I could say. "This kinda sucks, doesn't it," with a grimace on my face.

She smiles, giggles, "Ya, it kinda does."

"Nobody really says that to you though, do they?"

She rolls her eyes, "No." She pauses. Then she adds, "Maybe they think I haven't figured it out yet."

And we laugh uproariously. Huge, deep laughs. I am relieved beyond words that this is someone I can talk to. Renee seems relieved beyond words too.

"People don't want to scare you," I say.

She looks out the window for a moment to the deep blue, cloudless, sunny Santa Fe sky and says, without looking at me, "No, Jack, people don't want to scare themselves."

Oh. Right. Wow.

A few weeks later, Renee calls me from U.C.L.A. where she has been waiting for a heart. It's here. A little girl died in a car accident. Renee gets her heart. She tells me almost casually, but I understand. I remember what it's like when the emotions are gone from your voice. They are tucked so deep inside that nobody can see them in your face or hear them in your voice. Without a word to anyone, I race out of my office, tear out of the parking lot of Paramount, and drive as fast as possible to U.C.L.A.

I held Renee's hand right before she was taken into surgery. It was an honor. I was the last one to say goodbye because her family hadn't arrived yet by airplane. Still, there was something about it that felt like an honor to be trusted that I could provide her with a sense of security. Maybe because

I know how very, very hard it is to trust anyone. To let anyone reassure me. Yet, I tried, and Renee trusted me with her security. With her fear. Maybe I've never been trusted like that before. People know I'm trustworthy, but this is not that kind of trust. She didn't know me. Not really. Yet, she trusted me. The honor went to her for being able to do that. I felt somehow safe with her trust. I knew she was right to trust me. I had faith in myself. As though I had finally come full circle and went from patient to helper. I knew what I was saying. I knew what I was doing. I knew what she needed to hear and what I shouldn't bother with.

We were outside a set of double doors. Dim fluorescent lighting, nobody around. It doesn't seem right that before heart surgery Renee should be lying on a gurney in an empty hallway with bad lighting. Apparently, I'm past the point of thinking it's not right that she's here for heart surgery at all. I'm clearly more focused on the bad lighting. When I look down, I see the fear in her eyes. As though it's finally so real to her. I can see her thinking, "It's here." It's a strong feeling. Very pure. It blocks out anything you have ever thought, done, felt, or seen. As though it is the most important and true realization you will ever have. And it is horrifyingly lonely. Nobody is there with you, no matter how many people are around you. I remember that moment of true fear despite the fact that I was bombed out of my mind on Xanax at the time, which reminds me . . . I lean down and tell her I'll see her when she's done.

As they wheel her away, after I let go of her hand, she giggles. After the door closes and she is gone, her sister looks at me, confused, and asks, "Why did she giggle?"

"Because the last thing I said to her was 'tell them to give you massive amounts of drugs immediately'."

I also reminded her how to poo after her surgery. You can't push because that would hurt your chest. You sit on the toilet and breathe in and out as deeply as you can. And it works! It's like this little miracle of excrement! Who knew pooping could be so easy? That's what she really laughed at, but I didn't feel like telling her sister that my last words to Renee were about taking a shit.

After I watched Renee have a heart transplant, I stopped helping other heart patients. I got scared. What if someone I was trying to help died?

Someone I had gotten close to like Renee? How could I handle it? I've felt shitty that I stopped helping people because I know how selfish it is. I wish I was above it. I'm embarrassed that I'm not. Of course, the question looms in my head: What if people didn't/don't help me because they are scared that I might die?

Almost exactly six years post open heart surgery, I'm sitting in my apartment in Beverly Hills late on a Saturday night. Doing laundry. It's a little breezy outside, just the way I like it. The cat is sleeping on the oriental rug. Yes, I have a cat now. He is black and white. A tuxedo cat, clearly very sophisticated. In my ego-less state, I have named him Jackie. I am watching a repeat of an episode of "Six Feet Under." In the episode, there is a waiting room where people are sitting, waiting. Then there is the doctor telling the family Nate is alive,

Jackie

but may have stroke-related problems. They show Nate in a hospital bed, in a coma, attached to all the tubes. And I am sobbing. It pisses me off because it never fucking leaves my head, even after all this time has passed.

There are so many ways a heart can break.

I know that the heart is a strong muscle, but a fragile flower, held in the hands of those who love both its tenderness and its strength. It's not only the skilled surgeons—who cut out my heart and replaced its defective valve, then somehow miraculously started it up again—who have held my heart in their hands. It's also my parents and brother who hold my heart, each in their own way, and the cousins and aunts and uncles and nanas. It's also the gay friends, some confronting their own mortality in the face of AIDS, who brought a teddy bear to the hospital stuffed with their compassion. It's the parents' friends who hold vigil and send prayers of healing. It's the boss at work who says take all the time you need, I understand.

How many hands hold one broken heart? In the web of life, how many hearts can one heart touch?

WHAT COMES AT THE END of an extraordinary life like Jack's? The pain and heart-break of his family and dear friends. He himself experienced this pain when his friend Eric died. Jack was asked to give the eulogy at Eric's memorial; he could have been writing his own. That's why Jack's profoundly moving eulogy for Eric is the Afterword to Jack's own life.

One year ago today, someone who meant a great deal to me died. It's fitting that I am in Paris thinking of him because one of the many memorable experiences he and I shared over the eighteen years of being close was a week in Paris long ago.

I spent a week before the funeral writing and re-writing a typical eulogy. I had written about his family and their history, his educational achievements and professional accomplishments, the

Eric and Jack

many people in his life who loved him, and it was nice. Adequate. But, it wasn't really about the Eric I knew. So, in the middle of the night on a quiet red-eye flight heading to the funeral, I threw it away and decided to write who he was to me and why. It seemed selfish to write a eulogy that was only about me and him, but the only way I could honestly write about who he was—the only way to really honor him—was to do it that way.

It's very important to tell the people you love that you love them. That's not enough, though. Every once in a while, pull them aside, send a card, make a call, send an email—to friends/bffs/lovers/husbands/wives/parents/sons/daughters—and tell them WHY you love them. Risk that somewhat embarrassing moment of being a bit overly-dramatic and tell them why. Tell them the effect their being in your life has had on you. Tell them not only that they mean something to you, but why. In today's parlance, use your words.

Eric, wherever you are now, tonight in Paris I raise a glass in your honor. You were a royal pain in the ass most of the time, but you were worth every damn minute of it.

I met Eric when I was 24 years old and had just moved to New York City to finish post-grad school. One night after studying, I walked to a local bar for a drink. Sitting on the bar stool next to me was a very tall man who was smiling, moving his shoulders to the music a little, drinking a martini and not talking to anyone. I noticed that an enormous fur coat was in a pile on the floor near his feet. I said, "Your fur is on the floor. It's kind of gross down there." He turned to me, looked me up and down, paused, thought for a moment and then, leaning in a little closer, he very slowly said, "That's okay. I have many others."

Like most 24-year-olds, I thought I knew it all and had life all figured out. Eric immediately acted to disabuse me of that false notion. He would tear me down and then build me right back up over and over again. And I guess I let him because I knew he was right. Eric was equally critical and loving and, after a while, there didn't seem to be any difference between the two. Eric was simply brutally honest with those he cared about. If you did not want to hear a difficult truth, then you shouldn't ask Eric the question. He was rarely someone to candy-coat anything.

Eric taught me that the world can be a limitless place. He taught me to always try and face the truth. And he taught me that I should love myself even though I am very, very far from perfect. He taught me to judge people only by these things: their warmth, their sincerity, and their kindness. He used to say, "I don't care if someone is a ditch digger as long as they're interesting and kind-hearted." And he meant it. He really walked his talk.

Eric taught me about unconditional acceptance. Eric refused to be anything but Eric. If you were going to be in his life, you had to accept everything about him. His graces and his flaws. And there were many of both. He neither gloated about his successes, nor apologized for his flaws. But, he was just as capable of giving unconditional acceptance as demanding it. If he chose to be your friend, he would accept you unconditionally. That's not to say he wasn't honest and very often blunt about the things he didn't like or approve of, but he accepted the good with the not-so-good. He had a way of being able to see the best parts of people.

Being around Eric could be breathtaking. He was larger than life. He was over the top. Walking past the cafes on Madison Avenue on Manhattan's Upper East Side during brunch on Sundays was a chorus of "Hello, Eric" from everybody—from the bus boys at La Goulue to the ladies lunching at Le Relais. He was all flailing gestures, glamour, a full-length sable coat, and a martini or two or five. He enjoyed the finer things in life, had expensive taste, and loved artifice. I used to describe Eric as being "Auntie Mame on steroids." But, he was so much more than just the witty, stylish, funny, life of the party.

Eric had a kind and generous heart. And he was very sensitive. He didn't always show that part of himself because I think it was hard for him to be as sensitive as he really was. Eric was a very strong man, but not because he didn't let things hurt him. He was a strong man because he always tried to face any truth no matter how difficult and handle any amount of hurt that came along with it. He always said to me, "Jack, you must always face the truth. It is the hardest thing in life, but you must do it in order to grow." And if I wasn't facing a truth, Eric had no problem pointing that out to me.

Just before I turned thirty, I found out I needed open-heart surgery. Having been heavily influenced by Eric, I decided to have a thirtieth birthday party in Paris followed by the heart surgery back in the U.S. two weeks later. The doctors weren't sure I should be traveling. I told Eric and he said, "Fuck 'em. If you're gonna die, you should die in Paris." I sent out the invitations. While on the plane, I was looking out the window quietly and suddenly Eric was there in my ear, "I know you're very scared, Jack…" He continued for a while and I didn't say anything at that moment. He was pushing me to face my fear of the surgery, let it go and move on. There were a lot of amazing times with Eric over the years, but that week in Paris was really special. Eric demanded a lot from his friends. But, mostly he demanded that you face the truth and keep moving forward. "That's what you have to do in life, dear! Just move on, dear! Just move on!" he would say to anybody and nobody after two or three martinis.

Eric had that rare ability of being able to combine the exuberance of a child with the wisdom of an old soul. He was sort of a combination of the Buddha and Diana Vreeland. It's very easy to lose one's sense of wonder as we grow up. It takes more and bigger and better to give us that same feeling. We lose that beautiful childhood trait of happiness-for-no-reason. Eric never did. Eric never lost that sense of wonder. Despite a rich life full of diverse and unique experiences, Eric could always find joy in simple things. He never, ever lost the ability to be excited. And he also never lost the ability to find serenity in an extremely simple moment. In NYC, we would often take our respective books, whatever each of us was reading at the time, and meet in a quiet café. We would just sit together, reading our books, drinking our coffee while discussing the books and life in general. Sometimes when there was silence, I would steal a look at him and he would be deep into his book or people watching with a little smile of serenity and peace on his face. I loved when I saw him like that.

Eric was a very complex person in so many ways. He was challenging, exhilarating, infuriating, frustrating, and loving. But, to me, the Eric that I have always held in my heart and will always hold in my heart is a very simple man. When you strip away all the artifice, the masks, and the full length sable coat, when the caricature is gone, what you have left is a very kind, emotionally generous, sensitive, extremely wise, almost child-like man with a huge heart. I am a better person for having known him. And I don't think I will ever meet anyone like him ever again.

None us will ever meet anyone like Jack again in this life. So raise your glass in farewell to one whose heart, though physically flawed, was large enough to hold us all.

Drawing of Babba by Michael Brown

ACKNOWLEDGMENTS

—⌒

WHILE THIS BOOK IS FOCUSED on Jack's "heart thing" and the wild ride he took during the time he was defying (or dealing with) its existence, it is also a celebration of his unique and memorable life.

I want to acknowledge Jack's family: his mother, Linda Marie Drew; her sister, Jack's Aunt Bev; his father, Marny Freedman and his wife, Kim Phuong Nguyen (Jack called her his "big sister"); his brother, Nicholas Freedman; his nephew Dom; and his beloved grandmother Babba Fannie; Jack's Aunt Mil (Mildred Broudy), Aunt Freda (Driben), and Uncle Norm (Hirsch); cousins Moriah Buff, Lisa Steinberg, Dan Hirsch, Auntie Lanie, and Uncle Norm (Freedman).

Jack's good friends were vitally important to him. Not all of them are mentioned in the book, but deserve to be acknowleged. They include (in no particular order): Lady Paddy Hague, Countess Nora, Joanna Wasiutynski Wesson, Svend Littauer, Magda Fuentes, Roy Bailey and his husband David Hernandez, Rob Nichols, Lisa Spinelli, Monique Salazar, Simone Grace Myara-Dorrough, Theresa Page, Brent Pawlecki, John Gadd, Sj Miller, and Linda Mateyka.

There are many others in photos with Jack, arms around each other and smiling broadly, whose names I could not uncover. (Oh for the days when people wrote names on the back of actual photographs. I have not credited the photos since Jack's not around to tell me who took them; if you would like to be credited, please contact parvati@parvatimarkus.com.)

Finally I'd like to acknowledge the divine spark within Jack's heart—the non-physical heart, which never had an electrical or valve problem—the heart that radiated the love in which we all delighted.

Made in the USA
San Bernardino, CA
14 January 2018